Profiles of a Province

Profiles of a Province

Studies in the history of Ontario

A collection of essays commissioned by
The Ontario Historical Society
to commemorate the centennial of Ontario

Edited by Edith G. Firth

Ontario Historical Society
Toronto
1967

Printed in Canada by The Bryant Press Limited

Contents

Part II The Political Scene

Part III Aspects of Ontario's Economy

Preface

The celebrations associated with the one hundredth birthday of the Dominion of Canada have occupied the centre of the stage during 1967, and rightly so, for the Dominion that came into being a century ago was a bold, imaginative experiment in political engineering that is gradually becoming recognized as an important event in modern world history—the founding of a mighty nation whose industrial and artistic maturity are fittingly expressed in the World's Fair in Montreal, Expo 67.

These festivities honouring the centenary of the Dominion of Canada should not completely obscure the fact that not one, but three, political entities came into existence on July 1, 1867 in British North America—the provinces of Ontario and Quebec as well as the Dominion. True, the Dominion was a completely new creation, while the province of Ontario, despite the newness of the name, was a functioning regional community, the reality of whose existence was confirmed by the creation of the province. Ontario was the continuation of an earlier colony, Upper Canada, whose beginnings went back another seventy-five years; although it had been merged with Lower Canada in 1841 the union had not effaced the distinctive qualities of the community along the Great Lakes and upper St. Lawrence River, but only intensified them.

The people of Ontario, proud of their heritage as Canadians, have participated in the festivities to help make 1967 a year of rejoicing and of national rededication. But, equally, this year completes a century in the life of the province, during which Ontario has made tremendous advances. This centenary offers a convenient point to review and assess the many accomplishments of the province and its people. In this volume are examined some of these achievements in Ontario's progression from pioneer loyalist colony to powerful modern industrial and cultural community, or, as one author has phrased it, its advance from Outpost to Empire.

Profiles of a Province was conceived as a collection of essays that reflected the areas of special interest of the authors. All except three were especially prepared for this collection by scholars whose fields of study, taken as a group, cover the various periods of Ontario's history and a wide range of subjects. Inevitably, even though the articles represent a broad cross-section of current researches in the field of Ontario history, they leave many important aspects untreated. The number of possible subjects is simply too vast; a collection that aimed at being comprehensive would have necessitated a number of volumes. Because each author was given a free hand to treat his subject in his own way, the articles represent a considerable variety of approaches and presentations. To a surprising degree, however, the result is a reasonably well-rounded, integrated, comprehensive group of essays, which have been arranged in four parts according to their main themes. The Ontario Historical Society counts itself fortunate to have secured the support and assistance of so large a group of gifted and devoted contributors. It thanks these contributors for their excellent presentations, as well as Miss Edith G. Firth, head of the Canadian History and Manuscript Section of the Toronto Public Library, who acted as editor and superintended the volume through the press.

A perusal of the articles shows that even before the present province was established, an Ontario community with a definite, distinct regional character had evolved. On the political side, both Tory and Reform movements had abandoned extremist positions in favour of moderate, gradual constitutional reforms and responses to the needs of an industrializing community. Both had also perfected the organizations and structures of the future national and provincial parties. Despite a short-lived flirtation of the Radicals with American ideas, the Ontario of 1867 scorned republicanism and equated democracy with mob rule, and its citizens, depending on the circumstances, were either latently or openly anti-American. The laws, institutions, and traditions of the colony were British. Finally, the union with Lower Canada helped to weld the future province into a sense of its being a distinctive community, differing in interests, outlooks, and needs from its Lower Canadian partner. This regional or sectional feeling inspired its political leaders to evolve a new constitutional framework that would provide home rule for the Ontario community as a province in the new Dominion of Canada.

Ontario had also developed into a distinct economic community by the time of Confederation. By 1850 it possessed vigorous, buoyant, burgeoning cities, a prosperous staple export economy, thriving manufacturing plants and financial structures, and an adequate system of transportation by water and land. These were further expanded and improved during the 1850's through the building of railways. To preserve the autonomy of this economic region the statesmen of 1864–67 created a federal system under which existing material benefits could be maintained and extended within the province of Ontario, while at the same time the province could aspire to win an economic hegemony over the vast free trading area of the Dominion of Canada. Implicit, too, in the economic development of the Ontario community was a sizeable degree of state aid and control, unaccompanied, however, by a concern for the long-term welfare of the public, or the proper care of the natural resources.

The Upper Canadian experience had also moulded a distinctive society and personality. The community was strongly Protestant, pluralistic, disposed towards voluntarism, and opposed to religious privileges and state-supported churches. The people were serious, pious, sabbath-observing, pragmatic, frugal, puritanical, and interested in causes for human betterment like temperance, Indian and foreign missions, and the anti-slavery movement. Their architecture, painting, and literature were not profoundly original, but they reflected confidence in the worth of the community and a contented acceptance of established values.

During the century that followed, the province continued many of the patterns established by the previous colony. Post-Confederation leaders, Oliver Mowat in particular, epitomized the qualities of slow, gradual, practical reforms, the distrust of bold or radical solutions, a cautious but progressive approach to the needs of an industrializing, urbanizing society, a strong pro-British even imperialist sentiment, and a determination to maintain Ontario's rights to remain a distinct community within the Canadian Confederation. The personalities and works of later figures like J. P. Whitney, N. W. Rowell, and Mitchell Hepburn continued to reflect similar tendencies. Particularly in the career of N. W. Rowell one may discern the persistence of such traditional socio-religious virtues as earnestness, industriousness, application, temperate habits, and a sincere concern for the improvement of society.

The expectations at Confederation of continuing industrialization and diversification were fulfilled as southern Ontario became an industrial, commercial, and financial heartland of the transcontinental Dominion, and the province secured territories to the north and west that tripled its original area. The concept of the state as provider of material aid and facilities was reflected in the establishment of the Ontario Northland Railway and the Hydro-electric Power Commission as public utilities. State regulation has moved into setting industrial and labour standards, conserving natural resources, and providing support for the underprivileged. The religio-educational values of the earlier period were carried forward in the steadily-improving system of public education, created and guided by Dr. Egerton Ryerson in a non-denominational but Christian direction. Only in the field of the arts, to judge from the article on Ontario's literature, has the province possibly failed to fulfil its earlier promise.

Have the developments of the past century maintained or diminished Ontario's regional character? Certainly the modern province, thanks to its growth and diversification, has become less homogeneous than was the community that gained provincial status in 1867. Still, while no one would dispute the real differences that exist among such districts as the St. Lawrence valley and the Lakehead, or the minefields of the Canadian Shield and Metropolitan Toronto, the extent of their diversity can be exaggerated. The British background of language, laws, and institutions inherited from the older colony continues to unite Ontarians, as well as the works of successive provincial governments—the framework of local and municipal institutions, the schools system, common wage and work standards, the province-wide system of welfare services. Improving transportation media have reduced the effective distances between sections of Ontario, while technological developments have undermined localisms and integrated diverse sections, linking city and countryside, and southern with northern Ontario. The diffusion of common literary, cultural and artistic standards (largely fashioned in, and disseminated from, Toronto) is facilitated by the rising levels of education and increased leisure. Thus the different sections of the province are being increasingly unified and perpetuated as a distinct region.

Yet the regional sense, of being a part of a distinct entity known as Ontario, lacks the emotional quality of a century ago that inspired the establishment of the province, or that threatens Confederation today. Indeed, the regionalism of Ontario is often so closely identified with Canadian nationalism that many Ontarians fail to regard

Ontario as a region at all and equate the larger Dominion with the purposes of Ontario. This view comes easily to Ontarians, seeing that the province comprises one-third of the population of Canada, the national capital is in Ontario, and federal programmes of national integration have almost invariably favoured Ontario's regional interests. The inhabitants of other regions of Canada, all too often, have accepted this identification and accused Dominion governments of designing their programmes too much in conformity with the interests of Ontario, and insufficiently in tune with those of the western provinces, the Maritimes, or Quebec.

Is not this view which identifies Ontario with the Dominion, simply another manifestation of Ontario regionalism, an outlook characteristic of the province which differentiates it from the other sections of Canada? In fact, the domination of the federal state by Ontario has been exaggerated; more often than not, Ontario has returned opponents rather than supporters of federal governments to Parliament. The programmes of economic integration were conceived in the interests of national consolidation, to give reality to Confederation, and the benefits to Ontario were incidental to those objectives. Increasingly, Ontario has recognized its benefits under Confederation and shown a willingness to assist less well-endowed parts of Canada, or regions adversely affected by those policies that have been so helpful to Ontario. As Professor Innis observed over thirty years ago, in his article reprinted below, "An empire has its obligations as well as its opportunities." Ontario has been the willing ally and partner of the national government, prepared to identify its own interests with the preservation of a healthy Confederation, ready to co-operate to achieve the purposes of Canada, and more willing than most to submerge its own views in the face of the common good. Provincial rights found their earliest home in Mowat's Ontario, but the 'home rule' status achieved at that time has proved sufficient to Ontario's needs and aspirations. During the present century a prosperous, contented Ontario has been the Dominion's staunchest support against external threats of conquest or absorption, and against internal forces of division and disruption.

In publishing *Profiles of a Province* the Ontario Historical Society seeks to pay its respects to the great province, aspects of whose history and achievements it has studied since its founding. By this volume it hopes to place in truer perspective many of the key developments that have shaped Ontario and to help identify the basic characteristics of the modern province. It aims also to assist future scholars by answering some questions with these studies, and posing others. Finally, it hopes that this volume will reach the citizens of Ontario—particularly the young people in the schools—and make them aware of the glorious heritage bequeathed them by earlier generations of Upper Canadians and Ontarians, to the end that they will take a just pride in that heritage and be inspired to emulate the achievements of those who have gone before.

MORRIS ZASLOW
Past President, Ontario Historical Society

List of Contributors

FREDERICK H. ARMSTRONG is Assistant Professor of History at the University of Western Ontario.

MARGARET A. BANKS is Law Librarian at the University of Western Ontario.

R. N. BEATTIE is Records Administrator of the Hydro-electric Power Commission of Ontario.

PAUL G. CORNELL is Professor of History at the University of Waterloo.

A. MARGARET EVANS is Assistant Professor of History at the University of Guelph.

W. S. GOULDING is a Professor in the School of Architecture, University of Toronto.

FRED COYNE HAMIL is Professor of History at Wayne State University.

J. RUSSELL HARPER, formerly Chief Curator of the McCord Museum, McGill University, is lecturing in Canadian art history at Carleton and Sir George Williams Universities.

BRUCE W. HODGINS is Assistant Professor of History at Trent University.

NEIL C. HULTIN is Assistant Professor of English at the University of Western Ontario.

CHARLES W. HUMPHRIES is Assistant Professor of History at the University of British Columbia.

H. A. INNIS, who died in 1952, pioneered in the study of Canadian economic history, and was one of Canada's outstanding scholars.

FRED LANDON, formerly Chief Librarian and Professor of History at the University of Western Ontario, was awarded the Tyrell Medal in History, and the Cruikshank Medal. He is a past president of the Ontario Historical Society.

FATHER NEIL MCKENTY, S.J., formerly on the staff of Regiopolis College, is the author of *Mitch Hepburn*.

WILLIAM H. MAGEE is on the staff of the Department of English at the University of Alberta.

JOHN S. MOIR is Professor of History at the University of Toronto (Scarborough College) and is President of the Ontario Historical Society.

FLORENCE B. MURRAY is a Professor in the School of Library Science, University of Toronto.

EDWARD PHELPS is Collections Librarian at Brock University.

MARGARET PRANG is Associate Professor of History at the University of British Columbia.

GEORGE W. SPRAGGE, formerly Archivist of Ontario, has been awarded the Cruikshank Medal for distinguished service to Ontario history.

C. P. STACEY, O.B.E., is Professor of History at the University of Toronto.

ROBERT M. STAMP is Assistant Professor in the History of Education at the Althouse College of Education, University of Western Ontario.

J. J. TALMAN is Chief Librarian, University of Western Ontario.

S. F. WISE is Chief Historian in the Historical Division of the Canadian Forces Headquarters.

R. I. WOLFE is Associate Professor of Geography at York University.

MORRIS ZASLOW is Professor of History at the University of Western Ontario, and a past president of the Ontario Historical Society.

PART I

The making of a province

The United Empire Loyalists

J. J. Talman

In a brief paper such as this on a subject which has been covered voluminously we cannot do better than confine ourselves to trying to find answers for some of the questions that come to mind regarding the United Empire Loyalists. Why were they loyal? What kind of people were they? Where did they come from? How many were there? What was the immediate effect of their migration? What were the long-term effects? Is the Loyalist background of the province of Ontario still significant? Were the Loyalists who came to that part of Quebec which became Upper Canada different from those who went to Nova Scotia? Our answers in this paper must generally be limited to the present province of Ontario.

To answer our first question, a person who wishes to discover the Loyalists' views on loyalty has not an easy task as he is hampered by lack of evidence. Lorenzo Sabine, the mid-nineteenth century New England historian, was one of the earliest to point out this fact when in 1864 he wrote: "Men who, like the Loyalists, separate themselves from their friends and kindred, who are driven from their homes, who surrender the hopes and expectations of life, and who become outlaws, wanderers, and exiles, – such men leave few memorials behind them. Their papers are scattered and lost, and their very names pass from human recollection." Two competent early Canadian historians, William Canniff and Judge J. F. Pringle, discovered the same paucity of records. The latter, in 1889, complained of the great dearth of the "records of the services, the labours and the sufferings of the U.E. Loyalists both before and after their coming to Canada."

Some historians have tried to explain the movement of the Loyalists to what became Upper Canada as a simple migration of people looking for better land. Others have suggested that they were those who believed that the mother country would subdue the rebellious colonies and therefore, "having bet on the wrong horse," were forced to leave. Doubtless there were Loyalists who fitted these descriptions. At the same time it must be recognized that many were loyal out of a genuine loyalty to the Crown. They were Americans who wished to live under a king; as Edward Winslow put it, "zealots in the King's cause." On the other hand many *bona fide* Loyalists had been in America a very short time and were practically transients as far as the thirteen colonies were concerned.

The question as to what kind of people the Loyalists were and where they came from may be readily answered. As far as Upper Canada was concerned they did not represent the royal officials, the large landed proprietors, the professional classes or the wealthy classes of the thirteen colonies. Exceptions, of course, stood out. The Johnson and Jessup families had held large estates in New York. The Reverend John Stuart and the Reverend John Bethune were clergymen. But in over six hundred claims recorded in the Ontario Bureau of Archives *Report* for 1904 not a single lawyer is to be found and there are only two doctors in the group. That the Loyalists who settled in what became Upper Canada were not men of property is shown by a letter from Quebec dated January 29, 1786, written by Lieutenant Governor Hope to the commissioners investigating Loyalist claims. He protested because the commissioners were determined to hold their sessions in Halifax and expected claimants even from the western parts of Quebec to make their way there to present their claims. Hope wrote:

> The Loyalists in the Province with a few exceptions do not consist of Persons of great Property of consequence. They are chiefly landholders, Farmers and others from the Inland parts of the Continent, many of whom very early quitted their homes and Possessions to join the Royal Standard, the rest have been forced to abandon them and take refuge under his Majestys Government. . . . A small compensation for their Losses would restore to the great part of them all the Comforts and Conveniences they have lost.

Colonel Thomas Dundas, one of the commissioners investigating Loyalist losses, likewise wrote in 1787 to Lord Cornwallis that the settlers up to that time were "mostly farmers from the back parts of New York province."

The description of Loyalist immigrants to the present province of Ontario cannot be projected to describe the Loyalists of New Brunswick. Mr. Gerald Keith of Saint John has generously supplied the writer with a list of the names of some of those persons registered as Freemen of Saint John in 1785, together with the names of others who were thereabouts. He has found six physicians, twenty-four persons described as "esquires" (many of whom were lawyers), nineteen described as "gentlemen" and many others whose biographies record the holding of high positions in the thirteen colonies.

The conclusion seems clear. The Loyalist party in the thirteen colonies was made up of all sorts and conditions of men but with rare exceptions only Loyalists of humble origin found their way to what became Upper Canada and later Ontario.

The question of the number of Loyalist immigrants to Upper Canada is not so easily answered. The number actually was lower than is generally believed. In 1786 the official record of "the Number of Loyalists settled in the Upper Parts of the Province of Quebec" was 5,960. In 1791 the population, which by then included many non-Loyalists who quickly joined the Loyalist movement and within a few years became almost indistinguishable from it, had risen to only 10,000. This was the estimate of a select committee of the House of Assembly of Upper Canada in 1838. It is true that immigrants who fulfilled the technical requirements necessary to receive Loyalist land grants were recognized if they arrived by July 28, 1798. Nevertheless, the first flood of Loyalists who came to Canada soon after the peace totalled approximately 6,000.

What was the immediate effect of the Loyalist immigration? The Loyalists brought to Canada a tradition of freehold tenure of land, English law, and representative legislative institutions, which was soon reflected in their applications to the administration. They found the Quebec Act of 1774, providing as it did French civil law, guaranteeing the feudal system of land tenure, and no legislative assembly, to be entirely inadequate. The Loyalists were Tories but they were not prepared to surrender the political privileges they had gained before the revolution.

Two letters which show clearly what the Loyalists had in mind were sent in December, 1786, to Sir John Johnson from the magistrates at Cataraqui (Kingston) and Oswegatchie (roughly the north shore of the St. Lawrence to Brockville), signed by such representative Loyalists as Neil McLean, Jeptha Hawley, Peter Van Alstine, Michael Grass, Justus and Thomas Sherwood, John and Daniel Jones and others. The recommendation which both these letters described as "of the most importance" was that the system of land tenure should be altered and put on the same footing as it was in Nova Scotia and New Brunswick. Surprisingly enough, the traditional view that the first and foremost demand of the Loyalists was for an elected assembly is not borne out by the records.

The Loyalists in Upper Canada were not for long marked apart as a separate group. Within a very few years bitterness died out and inter-marriage between the Loyalists and the other Americans who followed close on their heels made the groups indistinguishable. As early as June 30, 1785, a Canadian Loyalist complained to a traveller that a great many people, not Loyalists, had settled near Johnstown, the heart of the Loyalist country; and added that it was very hard they should meet with the same encouragement as those who had fought in the war and lost all their possessions.

In 1788 the Reverend John Stuart of Kingston wrote to Bishop William White about the great influx of inhabitants from the American frontier "with melancholy complaints of Taxes, Poverty & Tyranny." A year later he wrote further, "This country continues to receive a great accession of strength by Emigrations from your States."

The long-term effects of the Loyalist immigration are intangible and hard to measure. Among the descendants of Loyalists the tendency has been to assume that since their ancestors were loyal in 1776 it automatically followed that they and their descendants were always loyal, especially in 1812 and 1837. But this conclusion did not necessarily follow. In fact, on June 27, 1816, the Executive Council of Upper Canada decreed that no petitions for land from sons and daughters of United Empire Loyalists would be received unless accompanied by a certificate from a magistrate in Quarter Sessions, signed by the chairman and clerk of the peace, that the parent maintained his loyalty during the war of 1812 and was under no suspicion of aiding or assisting the enemy. If the petition was from a son then of age his certificate had to show that he himself was loyal during the war and "did his duty in defense of the Province"; and if from a married daughter of a United Empire Loyalist, "that her husband was loyal, and did his duty in defense of the Province." In view of this regulation it can certainly be assumed that all

Loyalists who secured grants after the war of 1812 had proved their loyalty during it. But it cannot be assumed that no persons of Loyalist ancestry were disloyal in 1812.

In fairness to the record of the Loyalists it must be said that Lieutenant Governor Gore was confident in 1812 that "those persons who served in the American War and their descendants" would be opposed to the Americans in event of war. Certainly disaffection was not as prevalent in those parts of Upper Canada which had been settled by Loyalists as in other parts, although even in Leeds county, which was predominantly settled by Loyalists, there were some exceptions.

To trace important Loyalist influences in Upper Canada after 1815 is a difficult task. Egerton Ryerson recognized this fact when he wrote in 1880 "with the close of that war [of 1812-1815] terminates the history of the United Empire Loyalists of Canada as a distinct and controlling class of inhabitants."

Interest in the Loyalists revived in the middle 1850's. In 1855 the Toronto *Globe* printed an editorial on the ignorance in Canada West concerning the "Loyalist Fathers". The editorial said, in part: "Here, then, we are, in the sixty-second year of our being in Upper Canada, with the only men who could accurately inform us, fast dying, if not already dead, all but grossly ignorant of our provincial parentage and birth." The writer of the editorial suggested that Egerton Ryerson, the Superintendent of Education, might write the story. According to Ryerson, during the next five years newspapers and public men of different parties urged him to write. Out of this pressure grew his two-volume work, *The Loyalists of America and Their Times* (Toronto, 1880).

Another individual who promoted the cause of the Loyalists was William Hamilton Merritt. In 1859 he circulated a petition asking that the Legislature pay more attention to the history of Upper Canada. Other petitions followed and J. P. Merritt received an appointment to uncover Upper Canadian documentary material in Britain. Soon afterwards George Coventry was enlisted in a similar task. In 1861 these last two men, and others, organized a provincial historical society with the name "Upper Canada Historical Society." In 1869 the body appears to have been called the "Canada Historical Society" and in 1875 the "British North American Historical Society." J. P. Merritt was president of the last named. Although these associations cannot be said to have been highly successful their very existence suggests that there was a rise in interest in the history of the province at the time.

The centennial celebrations at Adolphustown, Toronto and Niagara in 1884, as centennials will, did much to keep alive the interest in United Empire Loyalists which had developed at mid-century. Twelve years later on February 28, 1896, the United Empire Loyalists' Association of Ontario was organized with the object of preserving such Loyalist records as were still available and of "keeping light the spirit of loyalty."

The Ontario Bureau of Archives *Report* for 1904, referred to above, made available a large collection of important documentary material relating to Loyalist claims and in this way advanced the aims of the United Empire Loyalists' Association.

Further recognition of the Loyalists came in 1909 with the creation of the Ontario coat of arms with its motto: "Ut incepit fidelis sic permanet." The story of the adoption of this motto was told by Dr. George Spragge in 1959 in *Ontario History*, volume LI, number 1. He records that in 1907 the Honourable James P. Whitney, Prime Minister of Ontario, proposed that the province should have a crest befitting its dignity. A Royal Warrant, issued February 27, 1909, prescribed the crest and motto. Subsequently, in a letter of May 10, 1910, Whitney told Miss I. K. Farlinger of Morrisburg that E. M. Chadwick, the compiler of *Ontarian Families* (2 vols., Toronto, 1894-8), had designed the crest and supporters and suggested the motto, which obviously alludes to the founding of the province by the United Empire Loyalists.

The original seal of Upper Canada, which as Dr. Spragge said "may well be regarded as the provincial coat of arms", had contained no references to loyalty. The two cornucopia "charged with fruits & corn" which were part of the design may have suggested the hope that the Loyalists were coming to a land of plenty although the well-authenticated "hungry year" belied such a theory. A calumet, or pipe of peace, also on the seal, paid tribute to the Indian allies of the Crown.

The lists of names in the *Canadian Parliamentary Companion* (the name varies) for 1883 enable us to measure, to a degree, Loyalist influence in government a century after the Treaty of Paris. Ten per cent of the members in both the House of Commons and the Ontario Legislature gave some indication of United Empire Loyalist ancestry. Fifty years later, in 1933, the percentage in the House of Commons had gone down to something over six per cent. In Ontario the figure went up to eleven per cent. No party had a monopoly of Loyalist members. A century and a half after the migration Loyalist ancestry was evidently still considered worth noting.

The *Canadian Parliamentary Guide 1966* showed no member of the House of Commons as being of Loyalist ancestry though in many cases other ancestries are shown. Clearly some members would qualify but presumably did not consider the information of political significance. The Legislature of Ontario has four United Empire Loyalist representatives, a reduction from the nine in 1933.

With a decline in Loyalist influence in government apparently revealed in the foregoing statistics we may ask "What now remains of the Loyalist tradition?" Professor A. R. M. Lower expressed the view in his *Canadians in the Making* (Toronto, 1958) that modern Ontario is "not a 'Loyalist' province like New Brunswick." On the other hand the Royal Commission on Canada's Economic Prospects, of which Mr. Walter Gordon was Chairman, stated in November, 1957: "Only a casual visitor bemused by the metropolitan bustle and the concentration of immigrants in Toronto could entirely fail to glimpse those levels of the city that still bear the impress of the back concessions of old Ontario, of the early Loyalist settlers and of the Methodist circuit riders."

The United Empire Loyalists' Association of Canada with many branches across the nation today keeps alive the record of the Loyalists. Their coming was a significant fact in Canadian history and their contribution cannot be gainsaid.

BIBLIOGRAPHICAL NOTE

The Dominion Council of the United Empire Loyalists' Association of Canada compiled a *Bibliography of the United Empire Loyalists at the Toronto Public Library,* in September 1966. This publication lists 144 items. Many of these are brief while others deal with specific persons or topics.

There are a few useful general histories. Although the work was published in 1914, William Stewart Wallace, *The United Empire Loyalists; A Chronicle of the Great Migration* (Toronto, 1914), provides a brief and well balanced account of the Loyalist migration to the Maritimes and the present province of Ontario, which is well worth reading today.

The introduction written by James J. Talman to *Loyalist Narratives from Upper Canada* (Toronto, 1946), attempted a critical judgment of the Loyalist movement. The narratives, though not by first generation Loyalists cover a wide range.

Ernest Alexander Cruikshank, ed., *The Settlement of the United Empire Loyalists on the Upper St. Lawrence and Bay of Quinte in 1784* (Toronto, 1934), supplies a rich concentration of documents, largely official.

Since most Loyalists in Upper Canada come from New York, Alexander Clarence Flick, *Loyalism in New York during the American Revolution* (New York, 1901), gives much of the Upper Canadian Loyalist background.

Adolphus Egerton Ryerson, *The Loyalists of America and Their Times: from 1620 to 1816* (2 vols., Toronto, 1880), is an uncritical eulogy.

Lorenzo Sabine, *Biographical Sketches of Loyalists of the American Revolution, with an Historical Essay* (Boston, 1864), though printed over a century ago is still a valuable work.

Hazel (Chisholm) Mathews, *The Mark of Honour* (Toronto, 1965), is a recent work which traces the careers of the Chisholm, Park, Thomson and Rose families. Since Mrs. Mathews describes the treatment of these Loyalist families in great detail her book is of general value as other Loyalists were treated in the same way.

The Reform Movement in Upper Canada

Fred Coyne Hamil

The Reform tradition in Upper Canada was forged from native materials and the political ideas emanating from Great Britain and the United States. The mother country had been committed, since the reaction from the premature Puritan Revolution of the seventeenth century, to a slow and traditional advance towards the realization of a democratic state within the framework of a limited monarchy. By the end of the eighteenth century the machinery of the cabinet system was being perfected, and sovereignty was rapidly passing to the House of Commons. But that body, until the implementing of the Parliamentary Reform Act of 1832, represented a narrow oligarchy of the rich and the titled. The American colonists, on the other hand, with the same constitutional heritage to begin with, carried on the radical principles of the Puritan Revolution, taking what they needed from the Glorious Revolution of 1688, the Bill of Rights, and the works of John Locke. That way led them to independence; to a republic with separated powers and a wide extension of the elective principle; and in time to Jacksonian democracy. In the minds of the Reformers of Upper Canada, American institutions and the elective system fought for supremacy with the ideas of English reform and the cabinet system.

The seeds of political reform in Upper Canada were sown in the fertile soil of a frontier population that was American in origin and nonconformist in religion. The province was an isolated outpost of the British Empire, its constitution contained in the backward-looking Constitutional Act of 1791. By the beginning of the nineteenth century it had come to be governed by an entrenched oligarchy of Loyalist and British officials, chiefly adherents of the Anglican Church, which was responsible only to the Colonial Office in distant London. Inevitably the government's exclusive patronage in the distribution of lands, public offices, and other rewards and honours, gave rise to inequities, abuses and discontent. After the war of 1812 the growing alienation of the people from their rulers was hastened by the pretensions of the Church of England that it was established in the province, with sole right to the clergy reserves and the control of education; and by the decision that settlers who had come in from the United States since 1783 were aliens. Added to this was a series of unpopular and sometimes arbitrary acts by the lieutenant governor and the ruling clique, especially during the administration of Sir Peregrine Maitland. In time, requests for redress of specific grievances were followed by demands for reform in certain departments of the government, and finally for a radical change which would lead to democratic self-government.

Radical leaders, most of them from the United Kingdom, appeared early, to take advantage of the prevailing discontent for their own purposes. They saw at once that the two democratic institutions, the township meetings and the Legislative Assembly, might be exploited just as similar institutions had been in England. The township meeting was established by a provincial act in 1793, to elect once a year the minor local officials. But it could be used by the people to exercise their right to assemble and petition for redress of grievances; and it could also constitute the basic unit for any kind of organization of the people to bring pressure on the government. The Legislative Assembly was composed of the people's elected representatives, but its powers were greatly circumscribed by the executive's control of the Legislative Council, as well as a major part of the revenues. The Assembly must be inspired to fight for the full power of the purse; then it could direct this weapon against the executive, and the Legislative Council. Constitutional reform would eventually take the form of a demand for popular control over either of the councils or both of them, on principles derived from Great Britain or the United States.

A demagogue appeared before the war of 1812 in the person of the Irish Judge Robert Thorpe, who openly invited the people, and the grand juries that appeared before him on his judicial circuits, to tell him their grievances. At the same time, Thorpe was telling the Colonial Office that he was fully aware of the miseries resulting "when the people are taught to interfere", and that his efforts were designed to keep them from meeting in every county to prepare grievance petitions to the king. In his attack on the governing clique, Thorpe induced his radical friends in the Assembly to investigate the various government offices. Surveyor General Charles B. Wyatt readily produced the books of his department on demand, without requesting permission of Alexander Grant who was administering the government, justifying this unusual procedure with the extravagant statement that the Assembly was "paramount in government."

It was evident to Thorpe and his followers that the Assembly could not in fact be paramount unless it acquired control of the purse. Following his election to that House early in 1807, Thorpe tried to induce the members to assert a claim to all provincial revenues, including the duties collected under imperial acts. They refused to do so; and Thorpe told them they were submitting to taxation without their consent, and were in fact giving up their freedom. After he left the province others took up the task. It is significant that the chairman and secretary of a public meeting of Thorpe's supporters in York county, which was held to give him aid, reappeared as active adherents of William Lyon Mackenzie two decades later, thus bridging the gap between the pre-war agitation and the Reform movement of the 1820's. A landmark was also established by Thorpe and his friend Joseph Willcocks, with the *Upper Canada Guardian*, the first independent vehicle for public communication in the province. Thorpe had earlier warned the Colonial Office that a newspaper was in project, which would soon "blow up the flame." It died with the outbreak of war in 1812, but after the peace it was followed by an ever-increasing number of newspapers of various political hues. Without newspapers and public meetings the Reform movement could not have existed.

Robert Gourlay came to Upper Canada in 1817, with a long record of agitation in Great Britain. For Upper Canada he was the first great agitator, demagogue, and organizer, who taught the people how to make their power felt. Gourlay was the first to make use of township meetings; he not only called them for the election of delegates to his District conventions, but also to adopt resolutions and addresses. Attorney General John B. Robinson sought in vain to find some legal justification for suppressing such meetings, but there were many who believed they were unconstitutional. A Gourlay supporter gave them enthusiastic praise; to him they were "the life and soul of liberty, the horror and dread of tyranny and oppression." Some years later on September 30, 1834, the Tory *Toronto Patriot* put it differently. "A Township meeting," it declared, "is a picture, in miniature, of Democracy or mob government." But the government feared even more Gourlay's provincial convention, a device associated with the French and American revolutions and with British radicalism; and the Assembly was jealous of what it regarded as an unconstitutional rival. Although the Convention Act passed in the fall of 1818 was repealed after two years, conventions were not again used in Upper Canada, except locally to nominate candidates for the Assembly.

After the passage of the Convention Act, Gourlay called on the people to revert to township meetings for the purpose of instructing their official representatives as to their wishes. He told them they must insist on the right of the Assembly to initiate all money bills. By holding the purse strings, he said, "every desirable object might be obtained without petitioning." Gourlay was removed from the scene a short time later, but his influence was felt in the Assembly elected in 1820, which showed a desire to extend its control over the revenues, and to keep the executive dependent on it for yearly appropriations. To Christopher Hagerman this "savored much of democracy," and democracy was like a serpent "twisting round us by degrees," which must be crushed in the beginning.[1] In Lower Canada at this time the Assembly and the executive were locked in a struggle over the control of the purse.

William Lyon Mackenzie, a Scot like Gourlay, entered the political arena in 1824, when he began publication of the *Colonial Advocate*. Unlike Gourlay, who disclaimed any wish to change the constitution, Mackenzie had many suggestions for changes in every department of the government; his ideas included schemes for colonial representation in the imperial parliament, and for a federation of the Empire with colonial self-government in internal affairs. As early as the summer of 1824 he seemed to be advocating the English cabinet system for the province. The executive of Upper Canada, he wrote, should be removable at the will of the nation as expressed in parliament, as was done in England; and the governor should only appoint to office "with the advice and consent" of the Assembly. Mackenzie insisted that the colonies must have the British constitution in all its purity, including an

[1] Kingston *Chronicle*, Dec. 28, 1821, Jan. 11, 1822.

administration "responsible to our parliament for its conduct."[2] On February 3, 1825, he pointed out in the *Colonial Advocate* that with control of all the revenue the Assembly could force the executive to seek annual appropriations; and this would give the Assembly the same powerful weapon wielded by the House of Commons, with which it could control the appointment and also the conduct of the more important government officials. Any misapplication of funds, he explained on December 22, could be met by a vote of censure on the "responsible advisers or cabinet" of the governor, and as a last resort, by a refusal to grant the supplies. The governor could counter this by dissolving parliament and appealing to the people in a general election, but if the new House continued to withhold the supplies he would be compelled to change his councillors, "for the voice of the province respecting administration must be attended to."

It is evident from Mackenzie's later writings that, like most people of his time, he did not fully understand the actual procedure of the cabinet system. He said nothing at this time about the necessity for members of the cabinet to have seats in the Assembly; indeed he consistently opposed all government officials or placemen, regardless of rank, sitting in the House. No doubt he was influenced by the lack of understanding of the cabinet shown by Blackstone, Hallam, and other writers. In December 1825, when Mackenzie was attempting to ingratiate himself with Lieutenant Governor Maitland, in hopes of getting some government patronage for himself, he wrote: "To withhold the supplies, because the other branches of the legislature will not submit to be dictated to by the House of Assembly, so as to alter the existing law of the country at the mere pleasure of the latter, is unconstitutional, destructive of the balance of power contemplated by the constitution, and the first step towards anarchy, revolution and civil war." Thus Mackenzie made it clear that he was interested in the power of the purse only to insure the proper application of provincial funds. For a brief period he had seemed to grasp the importance of the cabinet system as an answer to the province's ills; after this, until the Baldwins brought forth the idea of Responsible Government, Mackenzie devoted himself to suggesting remedies for each of these ills in turn.

Nevertheless, control by the Assembly of all the revenue, and the resulting power to bring the executive to terms by refusing to grant the supplies, remained a principal objective of the Reformers. In 1831 Upper Canada shared in the success of the lower province by securing the surrender of the Crown duties. While this matter was in progress, Attorney General Robinson had warned the Colonial Secretary that such a surrender would leave the government dependent on the Assembly for supply bills, and that those who paid would also appoint. "We shall slide rapidly into a republic," he wrote, "or rather into the turbulence of a democracy. . . ."[3] This danger was obviated by the permanent Salary Bill passed by the Tory Assembly. Mackenzie raged at this "everlasting Salary Bill", by which the Assembly relinquished a principal part of the power it had so long fought for. In 1835 the Colonial Office was even prepared to give up the casual and territorial

[2] *Colonial Advocate*, Aug. 19, 1824, Oct. 7, 1824.
[3] C.O. 323/163, Memo. to Hay, Dec. 13, 1830.

revenues, under certain conditions; but the conflict between Sir Francis Head and the Assembly delayed this.

Robert Baldwin once stated that his own opinions on Responsible Government had been imbibed from his father, Dr. William W. Baldwin. For his part Dr. Baldwin gave credit to his son for suggesting to him the principle "in its distinct shape", during private conversations in August, 1828. Mackenzie's writings may well have contributed to it, and perhaps even the events in Lower Canada. An anonymous *Mémoire*, probably written by the French nationalist Pierre Bédard, and published in Lower Canada in 1814, had suggested that the governor call to his councils the leading members of the majority party in the Assembly, and that a number of government offices as well as seats in the Executive Council be reserved for them, with the understanding that they should remain in office only so long as they retained the support of the majority in the Assembly. Louis Joseph Papineau, Speaker of the House, was offered a seat in the Executive Council several times, but quarrels with the governors prevented him from accepting. Although the object of the governors was to increase their influence in the Assembly, such an arrangement might have prepared the way for Responsible Government.

Dr. Baldwin advanced the first tentative suggestion of his new principle in the petition on behalf of Judge John Willis, which was addressed to the British government and adopted at a public meeting held at York on July 15, 1828. A clause in the petition asked for the passage of a provincial act which would provide a procedure to make the government of Upper Canada constitutionally responsible, "not only by the removal of these advisers from office, when they lose the confidence of the people, but also by impeachment for the heavier offences chargeable against them." Here the idea of punishment is seen warring with the principle of the English cabinet. In an anonymous article, probably written by Dr. Baldwin, which appeared in the *Upper Canada Herald* on October 14, 1829, the same confusion is apparent. The author noted that under the prevailing system of "practical responsibility" the executive could not perform any act "without those who *may be injured* thereby, having a constitutional right to call some person to account for it". The governor of a colony could be punished only by the British government for the misuse of the powers delegated to him; but his councillors, on whose advice he acted, could be brought to account by the process of impeachment in the provincial legislature.

The Reformers generally were mistaken in thinking that the governor had to seek the advice of his Executive Council, or to act upon it; and that impeachment was a necessary adjunct to Responsible Government. Impeachment was the ancient weapon of the British parliament against the king's advisers when it could not attack the king himself, but it had been rendered obsolete for this purpose by the development of cabinet control. It had never been used in Upper Canada, although long among the Reformers' demands. To facilitate its use against individual councillors the writer suggested that they should be required to sign the advice they gave, as privy councillors in England had to do under the Act of Settlement passed in 1701. Dr. Baldwin had suggested the same thing; all the governor's acts, he thought, should have "the character of local responsibility by the signature of some member of this ministry." Both writers seem to have been unaware that the clause cited in the Act of Settlement was repealed in 1706, thus making possible that secrecy and unanimity so essential to the modern cabinet system. This misunderstanding is not surprising when it is seen that in 1806 both houses of the British parliament held to the view that the cabinet had no collective responsibility, and was merely a convenient committee of the Privy Council, every member of which was individually responsible and liable to impeachment for his advice to the king. As late as 1827 the historian Henry Hallam observed that the existence of the cabinet made it difficult to assign responsibility to any particular minister, so that he could be impeached. To most people "responsibility" meant legal responsibility to punishment. .

In England the cabinet system of government was not fully understood until after 1832, because of the continued influence of the king and the absence of rotation in government of the two parties. Dr. Baldwin was making an original suggestion when he propounded the principle of Responsible Government for Upper Canada. As chairman of the Constitutional Committee established to further the Willis petition, he wrote to various government leaders in England and influential persons in Lower Canada explaining what he meant by Responsible Government. He now thought of a local ministry responsible to the Assembly and removable by the governor whenever public confidence was denied it, as manifested by the majority in that House.[4] The anonymous writer in the *Herald* recommended that the Executive Council be transformed into a cabinet consisting of seven heads of departments, who would also sit in one or other of the two houses of the legislature, as in England, "and the *principle thoroughly established* that resignation of office must follow the loss of parliamentary majority."

The *Herald* writer had begun his article with the statement that "the first principle of every constitution" is self-government. He then proceeded to use this axiom to prove that the colonists must have the general right to govern themselves, since they were not represented in the imperial parliament; and that the latter retained only those special powers over the colonies necessary to govern the Empire as a whole, in particular those relating to defence and the regulation of commerce and navigation. Thus the British parliament might pass an act imposing duties for the regulation of commerce, but the revenues derived from such duties belonged to the colonists who paid them, and could be appropriated only by their representatives. In this way the writer gave constitutional justification for the demand in the colonies for complete control of the purse, and showed how Responsible Government meant self-government in internal affairs alone, without separation from the Empire.

Mackenzie gave support to the principle of Responsible Government, although he had already been attracted to the American elective system. In January 1828, during his campaign for nomination to the Assembly from York county, he included in his platform the election of magistrates in township meetings. During the next few months he and the more radical Reformers began to urge that the Legislative

[4] Toronto Public Library, Baldwin Papers, Dr. Baldwin to F. C. Latt, Dec. 27, 1828.

Council be elected, and that township elections be extended to cover higher officials; some even demanded that the governor be elected.[5] Mackenzie's trip to Philadelphia and Washington in June, 1829, which was widely suspected to be subversive in nature, did at least confirm his admiration for the democratic institutions of that country. From this moment he seems to have become convinced that however desirable Responsible Government might be, it was necessary to make the Legislative Council elective, and to extend the same system to all the public offices. However, as he wrote privately, he thought it wise not to publicize these views too suddenly.[6] All pretence was cast aside in January 1832, following his expulsion from the Assembly; and he and many other Reformers came out openly for the elective system. To the supporters of the government it seemed clear they intended "to assimilate our institutions more nearly to those of the United States, and gradually prepare us for becoming an integral part of the Republic. . . ."[7] Already in 1830 a Tory had written: "So they creep upwards from Pound Keeper to Constable, Magistrates, then the Councils, and next the Governors."[8] The deadly disease of democracy was spreading beyond the township, as it had done in the old American colonies.

"The people cry out for an elective council and an elective magistracy", Mackenzie told Lord Howick while in England in 1833. But this was not for the sake of change, he said; only because of the misuse of the Crown's prerogative. Now that it seemed he would be successful in his other objectives Mackenzie stated it would not now be necessary to change the Legislative Council – except its membership.[9] He renewed his demand for elective institutions after his return to Upper Canada in the fall of 1833, when his hopes were disappointed; and he admitted that he had been foolish to waive the question.[10] Events in Lower Canada, where Papineau and his party had made an elective Legislative Council their prime objective, strengthened Mackenzie in his stand. The Assembly of Lower Canada in this year addressed the British government, requesting a national convention to consider the abolition or election of the Council; and an elective Council was stressed above all other demands in the Ninety-two Resolutions adopted by the Assembly in 1834. The same request was made by the Nova Scotia Assembly in 1834.

Egerton Ryerson and the Methodist Conference made their peace with the government in 1833, and were lost to the Reform movement. Several of the leading Reformers, dismayed by Mackenzie's reckless actions, and the strength of the opposition to Reform, temporarily withdrew from politics. Dr. Baldwin and John

[5] *Gore Gazette*, Dec. 20, 1828; Mackenzie to John Neilson, March 23, 1829, in *The Selected Writings of W. L. Mackenzie 1824-1837*, ed. Margaret Fairley (Toronto, 1960), pp. 284-6; *Colonial Advocate*, Apr. 30, 1829.

[6] Referred to by George Ryerson in letter to Mackenzie, July 6, 1831; Ontario, Department of Public Records and Archives, J. B. Robinson Papers, Private Letters, 1813-35.

[7] Kingston *Upper Canada Herald*, Feb. 15, 1832.

[8] Ontario, Department of Public Records and Archives, Macaulay Papers, R. Stanton to J. Macaulay, March 17, 1830.

[9] C.O. 42/417, Mackenzie to Howick, March 20, 1833.

[10] C.O. 42/430, Mackenzie to Hume, Dec., 1835 (clipping from Toronto *Correspondent and Advocate*, n.d.)

Rolph refused to act as delegates to the Metropolitan District Nominating Convention held at Toronto in February, 1834, where an elective Legislative Council and Responsible Government were included in the pledges demanded of the candidates.[11] In December of that year following the victory of the Reformers at the polls, the Canadian Alliance Society was formed at Toronto, with the radical element in control. With its many branches formed throughout the province, the Canadian Alliance marked a further step in the advance of party organization by the Reformers, which had begun in 1827 with the Alien Central Committee and its network of corresponding committees. The Canadian Alliance favoured an elective Legislative Council and Responsible Government, as well as a written constitution and the ballot.[12] The *Seventh Report on Grievances*, issued in the spring of 1835 by the Assembly committee headed by Mackenzie, gave strong support to an elective Council, although Responsible Government was also stressed.

In 1835 the Reformers also succeeded in getting the passage of a new Township Officers Act, which went into effect in January 1836, providing for the election of three commissioners in each District to supersede the justices of the peace in control of the township officers. The more reactionary Tories regarded the Act as republican in nature. It would prove to be, one of them told a friend, "the great schoolmaster to educate our population in the principles and practice of democracy". Mackenzie said he hoped soon to see every township electing by ballot its magistrates and postmaster; and he expressed confidence that the pressure of public opinion would eventually secure them an elective Legislative Council, because Responsible Government alone would not suffice.[13]

With the arrival of Sir Francis Bond Head in January, 1836, the whole emphasis shifted temporarily from an elected Legislative Council to an Executive Council responsible to a majority in the Assembly. The Colonial Secretary had stated, in his instructions to Head, that the old principle of a practical or legal responsibility must be maintained, under which the governor was "most fully responsible for his official acts" to the British government. In carrying out the expressed desire of the Whig ministry to have the Assembly brought into closer harmony with the executive, while the constitution was kept inviolate, Head appointed Robert Baldwin and two other leading Reformers to the Executive Council. However, the councillors resigned in a body when Head insisted that its purpose was only to serve him, and that he did not have to consult it unless he wished to do so. The new lieutenant governor had quickly sensed that the issue of Responsible Government was the deadliest foe of the established system of government. Now, purposely misinterpreting its essential principles, he charged that the Council was demanding that he turn over to it all his power and patronage, which would leave the people defenceless. "For in the confusion between the governor and an oligarchy composed of a few dominant families, shielded by secrecy, would not all tangible responsibility have vanished?" he asked.

[11] *Colonial Advocate*, March 13, 1834.
[12] *Correspondent and Advocate*, Dec. 18, 1834.
[13] *Christian Guardian*, Dec. 9, 1835; *Correspondent and Advocate*, Dec. 3, 1835; Toronto Public Library, William Allan Papers, J. Macaulay to W. Allan, Dec. 12, 1835.

In this way Head adroitly presented himself as the sole protector of the people against the greed and oppression of the hated Family Compact, which had long ruled through the Executive Council. He carefully concealed the fact that under Responsible Government this Council would become a cabinet responsible to the majority of the people's representatives in the Legislative Assembly, and would no longer be the tool of the oligarchy. From this position he never allowed himself to be diverted; and he proudly compared himself to the weasel, which he said always struck at the jugular of the rat and never let go until it was dead. The Assembly, forced to meet the governor on his own terms and take up the defence of Responsible Government, was finally driven for the first time to the drastic resort of withholding the supplies. Seizing his chance, Head countered by refusing to grant the contingencies and reserving all money bills, then blaming the resulting financial and economic troubles on the Assembly. Following the dissolution of parliament, a general election was held in June, with the governor personally appealing to the people to vote for government candidates, on the ground of loyalty and economic advantage. The only issue, Head repeated many times, was whether the people wished to keep their monarchical government, or separate from the Empire and form a republic. The result was a triumph for him and the Tories, and a great defeat for the Reformers. Responsible Government was repudiated along with American democracy and republicanism. Nevertheless, in order to win this victory Head was forced to make use of the democratic processes that he abhorred.

Robert Baldwin had gone to England after resigning from the Executive Council, to present the case for Responsible Government. In Upper Canada the more moderate Reformers had gained the upper hand in the declining Canadian Alliance Society, and at the end of May it was transformed into the "Constitutional Reform Society of Upper Canada", with Dr. Baldwin as president. Its objects included both "responsible advisers" and a reformed Legislative Council, although at first Dr. Baldwin continued to stress the former. However, on September 2 Dr. Baldwin wrote to Robert that he now believed it would be necessary to have a "new modelling" of the Legislative Council, or it would never cooperate with the country.[14] Similar opinions were expressed by the Reformers' friends in England. One of them declared that Responsible Government could never be kept without a radical change in the Legislative Council. "It is your second chamber which gives undue power to your officials," another wrote, "and until it is *radically* cured you will have no good government."[15] On October 10 Dr. Baldwin became president of "The City of Toronto Political Union", which had the same objects as the Constitutional Reform Society of Upper Canada. However, as Dr. Baldwin informed Robert a few days later, the principal objective was the passage of a bill to make the Legislative Council elective. No doubt, he observed, a Responsible Executive Council in its day would have given an opportunity for the Legislative Council "to drop into a mode of proceedings more in harmony with the people – but that disappointed . . . has rendered the claim of an Elective Legislative Council loud and extensive

[14] *Correspondent and Advocate*, June 1, 1836; Toronto Public Library, R. Baldwin Papers, Dr. Baldwin to Robert Baldwin, May 30, July 18, Sept. 2, 1836.
[15] *Constitution*, Nov. 23, 1836; Montreal *Vindicator*, Sept. 27, 1836.

through the Province".[16] In the absence of his son the old Doctor had fallen under the influence of the radicals.

Robert Baldwin never lost faith in Responsible Government as the salvation of his country. Unable to gain an audience with the Colonial Secretary, he was forced to put his arguments into a letter, which was dated July 13, 1836.[17] Responsible Government, he wrote, was "nothing more than having the Provincial Government, as far as regards the internal affairs of the Province, conducted by the Lieutenant Governor (as Representative of the paramount authority of the Mother Country), with the advice and assistance of the Executive Council acting as a Provincial Cabinet, and composed of men possessed of the public's confidence, whose opinions and policy would be in harmony with the opinions and policy of the Representatives of the people." The appointment of the provincial cabinet, he explained, and its continuance in office, would be dependent upon the support of the majority in the Legislative Assembly; and the members of the cabinet would also sit in one or other of the two houses of parliament. Such a system followed the practice in Britain and did not require any departure from the constitution.

With the same reasoning Robert Baldwin rejected the arguments of those who would either abolish the Legislative Council or make it elective. He believed the institutions of the colonies should correspond as nearly as possible to those of the mother country. While admitting that most of the Reformers of Upper Canada thought it would be ultimately necessary to make the Council elective, he expressed the belief that they would be willing to set it aside until the constitution had been fully tested by British principles. He himself was convinced that the establishment of an elected Legislative Council, which would represent the people and no longer be subservient to the executive, could never supersede the necessity for Responsible Government. On the other hand, the denial of the latter would drive the people to seek a much greater extension of the elective principle, even to the governor and the Executive Council. Then American democracy might be joined with republicanism at the expense of the British connection.

These arguments failed to convince the British government that Responsible Government was necessary, or even compatible with the status of a colony. Russell's Ten Resolutions, passed by the House of Commons in March, 1837, gave the final blow to the hopes of the Canadian Reformers; there was to be a continuation of the repressive course in Lower Canada, and of the old system of legal or practical responsibility. From this moment, the last of the moderate Reform leaders withdrew from politics to await better days. Only Mackenzie and a hard core of extreme radicals were left, to seek by force of arms what seemed impossible to attain by peaceful means within the Empire. Long predisposed to the elective system and American democracy in general, the radicals now felt obliged to embrace republicanism as well. But the great majority of the inhabitants of Upper Canada held true to the Loyalist tradition. With their help the insurrections in the two provinces

[16] Toronto Public Library, R. Baldwin Papers, Dr. Baldwin to R. Baldwin, Oct. 15, 1836. See also, regarding the two societies he headed, Dr. Baldwin's evidence of Dec. 7, 1836, before the committee of Assembly on Duncombe's charges, in C.O. 42/440.

[17] C.O. 42/434.

were quickly crushed, and the "Patriot" invasions repelled; and with them died the hopes of those who had turned to the American experiment for inspiration.

Responsible Government, although denied, was left as the only feasible goal of the Reformers who survived the debacle. Because it was a part of the British constitution it could be worked for by loyal subjects who desired democracy in government without republicanism; and self-government for the colonies within the Empire. When others faltered, Robert Baldwin held to his conviction that Responsible Government was the fundamental remedy for colonial ills; and that instead of separation it would serve to strengthen the ties of loyalty and affection with the mother country. When the rebellions roused the British government to the seriousness of the situation in the Canadas, and the liberal Lord Durham was sent out to investigate, it was Robert Baldwin's arguments that induced Durham to recommend Responsible Government with local control of internal affairs. Another decade passed before this recommendation was acted upon; but when it was, Robert Baldwin joined with L. H. LaFontaine in the united province of Canada to form the first ministry based on the principles he had so long worked for. In Upper Canada the principles of constitutional reform, in the British tradition, had won an enduring victory over the forces of reaction, and the forces of extreme radicalism. In the years to come American influences continued to flood over Canada, but the Reform tradition that had been worked out in Upper Canada helped to preserve the country's British character.

BIBLIOGRAPHICAL NOTE

The present study has been written to a large extent from contemporary newspapers and manuscripts. Among the latter, the Baldwin Papers in the Toronto Public Library, and the microfilms of the Colonial Office Papers in the Public Archives of Canada were of particular value. The basic published work on the Reform movement in Upper Canada is Aileen Dunham, *Political Unrest in Upper Canada, 1815-1836* (London, 1927; Toronto, 1963). Of the numerous other books, articles, or published collections of documents, the following more recent works may be given special mention:

Clark, S. D., *Movements of Political Protest in Canada, 1640-1840* (Toronto, 1959).

Craig, Gerald M., "The American Impact on the Upper Canadian Reform Movement before 1837," *Canadian Historical Review*, XXIX (1948), pp. 333-52.

———, *Upper Canada; The Formative Years, 1784-1841* (Toronto, 1963).

Mackenzie, W. L., *The Selected Writings . . . 1824-1837*, ed. Margaret Fairley (Toronto, 1960).

New, Chester W., "The Rebellion of 1837 in Its Larger Setting," Canadian Historical Association, *Report*, 1937 (Toronto, 1937), pp. 5-17.

Wilson, G. E., *The Life of Robert Baldwin* (Toronto, 1933).

An extensive bibliography of Upper Canada will be found in Gerald M. Craig's *Upper Canada.*

Upper Canada and the Conservative Tradition

S. F. Wise

Two streams of conservatism met and blended in the two generations of Upper Canadian history before the Union. One was that brought by the Loyalist founders of the colony: an emotional compound of loyalty to King and Empire, antagonism to the United States, and an acute, if partisan sense of recent history. To the conservatism of the émigré was joined another, more sophisticated viewpoint, first brought by Simcoe and his entourage, and crystallized in the Constitutional Act of 1791: the Toryism of late eighteenth century England. What Upper Canada received from this source was not merely the somewhat creaking intellectual edifice of Blackstone and Warburton, but a conservatism freshly minted into a fighting creed through Edmund Burke's philippics against the French Revolution. The joining of two intensely counter-revolutionary outlooks in a colony as peculiarly situated as was Upper Canada had powerful consequences for the Canadian conservative tradition.

It is not, of course, usual to think of Upper Canadian Toryism in relation to the Canadian conservative tradition. Its contribution has not been freely acknowledged by later Conservatives, and probably not even dimly apprehended by them. There are good reasons for this state of affairs. For one thing, John A. Macdonald dominates the history of Canadian conservatism. His long career, his creative association with great acts of nation-building, his extraordinary attractiveness and complexity as an individual, and the very brilliance and persuasiveness of his biographer, have made it difficult for us to see beyond him to the society that produced him, and that shaped his approach to politics. Secondly, the evil repute in which Compact Toryism is held has made it difficult for Conservatives, from the day of Macdonald onwards, to own that anything in their tradition could conceivably derive from a period prior to his coming. Thus the Conservative party dates its origin from the coalition of 1854, which is normally depicted as a grand rejection of the past by essentially forward-looking men, who turned to building modern conservatism from the foundations up. This is a harmless myth, and like other ancient monuments should doubtless be treated with reverent care. Since it is highly improbable, however, that anything said here will have the slighest destructive effect upon it, we propose to examine briefly some of the contributions made by Upper Canadian Toryism to the conservative tradition in Canada.

In doing so, it is necessary to acknowledge at once that much of that contribution was negative; that is, that the example set by the Family Compact in its exclusiveness, inefficiency, arbitrariness and occasional corruption had a salutary effect upon generations to come. High Toryism fell, once for all, with the system of government that had nurtured it; but its sins were recapitulated ad nauseam by succeeding generations of reform politicians. Thanks to their labours, and to those chroniclers and historians of Whiggish bent, it seems unlikely that the failings of the Compact will ever be forgotten; on this side of the ledger, at least, the historical record is complete. Nor is there any good reason why the record should be forgotten. Upper Canada's fifty years of oligarchic rule remain standing testimony to the weaknesses and dangers of government by an authoritarian and paternalistic élite.

But historians have a peculiar duty towards losers, not out of mere perversity, but because much is to be learned from them. This is the case with the conservatives of Upper Canada. Our reform tradition has telescoped the complexities of early conservatism into High Toryism, and has turned the phrase "Family Compact" into a term of political science, when it was nothing but a political epithet. The habit of viewing the first fifty years of Ontario's history as a political false start has obscured the essential continuity of Upper Canadian with subsequent provincial history, and has fostered the tendency to attach fundamental importance to the Rebellion and the Union as rejections of the colonial past, when they ought more accurately to be described as events which eliminated certain alternative lines of development, reform as well as conservative, implicit in the early circumstances of the colony. Beneath the polemics and violence which accompanied these events, beneath the clash of such personalities as Gourlay, Strachan, Mackenzie and Bond Head, beneath the struggles over constitutional change or clergy reserves, a provincial community was being born, and by 1841 it had taken on characteristics both distinctive and permanent.

In the building of the new Ontario society, conservative forces had been powerfully at work, and nowhere more so than in the sphere of politics. During Upper Canada's existence as a separate province, thirteen general elections were held, as well as a large number of by-elections. Although these elections have yet to be carefully analyzed, it is clear that their prime effect was to organize the population into its basic conservative and reform patterns. Since party, in the modern institutional sense, did not exist, political affiliations were quite fluid, and a sizeable body of electors shifted allegiance from election to election. Yet long before the Union, conservative and reform strongholds had emerged; areas from which the later Conservative and Liberal parties were to draw strength to the present day. The core of Tory support was in the eastern counties, the area of major Loyalist settlement, and in the towns, especially Kingston, Brockville, York-Toronto, Niagara and London. There was no significant variation from this pattern in the later Union period; indeed, there is a continuity between the electoral behaviour of colonial Upper Canada and the political geography of twentieth-century Ontario.

Conservative members were returned to the Assembly from ridings other than the eastern counties and the towns, but not quite so consistently. In the 1830's, the Tory cause was further strengthened by the addition of members from "frontier" constituencies, peopled by the recent flood of immigration from Britain. All this is to say that the political situation in Upper Canada was not invariably, or even normally, one in which a reform majority in the Assembly found its legislative programme blocked by the solidly Tory upper house. In the first few assemblies, political dissent was of little significance. A number of oppositionists were elected to the Fifth Assembly in 1808, and the habitual end-of-session absenteeism of the eastern county members seems occasionally to have given the opposition a temporary majority. There was no real unity of purpose among such men as Joseph Willcocks, Samuel Sherwood and David McGregor Rogers, however, and these early stirrings disappeared with the wartime election of 1812. From 1812 to 1824, the provincial house was once more dominated by conservative-minded members. By no means did this guarantee to the executive government an acquiescent and docile Assembly. Both the American Loyalist and English Blackstonian traditions emphasized the separate and distinctive functions of the popular assembly in the constitution. Conservative Assemblies, especially when led by men as able and articulate as Robert Nichol, were quite capable of kicking over the traces, as the 1816 Assembly did, for example, on the issue of land and immigration policy.

It might be argued that the conservatism of the early Assemblies reflected an electorate not yet awakened to its grievances, and content to elect men who could benefit the locality through their connections with government. The real beginnings of reform strength in the Assembly date from the election of 1820, and unquestionably some of the Reformers then elected owed their success to the agitation of Robert Gourlay. Yet it would be incorrect to say that as reform sentiment became province-wide, conservatism as a force in the Assembly melted away. In the five elections from 1824 to 1836, there were two reform and two conservative victories, while another resulted in a virtual stalemate. The house elected in 1824 was very evenly divided, although on some issues the government could still find a majority. The mishandling of the alien question by the provincial executive had much to do with the reform sweep of 1828, yet in 1830 the conservatives were back in the saddle again, though by a relatively narrow margin. The 1834 Assembly was reform, but there was a substantial conservative opposition. The Thirteenth Assembly elected in 1836 was decisively conservative in composition. In sum, these elections demonstrate that conservatism met the democratic test of the hustings in Upper Canada, and that even after the rise of reform, men of conservative outlook had at least one chance in two of forming a majority in the Assembly. Long before the day of Macdonald, thousands of provincial voters had become habituated to voting on the Tory side, and a substantial voting base for the future Conservative party had been firmly established by 1841.

It must not be imagined that the Tories elected to the later Assemblies were a solid phalanx at one with themselves and with the ruling élite. They were no more united than were the reformers. Relatively few conservative assemblymen were prepared to go down the line with the "pure" Tories of the Councils on every issue. This is not to say that High Tories were not elected. John Beverley Robinson and Christopher Hagerman were repeatedly returned, despite their close association with official policy, and virtually every Assembly contained a few Tories who followed their lead. Most conservatives, however, were unwilling to follow Hagerman when he championed the views of Dr. Strachan on such matters as the clergy reserves, the right to conduct the marriage ceremony, or the maintenance of the principle of primogeniture in cases of intestacy. Not even Hagerman would submit to official policies that conflicted sharply with the local interests he represented. Conservatives were frequently divided on banking legislation, the scale of appropriations for local services, proposals to tax unimproved lands in private hands, and hardy perennials such as the claims for war losses during the war of 1812; on these and other occasions, Tory assemblymen were at odds with the position taken by the official class. Members like Charles and Jonas Jones of Leeds and Brockville, William Morris of Perth, and Allan MacNab of Wentworth, all of whom have been identified with the Compact, took independent stands in the Assembly. On the whole, the brand of Toryism represented in the lower house was more moderate than that found in the councils; undoubtedly the need to get elected, and then to keep one's seat, helped to dilute High Tory principles. The lack of a constitutional connection between the Assembly and the other branches of government also encouraged independent behaviour in assemblymen, much as in the American congressional system, and allowed Tory candidates to distinguish themselves somewhat from government, although their reform opponents did what they could to obliterate this distinction in the minds of the electorate.

Undoubtedly the system of government under the Constitutional Act had something to do with swelling the ranks of conservatives in the assembly. Some moderate conservatives would have been quite as comfortable with the Baldwin reformers, had their business interests not induced them to retain official favour by maintaining some degree of orthodoxy on divisions. The permanence of officialdom, and the squeezing out of the moderate reform option in the 1830's, kept several men on the government side in politics. Perhaps the most prominent of these "business conservatives" was William Hamilton Merritt. Without the support of the provincial government, and of such figures in it as J. B. Robinson and John Strachan, Merritt's great undertaking, the Welland Canal, would have been impossible, and he trimmed his sails accordingly. Or was it his conversion to liberalism at the Union that is open to suspicion? In an intriguing correspondence with Robert Baldwin in 1840-41, Merritt admitted that he had never understood the principle of Responsible Government until he read Durham's Report, "but now that I see and feel the necessity of that measure being fully carried out in this province, no person can be more firmly devoted to aid in its accomplishment." He was aware of his reputation for "inconsistency in advocating Lord Durham's Report & not having supported the Reform Party heretofore"; interestingly enough, he denied this charge on the grounds of his past independent performance in the legislature on such issues as the dismissal of Hagerman and Boulton, in which he had joined his fellow

Tories in denouncing the interference of the imperial authorities! While it is quite possible that Merritt was a genuine convert, it is remarkable how nicely his conversion coincided with new directions in politics. To him, Responsible Government signified "the improvement of the St. Lawrence, a better and more abundant circulating medium, and unrestricted Emigration or at least on as liberal a footing as before the War of 1812": business objectives all, and much in keeping with the new Sydenham approach.

The thousands of recent immigrants from the British Isles who cast their first votes in the elections of the 1830's must have included many men of moderately liberal politics who, like Merritt, were forced by colonial realities to support Tory candidates. At an earlier time, the elector often could choose among five, six or even more competitors, but such smorgasbord politics diminished sharply after 1828. In many constituencies, the recent immigrant of Whiggish background found he had to choose between a Tory and a Mackenzie radical. "I feel myself fast growing a Tory", said John Langton, and many another must have made a similar choice.

If Upper Canada conservatism lacked uniformity and homogeneity, this is only another way of saying that it was an alliance of various groups, with different interests and outlooks. It is possible to express the nature of the alliance in several ways. A Tory of the time would certainly have said that conservative leadership came from the "respectable classes" in the community. In this sense, Toryism was the political expression of the province's small upper class, the people who considered themselves the natural leaders of society. For members of the professions, attachment to government conferred status and more tangible benefits. It is true that many reform leaders came from the legal and medical professions: John Rolph and William Warren Baldwin were members of both, while Dr. T. D. Morrison and the lawyers Robert Baldwin and Marshall Spring Bidwell testify to the lack of a Tory monopoly in this sphere. Yet most members of both professions seem to have been conservative. As for the military profession, its bias was instinctively conservative; among the hundreds of army and navy officers resident in Upper Canada on half-pay, a reform politician like Captain Matthews was very much a rare bird. Similarly, most landowners who thought of themselves as gentry, not farmers, were conservatives in politics. Yet, though the Tories were indisputably the representatives of the classes, to the dismay and mystification of reformers they were also able to win the support of many artisans and farmers, a phenomenon by no means confined to this period.

Merchants and other men of business were a special case. By and large, it was advantageous for them to be on the right side of government; as creditors, both their interests and their inclinations pushed them in that direction. Moreover, although the upper echelons of Toryism were almost exclusively bureaucratic in character, the official class proved reasonably responsive to the interests of the provincial mercantile community, and to the larger needs of St. Lawrence commercialism. Although there were exceptions, most substantial merchants, ship-owners and lumbering operators were Tory adherents, while many smaller tradesmen and shopkeepers tended the other way.

Early Toryism is usually associated with Anglicanism, and with the exclusive pretensions of the Church of England to the clergy reserves and to control over public education. This is not altogether an inaccurate impression, but it is a misleading one; obviously the Tories could not have achieved any measure of electoral success had they depended upon the votes of Anglicans alone. The situation has perhaps not been recognized in all its complexities. On the one hand, it is certainly true that for many years John Strachan spoke both for his church and for the executive government of the province upon religious policy, and that from first to last he never yielded an inch in his claims for the exclusive rights of the Anglican Church. Yet Strachan did not speak for all conservatives, probably not for a majority of Anglican laymen, and certainly not for the Tory politicians whose first concerns were to win elections and to keep their local supporters satisfied. Whatever the merits of Strachan's cause, from the political point of view his pronouncements were inept, and disastrously weakened the conservative alliance at some crucial stages in its history.

For an alliance, however precarious, did exist among Anglicans, members of the Church of Scotland and Catholics. There was not a great deal of difference, except in national origin, between well-to-do Anglicans and Presbyterians, and they met and mingled easily in society and business. All three denominations were united in their distrust of Protestant dissent, particularly that emanating from the United States. The clergy of all three churches were instinctively social and political conservatives; all believed that churches had a public role to play; and all accepted the principle that churches should support order and government through the promotion of public and private morality and the inculcation of ideas of subordination and of veneration for authority. Neither Presbyterians nor Catholics (with a few notable exceptions) objected to the principle of public endowment of churches, or to church control over public education. What they found objectionable was Strachan's insistence upon the exclusive jurisdiction of the Church of England in those spheres, and the style he chose to adopt in urging his case.

Nevertheless, an alliance, however fragile, was maintained politically among the members of the three churches, and was manifested in a variety of ways. Through the provincial government, the clergy of the Catholic Church and of the Church of Scotland were accorded a status not extended to the clergy of the sects. Grants of Crown land for churches, and small grants of public money for the support of clergy and schoolmasters, were made to both churches from an early date. Bishop Alexander Macdonell was made a legislative councillor; so were a number of Catholic and Presbyterian laymen. In the Assembly, spokesmen of the three denominations combined to defend their common viewpoint on such matters as the right to perform marriages, or to denounce the radical proposal to secularize the reserves and devote the proceeds to a system of secular education. It was only at the critical election of 1836 that the Tories opened their ranks to admit Ogle Gowan and his Orangemen to a full political partnership; prior to that time the Orangemen had been regarded with deep distrust, not only by the Catholics, but by non-Catholic Tories as well, precisely because of the danger they posed to the religious foundations of the conservative coalition. Bishop Macdonell's address to the Catholic and Protestant freeholders of Stormont and Glengarry in 1836, advising them to vote the conservative ticket, was remarkable testimony of the religious base of Toryism.[1]

Upper Canadian Toryism was an alliance, or rather a system of alliances, between the bureaucratic élite attached to the government of the province, and local élites and their followings. Although the alliance was held together in part by natural affinities arising from common social, economic and institutional outlooks, its chief bond was political. Only in the central arena of politics did the interests of all the groups that made it up intersect, and only through the political process could tangible satisfaction for these interests be forthcoming. In other words, in order to meet the needs of the conservative coalition, something very like the modern political party was required, and something very like it was created. Under the shelter of the 1791 constitution, the Tories constructed the first province-wide political organization in Upper Canada. While it might be technically incorrect to employ the term "party" to describe a system that lacked the modern party's distinctive trappings, yet in the crucial test of function there was a provincial Tory party long before the reformers had begun to organize themselves. The constitution of Upper Canada was doubled – outwardly, it was the usual formal structure of the British colonial establishment; inwardly, the apparatus of government was virtually identical with the apparatus of party. There was no need for the Tories to band together in any permanent fashion, as reformers began to do under the leadership of W. W. Baldwin, William Lyon Mackenzie and Jesse Ketchum in the late 1820's. Little wonder that reformers writhed at Tory hypocrisy when their party organizations were denounced as "factions". So long as the constitution remained unreformed, conservatives had no need for political associations outside it.

The building of the Tory party into the constitution can best be traced briefly in the history of the distribution of Crown patronage in Upper Canada, since the handling of patronage illustrates clearly the dynamics of the system. During Simcoe's tenure, the dispensing of patronage remained in the hands of the lieutenant governor, though even Simcoe distributed jobs and other favours partly on the advice he got from his principal officers of government. He used patronage for the explicit purpose of cementing to government the loyalties of the most "respectable" members of society, whose principles through emulation would then be broadcast throughout their localities. Though Simcoe's political objective was never departed from, inevitably it became intermingled with motives of private advantage as population grew and as the process of selection became more complicated. Continuity in government patronage policy came to rest with the officials, whose tenure was permanent in fact if not in law, even though successive lieutenant governors exerted ultimate con-

[1] This analysis of the religious base of Toryism deals with its leading elements. There was, of course, scattered support from members of other denominations, and a notable, although temporary accession of strength from Methodism following Egerton Ryerson's dramatic break with reform in 1833.

trol, and sometimes intervened directly in the process. Those officials of government who enjoyed the particular confidence of the lieutenant governor used their favourable position to benefit their friends in various parts of the province. As a result, a simple clientage or "interest" system took shape, and by the time of the war of 1812 it was so well-established that it was impossible for a young man to make his way up the ladder of preferment without the necessary connections.

The inner political history of Upper Canada is largely the history of warring interests, and of their rise and fall. Peter Russell's interest was paramount for the first decade of provincial history, and through him the fortunes of families like the Baldwins and the Willcockses were advanced. Russell's influence waned after the turn of the century, and at his death in 1808, since the politics of patronage were personal, the Russell interest collapsed, and with it the hopes and prospects of his clientage. The ascendancy of Judge William Dummer Powell dates from shortly after the arrival of Lt. Gov. Francis Gore. Through Powell's help, usually obtained through such local intermediaries as Richard Cartwright of Kingston or Dr. Solomon Jones of Augusta, a large number of people received places or other benefits from government. Dr. John Strachan and his protégé, John Beverley Robinson, were both in Powell's debt at early stages in their careers – something of an irony, since they combined to ease the Chief Justice out of his place at the centre of power and of the web of patronage shortly after Sir Peregrine Maitland took over.

As the clientage system ramified, as indeed it was bound to do, since every prominent official at York had at least some jobs or perquisites in his gift, it hardened into a complex network joining officials at the capital to interest groups in every locality, in a bewildering maze of inter-relationships. As early as the 1820's, and probably well before then, each community had a local oligarchy – in effect, a party machine – through which the provincial government dispensed its favours. In Kingston, for example, a group headed by John Kirby, John Macaulay and Thomas and George Markland advised the York officials on questions of patronage, and submitted nominations for justices of the peace, local court officials, commissions and promotions in the local militia, the issuance of licences, or the allocation of government contracts of one kind or another. In Leeds and Grenville, the Joneses and Sherwoods performed the same functions; everywhere, in fact, across the province a voluminous political correspondence was maintained between the central bureaucracy and local Tory personages, from district chieftains like Allan MacNab of Wentworth and Mahlon Burwell of the London district down to party wheelhorses like Thomas Mears of Peterborough and George Hamilton of Hawkesbury.

The Tory "party", then, was a quasi-official coalition of the central and local élites united for the purpose of distributing honours and rewards to the politically deserving. The system was certainly effective in building, maintaining and disciplining a conservative coalition for electoral purposes, although that was by no means its only function. On the whole, it worked fairly smoothly, despite the inevitable faction fights among local groupings over division of the spoils, and tussles among higher officials over jurisdiction and influence. Its operations strengthened the social, economic, religious and ideological bases of the conservative alliance in the most tangible way. Thus, in the Perth area, the Presbyterian William Morris was given a leading voice in the allotment of jobs; in the eastern counties Bishop Macdonell had for many years a free hand in dispensing patronage among the Catholic population; while in Kingston, Christopher Hagerman took care to see that his Presbyterian and Catholic constituents got their share of plums. Some of the most intricate balancing of competing group claims was done whenever new writs for the commissions of the peace were issued. Nominations for justices of the peace went up to York from the localities, and then were sifted by the law officers of the Crown before the new commissions went out. It is worth noting that John Beverley Robinson, among others, was quite prepared occasionally to accept the appointment of known reformers as J. P.s, usually when there was a shortage of competent Tory candidates.

But because the patronage system hinged upon personal relationships, and had little to do ordinarily with forms of merit other than the political, its operations led inevitably to abuses that in the long run hurt the Tory cause. Too frequently men of real ability were passed over, and became permanently embittered. Robert Nichol, William Warren Baldwin, and an assortment of Ridouts, Jarvises and Smalls were given jobs of a demeaning kind, either in terms of their competence, or in terms of their personal measurements of their merit; such incidents had something to do with the making of a few reformers. In the 1830's, hundreds of able new Upper Canadians found that the official avenues of preferment were closed to them; the system had hardened too much, had become too exclusive and too inflexible to make room for enough of them. Pluralism, the cosy practice of passing offices down from father to son, and the maintenance in office of incompetent or unreliable men were abuses of the second generation of Upper Canadian Toryism that provided weapons for reformers, and sharpened their desire to turn the rascals out, and to get rid of a form of government that could foster such a system.

Political patronage was hardly the invention of the Upper Canadian conservatives. Yet their use of it to build up a coalition was the central fact of provincial politics, and established a political climate that profoundly affected reformers as well. It is true that the reforms of the 1840's and 1850's did much to regularize public administration, and to rid the structure of local government of many of its more spectacular abuses. But it was no accident that the reform-inspired conciliar crises of 1836 and 1843-4 centred upon control of Crown patronage, even though, on each occasion, the issue was masked in the lofty principles of Responsible Government. Nor is it an accident, as students of the Baldwin papers know, that well over half the surviving Baldwin correspondence is devoted to questions of patronage. The Tories pioneered in the use of patronage to build party; the reformers, despite their rhetoric, learned the lesson well, and played the same game as intensely, and perhaps more skilfully, than had their conservative teachers.

The Upper Canadian Tories contributed to subsequent politics on quite other planes than patronage. In the field of public policy, their major legacy was the Welland Canal, and to a lesser degree the St. Lawrence canal system. The Welland was a collaboration between the energy and enthusiasm of private projectors like William Hamilton Merritt, and the readiness of conservatives, official and otherwise, to pledge the co-operation of government in an enterprise of great provincial importance. Both elements were indispensable to the completion of this remarkable project, which in the end became a government-owned facility.

The Tories, in entering into collaboration with private initiative in the development of the Welland and other canals, were responding to a general desire for public improvements, and in particular to the threat posed by the building of the Erie Canal, which, if not countered, would drain off the commerce of the province to the south and New York. It is important to emphasize, however, that conservative canal policy was not just a response to public pressure. In the lengths to which they were prepared to go in mortgaging the public credit, the Tories far outran the views of a large section of provincial opinion. At first, the reformers had been quite as enthusiastic as conservative assemblymen in their support for the Welland, but as the real difficulties of its construction and financing unfolded, they became more and more hostile towards it, and more and more suspicious of the ties between it and government.

Some Tory Assembly members did oppose the Welland Canal, usually as a result of the same regional considerations that influenced reformers from the eastern part of the province. Many easterners could not accept the argument that the Welland, as an integral part of the whole St. Lawrence system, would benefit the whole province and not just the merchants and farmers of the west. On the whole, however, most opposition came from reformers, from whatever region. Some of them, like William Lyon Mackenzie, were convinced that the canal was a great engine of Tory corruption and patronage, although an Assembly investigation under Mackenzie's chairmanship disclosed nothing but inefficiency. Most reformers thought that Upper Canada was too small for such an immense undertaking. "This great overgrown concern", said Marshall Spring Bidwell in the Assembly debates of January, 1834, was "consuming the life's blood of this young province." "Is all to be subservient to this great Moloch?", Peter Perry asked; it should be left to rot, in his opinion, as "a monument of the folly of the Legislature of Upper Canada." By and large, reformers took a democratic view of their relationship to their constituents, and as mouthpieces for local electorates tended to be more parochial in outlook than most conservatives. Consequently, public improvements for them meant chiefly roads and bridges for their own constituencies. Conservative members were more responsive to the commercial interests that formed so important a part of their political support, and while quite ready to play the politics of roads and bridges, were more open to the appeal of enterprises that were provincial in scope.

Here they were following the lead given them by the official Tory élite. The list of substantial provincial subscribers to Welland stock under the charter of 1825 was dominated by the names of men in the inner circle of power: J. B. Robinson, William Allan, J. H. Dunn, H. J. Boulton, D'Arcy Boulton, and Col. Joseph Wells. Repeatedly, during the ensuing years, it was the influence of these men, and others like Strachan, Hagerman, MacNab and John Macaulay, that rescued the Canal from final disaster. Vested as they were with responsibility for the whole province, largely unconnected with popular politics and thus relieved of the inconvenient necessity of assuaging the doubts of a local electorate, acutely conscious of the military, economic and political menace of the United States, the Tory élite backed the Welland Canal to the hilt as a measure vital to the security as well as the prosperity of all. Robinson termed the prospect of private gain from the Welland "quite a secondary consideration"; it was well he did, for none was made. "The grand object", he said, "was to overcome a great natural impediment to the prosperity of the better half of our country." There was nothing doctrinaire in the readiness of conservatives to use public credit to supplement, and eventually to replace private capital; in a country so short of fluid capital as Upper Canada, in the face of so urgent a public necessity, government had to step in. When the legislative commissioners, John Macaulay, W. B. Robinson and Absolom Shade, found that the Welland Canal Company was no longer equal to maintaining the canal, they recommended public ownership without a tremor, so that "the Canal should be thus rendered in name, as it always has been in fact, and must be in effect, a *national concern.*" Despite their inefficiencies and miscalculations, there was an undeniable statesmanship in the pragmatic conservative acceptance of the positive role that government must play in order to counteract the vulnerabilities of the Canadian economy and polity. The example they set was to be followed by the next generation of canal builders, and by the Conservative party in the years to come, whether the object involved was one of national importance, as with the Intercolonial and Canadian Pacific railways, or of provincial concern, as with Ontario Hydro. In this realm of public policy, both Macdonald and Whitney were legatees of the Upper Canadian conservatives.

When the Tories used the term "national" to describe projects like the Welland and St. Lawrence canals, they meant only that they were natural monopolies, affecting so vitally the common weal that they were, or should be, removed from the sphere of private relationships. In all other senses, "national" still meant "British" or "imperial", since the conservative still regarded himself as a member of the British nation. Yet the seeds of a separate nationalism were implicit in the Upper Canadian Tory's approach to the economic problems involved in public improvements, trade, and banking, for though he might justify a particular policy on grounds of imperial interests, it was the provincial stake he had chiefly in view. Joined to the concern for local interests was a deeply defensive cast of mind. To most Tories, though perhaps not to the aggressive and optimistic merchants, a canal like the Welland was a protective device, to be visualised in political, social and cultural contexts as well as in the economic.

It is at this point that the conservative economic policy intersected with the total structure of conservative values; values which have had an influence far beyond the bounds of party, and which indeed lie at the roots of Canadian national feeling. Conservatism is concerned with the preservation of arrangements deemed good. The more highly such arrangements are prized, the more strongly the conservative will react under challenge to them. Upper Canada, in conservative eyes, was not merely challenged, but was under a state of permanent siege; hence the conservative mind in Upper Canada was a mind beleaguered. While conservatism flourished in all the provinces of British North America, only in Upper Canada was it professed with such passionate conviction, because Upper Canada was vulnerable in ways which the other provinces were not. The apprehended threat from the large American-born element in the population, and the quite genuine danger, military, political and cultural, from the United States, made "loyalty" the crux of conservative attitudes. Loyalty did not simply mean adherence to the Crown and the Empire, although it started there. It meant as well adherence to those beliefs and institutions the conservative considered essential in the preservation of a form of life different from, and superior to, the manners, politics and social arrangements of the United States. To the Tory, American democratic republicanism was the worst possible form of government, since it tempted politicians to play upon the worst appetites of men. The Tory was ignorant of such subtleties in the American constitution as the system of checks and balances, or if he was not, considered that their effect was rather to weaken executive government than to check the turbulence inherent in democracy. The deistic founding fathers, in their rejection of the connection between religion and the state, had sacrificed the most effective brake upon public disorder, and paved the way for anarchy. While it was true that men created the institutions under which they chose to live, the conservative believed quite as strongly that institutions made men and made nationality. The American, shaped by his secularized and revolutionary democracy, was a being altogether different from the British American; and his society was moving along another road. The shape of things to come was to be seen in the cities of the United States: swollen by non-British immigration, torn by crime and violence, and governed by corrupt machines kept in power by demagogic appeals to mass envy and greed. How preferable it was to live under the stable, orderly and peaceful government of Upper Canada, with institutions that encouraged both private and public morality, and that cherished true liberty, personal independence and a decent respectability.

Loyalty, then, meant much more than political allegiance. It signified acceptance of the special character of life in Upper Canada. Any attack upon the beliefs and institutions that guaranteed that life was an attack upon the order of things that made the Canadian different from the American, and hence the Upper Canadian conservative reacted with peculiar vehemence against reformers, particularly those who were "soft" on the American question. The relation of these attitudes to the fostering of an intense local patriotism, or, as S. R. Mealing has put it (having in mind the Union period), a spirit of Ontario sectionalism which "survived the Compact's disintegration", is fairly clear. What has not been apprehended so clearly is the extent to which early conservatism was assimilated into the dominant attitudes of nineteenth century Canadian society, and how significant a part of present day patterns of thought derives from colonial Toryism. For this transformation to come about, the focus of loyalty had to be shifted from Britain to British North America. As has been suggested, that process was well under way before 1841. (It is remarkable, incidentally, how conscious such Upper Canadian High Tories as J. B. Robinson, William Macaulay, H. J. Boulton, George Markland and Christopher Hagerman became of their separate identities as Canadians when, at various times, they visited the centre of Empire, and discovered with a sudden shock how greatly Britain differed from their picture of it.) It was necessary, too, for the concept of loyalty to be broadened to embrace the party system and the idea of responsible opposition. That was to be the work of the next generation.

In certain ways, Upper Canadian conservatism was a major formative influence upon the nature of the reform tradition in the province. This was so not only in the sense that the failings of Toryism provided reformers with a platform and with a catalogue of grievances, but also, and quite as significantly, because the long conservative dominance, and the effect this had upon Upper Canadian habits of mind and political behaviour, eliminated radicalism as a major political alternative. The mainstream of reform is represented by Robert Baldwin and George Brown, not by Robert Gourlay, William Lyon Mackenzie and "Coon" Cameron; by a mingling of moderate political reformism and social and economic orthodoxy, not by across-the-board democratic radicalism; and by the observance of the proprieties in political discourse, rather than by the unfettered approach of the radical school. In all this, the reformers were adapting themselves to an environment largely created by early conservatism.

When, in the 1850's, a common political culture emerged in the Canadas, and the major parties, despite their surface antagonisms, came to be in agreement upon the fundamental assumptions without which a viable polity could not have existed, the foundations for a Canadian national feeling were laid. In the new synthesis, though both liberal and conservative traditions were considerably modified, it was the values of conservatism that gave coherence to the whole. In this context, it was Macdonald's function to extend the values he had inherited from the Toryism of old Ontario to the rest of the country, in company with those thousands of Upper Canadians who took part in the peopling of the West.

BIBLIOGRAPHICAL NOTE

This essay is largely based upon conclusions drawn from a variety of manuscript sources. Patronage questions, for example, are dealt with in such bodies of personal correspondence as the Powell and Baldwin Papers in the Toronto Public Library, the Strachan, Robinson, Jones and Macaulay Papers in the Ontario Department of Public Records and Archives, and, above all, in the Upper Canada Sundries in the Public Archives of Canada. Most writing on Upper Canadian politics is concerned with the reform side. Gerald M. Craig's *Upper Canada; The Formative Years, 1784-1841* (Toronto, 1963) contains the most balanced treatment of early conservatism yet published. Robert Saunders' paper, "What Was the Family Compact?" *Ontario History*, XLIX (1957), pp. 165-78, broke new ground, as did H. G. J. Aitken's stimulating study, *The Welland Canal Company: A Study in Canadian Enterprise* (Cambridge, Mass., 1954). The formation of local élites can be traced in E. G. Firth, ed., *The Town of York* (2 vols., Toronto, 1962-6) and R. A. Preston, *Kingston before the War of 1812* (Toronto, 1959); also in F. H. Armstrong, "The Carfrae Family, A Study in Early Toronto Toryism," *Ontario History*, LIV (1962), pp. 161-81. Preliminary studies of local elections include H. V. Nelles, "Loyalism and Local Power: The District of Niagara, 1792-1837," *Ontario History*, LVIII (1966), pp. 99-114 and S. F. Wise, "Tory Factionalism: Kingston Elections and Upper Canadian Politics, 1820-1836," *Ontario History*, LVII (1965), pp. 205-25. Aspects of Upper Canadian conservative values are dealt with in S. F. Wise and R. C. Brown, *Canada Views the United States: 19th Century Political Attitudes* (Seattle, 1967), especially chapters 2 and 3; and in S. F. Wise, "God's Peculiar Peoples," in W. L. Morton, ed., *The Shield of Achilles* (Toronto, 1968).

The Districts of Upper Canada, 1788-1849[1]

George W. Spragge

With the coming of the Loyalists into the western part of the old province of Quebec some means had to be devised for the government of this, as yet, very sparsely settled territory. So, on 24 July 1788 the Governor-in-Chief, Lord Dorchester, issued a proclamation dividing this territory into four districts, as shown on the first of the accompanying maps:

1. Luneburg, 'bounded on the east by the eastern limit of a tract lately called or known by the name of Lancaster, protracted northerly and southerly as far as our said Province extends, and bounded westerly by a north and south line, intersecting the mouth of the river Gananoque, now called the Thames, above the rifts of the St. Lawrence, and extending southerly and northerly to the limits of our said province, therein comprehending the several towns or tracts called or known by the names of Lancaster, Charlottenburg, Cornwall, Osnabruck, Williamsburg, Matilda, Edwardsburg, Augusta, and Elizabethtown.'

2. Mecklenburg, extending from the western limits of Luneburg to a north and south line intersecting the mouth of the River Trent at its discharge 'into the head of the bay of Quinty and therein comprehending the several towns or tracts called or known by the names of Pittsburg, Kingstown, Ernestown, Fredericksburg, Adolphustown, Marysburg, Sophiasburg, Ameliasburg, Sydney, Thurlow, Richmond and Camden.'

3. Nassau, extending westerly from Mecklenburg 'to a north and south line intersecting the extreme projection of Long Point into the lake Erie', and

4. Hesse, comprehending 'all the residue of our said Province in the western or inland parts thereof: of the entire breadth thereof from the southerly to the northerly boundary of the same.'

In assigning German names to these districts it may have been the intention to honour the royal family: Luneburg is taken from the former principality of Brunswick-Luneburg, part of the Kingdom of Hanover; George III's queen was Charlotte Sophia of Mecklenburg-Strelitz; and among the ancestresses of George III were a Countess of Nassau and a Duchess of Hesse-Darmstadt. G. C. Paterson,

[1] First printed in *Ontario History*, XXXIX (1947), pp. 91-100.

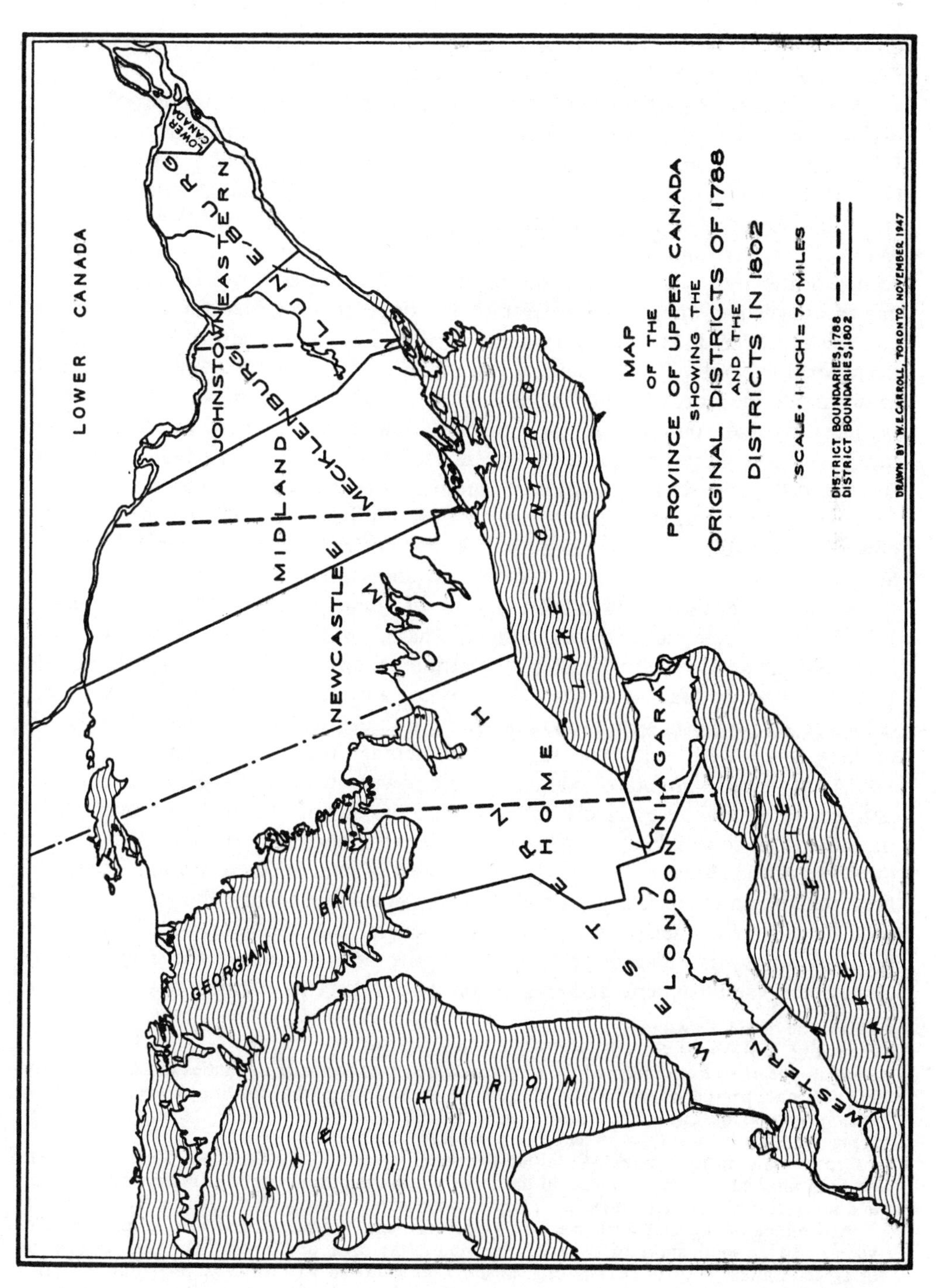

MAP
OF THE
PROVINCE OF UPPER CANADA
SHOWING THE
ORIGINAL DISTRICTS OF 1788
AND THE
DISTRICTS IN 1802
SCALE: 1 INCH = 70 MILES
DISTRICT BOUNDARIES, 1788
DISTRICT BOUNDARIES, 1802
DRAWN BY W.E. CARROLL, TORONTO, NOVEMBER 1947
LOWER CANADA
JOHNSTOWN
EASTERN
MIDLAND
MECKLENBURG
NEWCASTLE
HOME
NIAGARA
LONDON
WESTERN
LAKE ONTARIO
LAKE ERIE
LAKE HURON
GEORGIAN BAY

however, states that the districts were so named 'out of consideration for the large German element in the United Empire Loyalist population.'

For purposes of parliamentary representation and also for militia purposes these districts were divided by a proclamation of Lieutenant Governor Simcoe, dated 16 July 1792, into the nineteen original counties of Upper Canada: Glengary,[2] Stormont, Dundas, Grenvill,[2] Leeds, Frontenac, Ontario,[3] Addington, Lenox,[2] Prince Edward, Hastings, Northumberland, Durham, York, Lincoln, Norfolk, Suffolk,[4] Essex,[5] and Kent[6]. These divisions (the name 'Ontario' has been omitted) are shown on the second of the maps here reproduced. In this list of counties it will be noted that the names assigned to the counties west of Hastings are in order the names of the counties in England which border on the North Sea and the Straits of Dover, reading from north to south. For the several counties Simcoe named 'County Lieutenants', answering to the Lords Lieutenant of English counties, to whom was committed the organization and command of the county militia, and on whose recommendation the magistrates were appointed. It was not, however, until 1849 that the County succeeded the District as a division for municipal and judicial purposes.

From the formation of the districts in 1788 until 1841 the management of local affairs in each district was committed to the District Court of General Quarter Sessions of the Peace, composed of magistrates appointed by the Governor or Lieutenant Governor in Council. The system of municipal government by appointed justices was, of course, of British origin, where, until 1835, the rural districts of England were governed by the absolute patriarchal sway of the justices of the peace. But this system had also been introduced and developed in the American colonies: the Loyalists would therefore be accustomed to such a system. The powers of these courts were many and varied, and included much of the work later (after 1841) entrusted to municipal councils. Their powers included the erection and management of court-houses, gaols and asylums; the laying out and improvement of the highways; the making of assessments therefor and also 'to pay the wages of members of the House of Assembly'; the making of regulations to prevent accidental fires; the appointment of district and township constables; fixing the fees of gaolers, of town or parish clerks, and of pound keepers; the appointment of street and highway surveyors, and inspectors of weights and measures; the regulation of ferries; the establishment and regulation of markets in various towns; and the

[2] This is the original spelling.

[3] Consisting of Amherst, Simcoe, Wolfe and Howe Islands.

[4] Suffolk appears to have included the territory which now forms the counties of Middlesex and Elgin. It disappeared when the Act 38 Geo. III, c. 5, stating what townships were included in the various counties, was proclaimed 1 January 1800.

[5] Roughly, Essex included the present Essex and Kent counties.

[6] Except for a strip four miles deep along the south shore of Lake St. Clair, Kent county was north of the Thames, and included all the lands not in the possession of or reserved for Indians and not included in other districts. 'A large county surely', wrote C. C. James, 'but the voters [for members of the first Parliament of Upper Canada] were included in a strip four miles wide along the south shore of Lake St. Clair and in the town of Detroit.' 'The First Legislators of Upper Canada', Royal Society of Canada, *Transactions*, Sec. II, 1902, 113. For the exact boundaries see Simcoe's proclamation. (Fourth *Report of the Ontario Bureau of Archives* (1906), 176-181.)

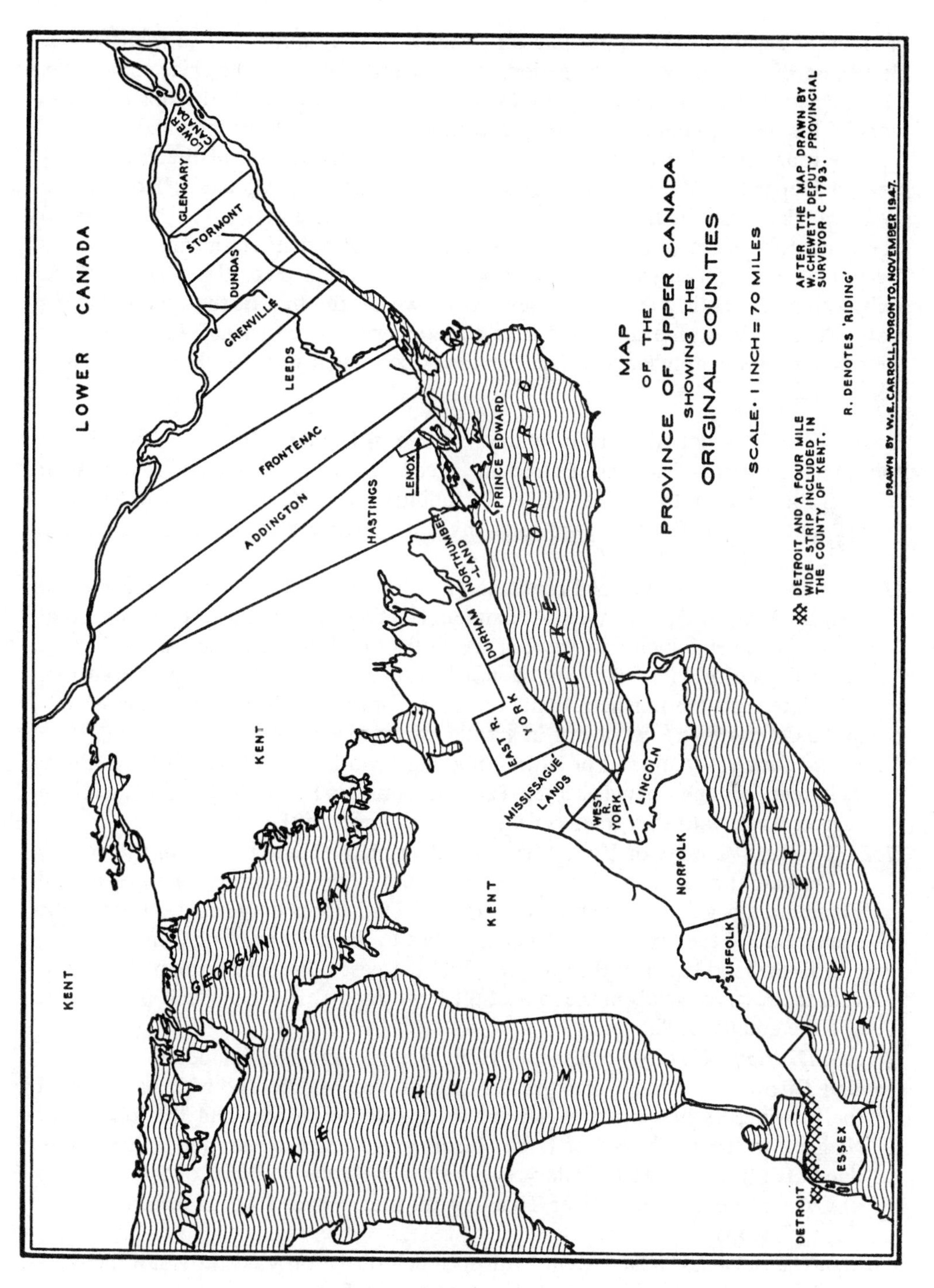
MAP
OF THE
PROVINCE OF UPPER CANADA
SHOWING THE
ORIGINAL COUNTIES
SCALE: 1 INCH = 70 MILES
DETROIT AND A FOUR MILE WIDE STRIP INCLUDED IN THE COUNTY OF KENT.
AFTER THE MAP DRAWN BY W. CHEWETT DEPUTY PROVINCIAL SURVEYOR C 1793.
R. DENOTES 'RIDING'
DRAWN BY W.E. CARROLL, TORONTO, NOVEMBER 1947.
LOWER CANADA
LOWER CANADA
GLENGARY
STORMONT
DUNDAS
GRENVILLE
LEEDS
FRONTENAC
ADDINGTON
LENOX
HASTINGS
PRINCE EDWARD
NORTHUMBER-LAND
DURHAM
EAST R. YORK
MISSISSAGUE LANDS
WEST R. YORK
LINCOLN
NORFOLK
SUFFOLK
ESSEX
DETROIT
KENT
KENT
KENT
LAKE ONTARIO
LAKE ERIE
LAKE HURON
GEORGIAN BAY

granting of certificates to applicants for licenses to sell liquor, and to ministers or clergymen of 'dissenting' congregations authorizing them to solemnize marriages. The districts of these early days were thus very important political divisions, for the work of the district councils affected very closely the daily life of the inhabitants.

The four original districts – renamed in the opening session of the first parliament of Upper Canada by 32 Geo. III, c. 8, the 'Eastern', 'Midland', 'Home', and 'Western' districts – had, by 1 January 1800, been increased by subdivisions to eight, the Johnstown, Niagara, London and Newcastle districts having been thus formed. These eight districts are described in the Act 38 Geo. III, c. 5, ss. vi, x, xviii, xxiv, xxv, xxxii, xxxvii, xl. They are shown on the first of the accompanying maps. At the same time the number of counties was increased and in some cases their boundaries were changed. The territories contained in these districts in 1800 were as follows:

Eastern District – Counties of Glengarry, Stormont, Dundas, Prescott, Russell.

Johnstown District – Counties of Grenville, Leeds, Carleton. (Carleton county, then altogether west of the Rideau River, including part of the present Carleton, Lanark, and part of Renfrew, was later divided into the counties of Carleton and Lanark by 4 Geo. IV, c. 5.)

Midland District – Counties of Frontenac (to which was added at this time the old county of Ontario), Lenox and Addington, Hastings, Prince Edward, 'with all that tract of country which lies between the district of Johnstown and a line drawn north sixteen degrees west from the northwest angle of the township of Rawdon, till it intersects the northern limits of the province, together with all the islands in the Ottawa River, wholly or in greater part opposite thereto.'

Newcastle District – Counties of Northumberland and Durham 'with all the lands in their rear, confined between their extreme boundaries, produced north, sixteen degrees west, until they intersect the northern limits of the Province.'

Home District – County of York: the east riding of the county (west of the county of Durham); and the west riding of the county (the townships of Beverly and Flamborough and 'so much of the tract of land upon the Grand River in the occupation of the Six Nations Indians as lies to the northward of Dundas Street, and all the land between the said tract and the east riding of the county of York, with the reserved lands in the rear of the townships of Blenheim and Blanford'); and the county of Simcoe.

Niagara District – Counties of Lincoln (four ridings) and Haldimand.

London District – Counties of Norfolk, Oxford and Middlesex, 'with so much of the Province as lies to the Westward of the Home District and the District of Niagara, to the southward of Lake Huron, and between them and a line drawn due north from a fixed boundary (where the easternmost limits of the township of Oxford intersects the River Thames) till it arrives at Lake Huron' (38 Geo. III, c. 5, s. xxxvii).

Western District – Essex and Kent 'with so much of the province as is not included within any other district thereof' (38 Geo. III, c. 5, s. xl).

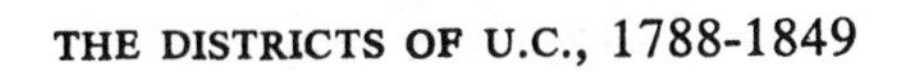

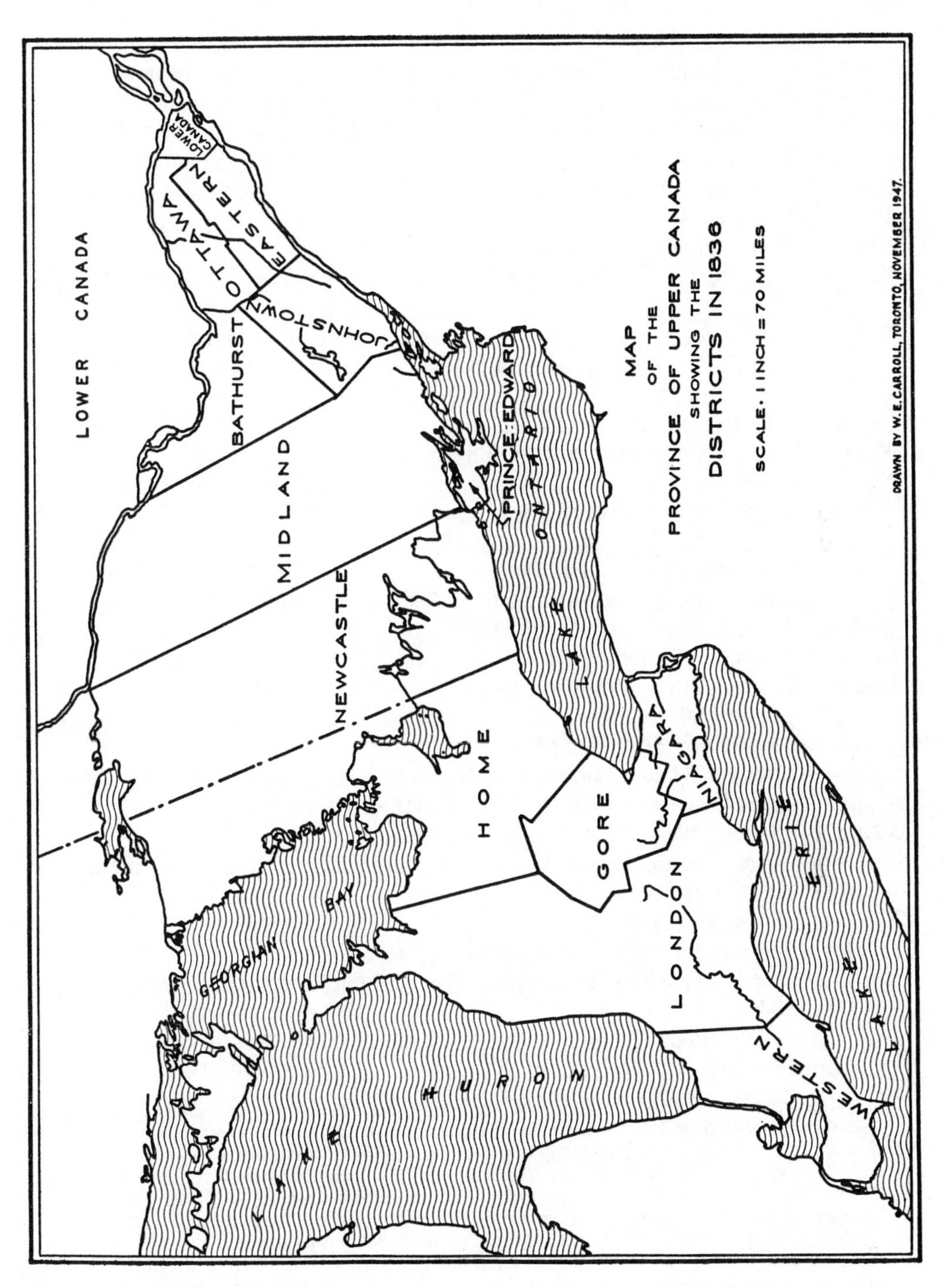
LOWER CANADA
LOWER CANADA
EASTERN
OTTAWA
JOHNSTOWN
BATHURST
MIDLAND
NEWCASTLE
PRINCE EDWARD
LAKE ONTARIO
HOME
GORE
NIAGARA
LONDON
WESTERN
LAKE ERIE
GEORGIAN BAY
LAKE HURON
MAP
OF THE
PROVINCE OF UPPER CANADA
SHOWING THE
DISTRICTS IN 1836
SCALE: 1 INCH = 70 MILES
DRAWN BY W. E. CARROLL, TORONTO, NOVEMBER 1947.

For some years the above districts remained unchanged, but, with an increase in population and wider settlement, demands arose for the creation of new districts. A few changes were made after 1820, but the greater number were made after 1835. The third map shows the districts in 1836. In 1849, when the county first became the unit of division for municipal and judicial, as well as for parliamentary purposes, there were twenty districts in Canada West. Their boundaries are shown on the fourth of our maps.

Eastern – Stormont, Dundas, Glengarry.

Ottawa – Prescott, Russell (Erected into a separate district in 1816 by 56 Geo. III, c. 2).

Dalhousie – Carleton (Erected into a separate district in 1838 from parts of the districts of Bathurst, Johnstown and Ottawa, by 1 Vic., c. 25.)

Johnstown – Leeds and Grenville.

Bathurst[7] – Lanark and Renfrew.

Midland – Frontenac, Lennox and Addington.

Victoria – Hastings (Erected into a separate district, 1837, by 7 Wm. IV, c. 31).

Prince Edward – Prince Edward (Separated from the Midland District, 1831, by 1 Wm. IV, c. 6).

Newcastle – Northumberland and Durham.

Colborne – Peterborough – then including Victoria (Separated from the Newcastle District, 1838, by 7 Wm. IV, c. 115).

Home – York – then including Ontario and Peel.

Simcoe – Simcoe (Provision was made by 2 Geo. IV, c. 3, s. 8 for this county to be declared a separate district under certain restrictions; it was proclaimed a separate district in 1837 by 7 William IV, c. 32).

Gore – Wentworth, Halton, and part of Brant (Formed out of parts of the Home and Niagara Districts in 1816 by 56 Geo. III, c. 19).

Niagara – Lincoln, Welland, and part of Haldimand.

Talbot – Norfolk and the remainder of Haldimand (Erected into a separate district in 1837 by 7 Wm. IV, c. 33).

Western – Essex, Kent and Lambton.

London – Elgin and a portion of Middlesex.

Brock – Oxford – including part of Brant (Erected into a separate district, 1837, by 7 Wm. IV. c. 30).

Wellington – Waterloo, Wellington, Grey and part of Perth (Erected into a separate district in 1838 by 7 Wm. IV, c. 116).

[7] It is somewhat disconcerting to find that the county of Carleton was erected into the district of Bathurst, and a little later to find that the county of Carleton was erected into the district of Dalhousie, the district of Bathurst being composed of the counties of Lanark and Renfrew. The explanation is that the county of Carleton after 1800 was composed of what is now part of Carleton county, Lanark county, and part of Renfrew county. This was proclaimed a separate district by the name of Bathurst, 13 November 1822 (*Upper Canada Gazette*, Nov. 28, 1822). Then, by Geo. IV, c. 5 (1824), Carleton county was divided into the counties of Carleton and Lanark, the area of Carleton being restricted to seven townships. In 1838 Carleton county was enlarged and erected into the district of Dalhousie, part of old Carleton county, viz. Lanark and the new county of Renfrew, retaining the name of the Bathurst district.

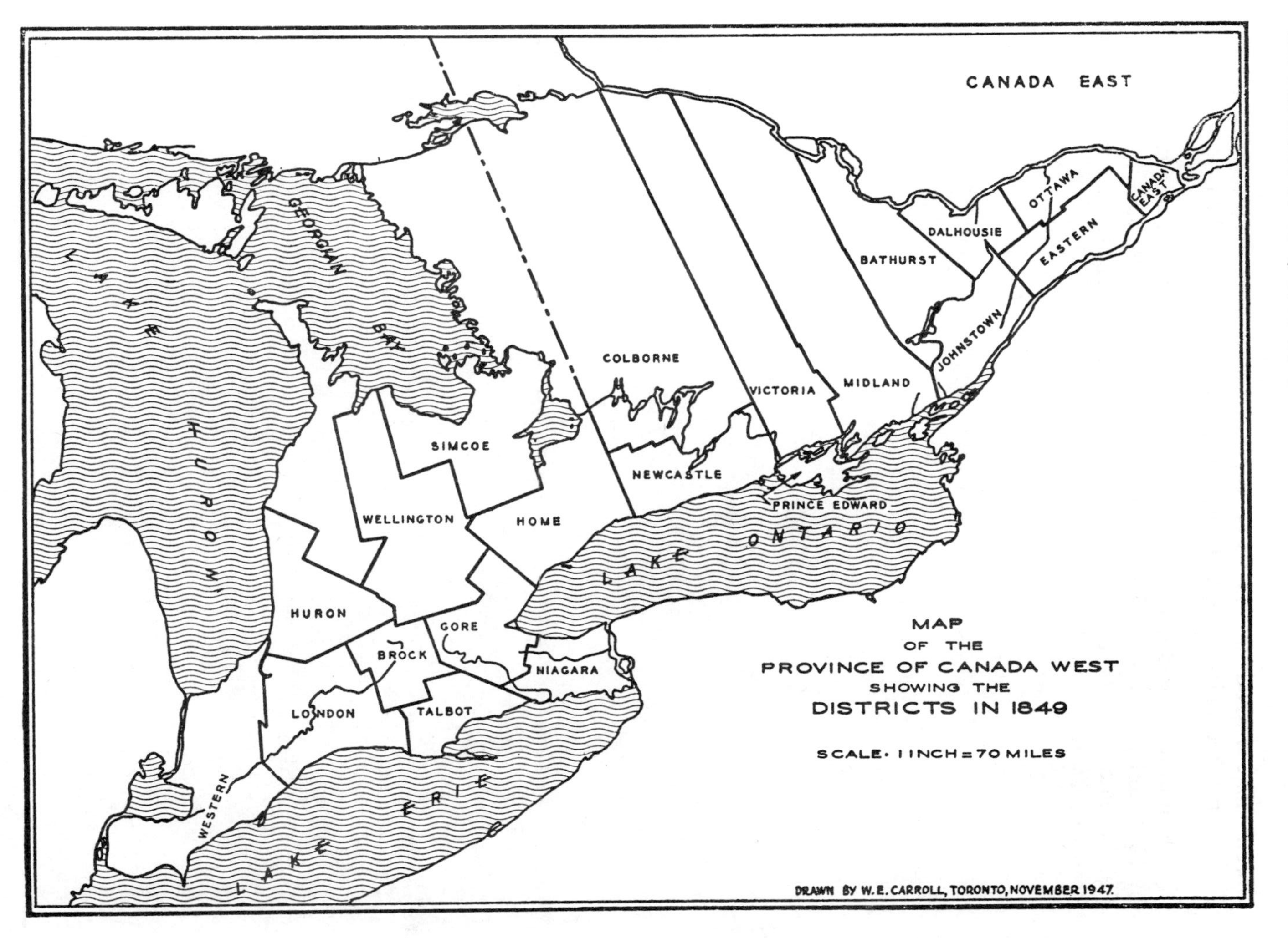
CANADA EAST
CANADA EAST
OTTAWA
DALHOUSIE
EASTERN
BATHURST
JOHNSTOWN
COLBORNE
VICTORIA
MIDLAND
SIMCOE
NEWCASTLE
PRINCE EDWARD
WELLINGTON
HOME
LAKE ONTARIO
GEORGIAN BAY
LAKE HURON
HURON
GORE
BROCK
NIAGARA
LONDON
TALBOT
WESTERN
LAKE ERIE
MAP
OF THE
PROVINCE OF CANADA WEST
SHOWING THE
DISTRICTS IN 1849
SCALE: 1 INCH = 70 MILES
DRAWN BY W.E. CARROLL, TORONTO, NOVEMBER 1947.

Huron – Part of Middlesex and all the organized portions of the present county of Huron (Erected into a separate district in 1838 by 1 Vic., c. 26).

The province ceased to be divided into districts in 1849. The change was made by 12 Victoria, c. 78, s. 2: 'The division of that part of the Province called Upper Canada, into Districts for judicial and other purposes, shall be and the same is hereby abolished.'

The Anglo-American Magazine Looks at Urban Upper Canada on the Eve of the Railway Era[1]

Frederick H. Armstrong and Neil C. Hultin

The greatest single development affecting the urban pattern of Upper Canada in the nineteenth century was the coming of the railway era in the mid-1850's. The canal building period had been important; it had created St. Catharines and Hamilton and had prepared the way for the development of Ottawa. But this change was nothing compared to that brought on by the railways twenty years later. Until the railways appeared, transportation had of necessity been by water wherever possible for the roads were poor at best, and in some seasons almost impassable. As a result, almost all the leading towns of the colony were ports, most of them on Lake Ontario, where population was concentrated and commerce had reached the greatest stage of development. London, surrounded by a rich agricultural hinterland, was the sole exception.

Access to water transportation gave a false sense of security, or of hope, to many towns that actually had few prospects for the future; Port Hope, Cobourg, Belleville, and others still possessed their own regions of domination and dreamed of spreading their influence northward over far wider areas. But by 1850 their fate had been decided. Improved steamers were making it easy to travel along the lake without touching at the smaller ports. Toronto, with its great natural hinterland, was well on the way to dominance, even if it was no longer the permanent capital of the United Province of Canada. A new pattern was emerging, but it took the railway revolution to make it obvious.

The first railway boom took place in the 1830's when no fewer than nine lines were chartered by the provincial Legislature; however, it came to a sudden end in the panic of 1837 and the decade-long depression that followed. Only one of the nine lines was completed, a ten mile by-pass line around Niagara Falls, and even that was not a true railroad since the cars were drawn by horses because of the steep gradients. But many of the suggested routes were logical ones, and when by

[1] The writers would like to thank their colleague Professor A. M. J. Hyatt for his helpful comments on the introduction.

the mid-1840's times improved the schemes were revived and another railway boom was under way. At first it moved slowly, but, stimulated by government aid under the Guarantee Act of 1849, development came rapidly. Soon three main railway lines snaked across the province. The Northern extended north from Toronto, to reach Aurora in 1852, Allandale (Barrie) in 1853, and finally, Collingwood on Georgian Bay in 1855; while the Great Western, which was opened from Niagara via Hamilton to London by 1853, reached Windsor in 1854. It was then extended eastward from Hamilton to join Toronto in 1855. Meanwhile, plans were being made for a connection between Canada West and the St. Lawrence cities, and by 1856 the Grand Trunk was completed from Montreal to Toronto.

These major lines were followed by a rash of little railways when the government made aid available to smaller projects under the Municipal Loan Fund Act of 1852. Soon each town had its pet railway scheme which the civic leaders were certain would lead it to metropolitan status and vast riches. The result was an orgy of railway building – most of it either premature or completely unsound. By 1857, when a new panic and depression brought construction to a virtual stop, the province was criss-crossed by railway lines, but it was virtually bankrupt, and suffering the inevitable hangover which follows a period of over-indulgence.

Railway construction, however, had far wider effects than just to place the province in debt, for it had created a completely new economic and social pattern. Henceforth the mere fact that a town was a good port was no longer sufficient to mean automatic prominence; it had also to be located on a major railway line to insure continued prosperity. Important centres which were bypassed by the railway declined into obscurity; villages that were well located on the new network grew into cities. The change was intensified by the fact that inefficient local industries which had been able to operate profitably because of poor communications were now wiped out and manufacturing began to be concentrated at certain strategic points. The colony that was soon to become Ontario had entered a new era.

Just as this change was beginning to take place in 1852 a new magazine was established at Toronto, the *Anglo-American,*[2] dedicated to improving the literary quality of the province in a rather folksy way, and edited by two enterprising figures, the Rev. Robert J. MacGeorge and Gilbert Auchinleck. Like so many similar journals its life span was short; by 1855 it had been forced to suspend operations. But during its brief three years' existence it provided an insight into both the literary interests and the urban development of part of Canada. The outstanding literary achievements of the magazine were the serialized publications of Gilbert Auchinleck's *History of the War of 1812*, and Catherine Parr Traill's *Forest Gleanings*. The magazine also published scientific articles, introduced the poet Charles Sangster, and, in keeping with the ambitions of its publisher, the Toronto bookstore owner Thomas Maclear, it attempted to counteract the influence of American magazines which were then so prevalent in the colony.

One of its special sections was a description of the cities of British North

[2] For details on the *Anglo-American Magazine* and its editors see Carl F. Klinck, ed., *Literary History of Canada* (Toronto, 1966).

America, at first entitled "The Cities of Canada" and then, after the few Upper Canadian cities had been discussed, "Cities and Towns of Canada". In the first few issues these vignettes were the lead articles, but they were afterwards supplanted by Auchinleck's *History*, appeared irregularly, and eventually vanished altogether. Except for the first two, on Toronto and Kingston, they were generally only a page or two in length and were to an extent constructed around a description of a picture that accompanied each article. Except for the article on St. Catharines which was signed "A. J.", all were unsigned and presumably were written by the editors.

The choice and order of subjects is interesting: Toronto, Kingston, Hamilton, Brockville, Port Hope, Cobourg, London, and St. Catharines. Toronto, as the locale of publication and the largest city, had the place of precedence, while Kingston, the old centre of commerce, still managed to follow it. But already the relatively new Hamilton appeared in third place and its predecessor and rival for the domination of the Head-of-the-Lake, Dundas, was not even included. Similarly in the Niagara peninsula, St. Catharines was discussed, even if it came last, whereas the old capital of the province, Niagara-on-the-Lake, long a ship-building centre, was omitted altogether. Obviously, the Welland Canal had replaced the old Niagara River route in the estimation of the editors in spite of the construction of the horse railway around the Falls. Some of the north shore towns were given short descriptions – Cobourg, Port Hope, and Brockville; but others, Belleville and Prescott for example, were overlooked, as was Bytown, soon to become Ottawa and the new capital. In the west, London, despite its inland location was discussed, but the older ports of Amherstburg and Sandwich were not. Beyond the confines of Upper Canada there were articles on Quebec, Montreal, Halifax, St. John, and Fredericton, which are not reproduced here; nor is the short note in Vol. I, no. 4 (October 1852) 289-91 on Brockville, which was little more than a description of the picture.

All the articles are written in a lively style and depict scenes of both rapid growth and great ambitions. Many of the hopes expressed were soon to be dashed by the new urban pattern which emerged with the coming of the railways. In most cases, however, the editors showed great perspicacity in their predictions. They carefully noted not only the factors which had led to the rise of the cities, but also those which ought to result in future growth, and, as was appropriate in a journal which hoped to direct British colonization to the province, described those conditions which the prospective emigrant would find attractive. Their most frequent complaint, one that is not surprising in a periodical that hoped to improve the cultural level of the population, was the lack of literary institutions in the province. Mechanics Institutes, the ancestors of the public libraries of today, were making their appearance, but there was little else.

In editing the articles it has unfortunately not been possible to reproduce the pictures that accompanied them. This has resulted in certain deletions from the texts, but in general the descriptions have not been greatly affected. Other sections of the articles, which were repetitious or dealt with points that would be of little interest today, have also been omitted. For ease in reading the conventional three dots which indicate such deletions have been omitted, but those who wish to examine the full texts are referred to the original articles. Footnotes have been avoided, but some explanatory notes have been added in square brackets as well as the dates for those buildings which are still in existence. The description of Toronto is from Volume I, number 1, July, 1852, 1-4; of Kingston, from Vol. I, no. 2, August, 1852, 97-101; of Hamilton, from Vol. I, no. 3, September, 1852, 193-5; of Port Hope, from Vol. I, no. 6, December, 1852, 481-2; of Cobourg, from Vol. II, no. 1, January, 1853, 17-18; of London, from Vol. II, no. 3, March, 1853, 241-2; of St. Catharines, from Vol. III, no. 2, August, 1853, 124-31. The "Smith's Canada" referred to in several places is William Henry Smith's *Canada: past, present, and future* (2 vols., Toronto, 1851).

TORONTO

It may be regarded as a high degree of local vanity – a species of Metropolitanism, closely allied to the pride of Cockaigne – which induces us to commence our series of illustrations of the cities of this portion of Our Most Gracious Majesty's Dominions, with a description of the place of our habitation. But, Reader, whatever the feeling which prompts this preference may be, you will, perhaps, readily concede that it is a most natural one. Dwelling in a city, whose every stone and brick has been placed in its present position, under the eye of many who remember the locality as the site of primeval woods, the region of swamp – of some who have seen the lonely wigwam of the Missasauga give place to the log-house of the earlier settler, and this in its turn disappear, to be replaced by the substantial and elegant structures of modern art – we feel that we are justified in yielding to the pardonable, if vain desire, of telling the wondrous metamorphosis of forty years. It is meet that we should rejoice over the triumph of civilization, the onward progress of our race, the extension of our language, institutions, tastes, manners, customs and feelings. In no spot within British territory could we find aggregated in so striking a manner, the evidences of this startling change; in none should we trace so strongly marked the imprint of national migration; in few discover such ripened fruits of successful colonization. The genius of Britain presides over the destiny of her Offspring – the glory of the Empire enshrouds the prosperity of its Colony – the noble courage and strength of the Lion inspires and protects the industry of the Beaver – the Oak and the Maple unite their shadows over breasts which beat in unison for the common weal.

We boast not superior intelligence, we claim not greater, nor even an equal share of, local advantages over the sister cities of our country, but we assert, in sincerity of belief and in justice to ourselves, a rapidity of growth and a stability produced by wholesome enterprize, as encouraging as it is remarkable.

Notwithstanding the disadvantage of its low situation, the effect produced on the mind when entering the Bay, and viewing the city from the deck of the steamer, is very pleasing and striking. Its spires and domes lighted up with the parting rays of the evening sun, the dark woods at the back, and the numerous handsome villas which flank the Bay, especially at its entrance, combine in creating an effective *coup d'oeil*. A most prominent object, at the eastern end, is the Gaol, by no means a picturesque or prepossessing one, but still it may be taken as an indication of the general substantial and appropriate character of the buildings, being a solid symmetrical mass of grey limestone sufficiently significant of its purposes; not, however, in the same sense as the traveller, who said he knew that he was in a civilized country whenever he saw a gibbet. The Light House on the point of the Peninsula, the Lunatic Asylum, Government Wharf, the Parliament Buildings, the spires of St. George's, Knox's, and St. Andrew's Churches; St. Lawrence Buildings, the City Hall and Trinity Church, all attract the eye.[3] The sites of the Anglican [St. James 1850-53] and Roman [St. Michael's 1845] Cathedrals and the direction of the main streets, may also be made out. It is not our purpose to enter into a topographical description, and we therefore pass to other topics.

The "Queen City of the West" has seen changes and vicissitudes in her time. All traces of these events it is true, are rapidly becoming extinct, recent as they have been; the few which still remain are not of sufficient interest to require any very extended notice. And it is well that it should be so. The absence of such evidences, to the curious investigator of a future age, will establish more fully the wonderful brevity of our transition state. But we may permit ourselves the indulgence of some reminiscences of the days that are past. Few who now stroll along the well boarded sidewalks of King Street, reflect upon the inconvenience attending this recreation to their grand-sires and grand-dames, who were compelled to tuck up their garments and pick their way from tuft to tuft, from stone to stone, and even to content themselves with an occasional dip in the puddle; but,

"Nothing is a misery
Unless our weakness apprehend it so,"

and spite of these little contrepieds, they would briskly do their shopping or call to enquire for Mrs. So-and-so and the darling little infant. It was no unusual sight to behold the heavy lumber waggon (Broughams were not then known,) sticking fast, up to the axle in the very middle of the Street.

It is certainly a source of regret that with all this magic advancement in the substantialities of condition and importance, so very little, comparatively, has been done to mark an equal progress in the higher qualities which adorn and accompany civilization. When one walks along King and Yonge Streets, and views with mingled feelings of surprise and admiration, the splendid Cathedral [St. James], the handsome St. Lawrence Buildings, and the princely stores already built or in the course of erection, the mind will naturally revert to the intelligence which designed, and the skill which is completing them; and a desire will as naturally arise to ascertain the character and extent of the institutions appropriated to the furtherance of intellectual pursuits. Alas! shall we confess it, in this we are miserably deficient. Not a solitary building is to be seen answering this description. There is not even a public library! In the St. Lawrence Buildings there is a very large and convenient room, appropriated as a reading-room, and kept well supplied with the current periodical

[3] The Light House (built 1806); Lunatic Asylum, at 999 Queen St. W. (1846-49); the tower only of St. George the Martyr (1844, rest burnt 1955); St. Lawrence Market (1849-51); and "Little" Trinity Church (1843), all survive today.

literature of the day – but that is all. Nor is there a room even devoted to the collection of specimens of art, or the fruits of genius. It may be said that we are unreasonable in this accusation, that the place is too young for such matters. But when we call to remembrance the work of this nature which has been done in smaller, less wealthy, and less important communities, we cannot refrain from expressing our conviction that much more ought to have been accomplished in Toronto.

Much to the credit of its promoters, there is a flourishing Mechanics' Institute, possessing a library worthy of better accommodation.

Within the past two years [1849], also, a Society has been organized, under the appellation of "The [Royal] Canadian Institute," which has for its object the promotion of literature, science, and art. Under the auspices of this Association, (which has been chartered,) a monthly publication is shortly to make its appearance, devoted to the cultivation of these pursuits. We hail this as a good omen of what we may shortly expect on a more extended and comprehensive scale.

We must also enter our protest against the injudicious manner in which most of the public buildings are "located," (to borrow a Columbian idiomatic term). The general effect of a fine proportionate building, however classical its style and elaborate its ornamentation, is completely destroyed by being crowded in among other less pretending structures, in an out-of-the-way place. Witness the result in the St. Lawrence Buildings – in the new Post Office [now 10 Toronto St.], a truly chaste and well-designed piece of architecture, poked away behind an uninteresting row of fire-proof windows. The same remark will apply to many others, but these examples will suffice.

The absence of large spaces, in the form of public squares, gardens and arrangements of a similar kind, is also most remarkable, and very much to be regretted. In a city whose local disadvantages, as far as public health is concerned, have been made the subject of frequent comment, we opine that the wisest policy would be to make a sacrifice of present wealth, for the purpose of future good.

The railroads to the north and west, and eventually to the east – the increasing means of water communication – the vast extent of cleared and highly cultivated farms around it, and the extending settlement of large tracts of land, point to a prosperous future for this city. We might expatiate on this and kindred topics to greater length, but we should only tire the patience of the reader, and exceed the proper bounds allotted to our subject.

KINGSTON

There are few circumstances better calculated to convey a correct impression of the progressive condition of this colony, than an occasional journey over Lake Ontario in one of the water palaces which now float on its surface. Fifteen hours, stoppages included, now constitute the utmost limit of time which the grumbling traveller can sanction for the performance of that journey which not very many years ago, as many are able to testify from personal experience, occupied commonly three weeks and occasionally a more extended period. The character of the country we pass in our trip to Kingston, is in pleasing contrast to the upper part or even the opposite coast of the Lake. A rolling surface, with frequent bold and projecting cliffs, vary the monotony of flatness elsewhere seen.

The approach to the blue city offers, to the contemplation of the visitor, a landscape of singular feature and pleasing aspect. The approximating shores of the Lake indented with numerous inlets, the islands scattered about before us, among which we glide with pleasant smoothness, the river stealing its way from behind the buildings and the distant prospect up the Bay of Quinte, cannot be regarded with indifference, and impart an air of romance to the whole view, of a most agreeable nature.

The geographical position of this city, clearly establishes its claim to be considered what it undoubtedly still is, the key-stone of military defence at this end of the Lake. The crumbling ruins of Frontenac mark the keen perception of the early French settlers, and the fortifications of Fort Henry [1836-42], unsurpassed in America, prove how well the Government understood its superior advantage in this respect.

On first landing from the steamer, the attention of the visitor is at once arrested by the peculiar sombre hue which everything around him seems to wear. It is impossible to divest the mind of a feeling that the inhabitants have put their city into half mourning; and it is a long time before the eye becomes familiar with this appearance, which is due to the bluish limestone, of which it is built.

But while we are startled by the uniform sobriety of colour, we cannot fail to admire the substantial character imparted to its buildings by the stone with which they are constructed. Lying on a bed of stone, the material is easily and economically obtained; indeed, in many instances, it may truthfully and literally be said, that the dwellings are hewn out of the rock. The care and finish with which the abundant stone has been wrought into form, is highly creditable to the parties concerned, and nowhere in Canada can a better piece of masonry be seen than that exhibited by the City Hall [1843], with the fortifications in front of it. The streets are laid out with as much regularity as the nature of the locality would permit, the situation being on a narrow and angular promontory, running out into the Lake, and forming the western bank of the Cataraqui [River].

Evidence is to be discovered of the successive checks which Kingston has received, from the external influences which have controlled its destinies, but we rejoice to think that its course is now onward, that under steadily increasing commercial relations, it will soon regain its wonted prosperity. At a time when between this point and Montreal and Albany, communication was infrequent and expensive, and scarcely a town existed to the westward, it rapidly assumed an importance which its physical advantages amply justified, and even at a later date, when the tide of emigration had set in strongly towards the west, it still retained its superiority over the other and newer cities, by becoming the place of trans-shipment for imports and exports. The war of 1812, while it disturbed, for a season, the mercantile enterprise of the place, brought with it other sources of wealth and influence. It now became the principal seat of military and naval operations, and the noble fortifications on Point Henry, with the large body of soldiery stationed there, were good reasons one would imagine, for making it also the seat of Government of the Province. After a season this result was compassed [1841-44], in spite of the outcry of its propinquity to a hostile frontier. Then it was that an impulse was given to it, which bid fair to render it the capital indeed of the West. This hope was, however, blighted and for a time the city felt severely the consequence of hasty and overstrained speculation. Nor was this the only adverse cause at work to mar its fortunes. The improvement in the navigation of both Lake and River, – the construction of the Canals on the St. Lawrence, by which vessels of considerable tonnage could pass directly through to Montreal; and latterly the discovery of the practicable navigation of the once dreaded Long Sault and other Rapids, – all tended to divert the stream of population and trade, and carry past its wharves and storehouses the merchandize and traffic at one time its almost prescriptive right. The want of a productive farming country in its immediate vicinity, has, doubtless had the effect of deterring emigrants from selecting this as a halting point; but a little previous information, or a pause of investigation, which it is true few can afford, and many more are unwilling to make, – would satisfy the seeker after a home, that although not close around the city, there is within a reasonable distance of it, one of the most magnificent agricultural districts in the Province. If the Canal navigation brought with it detriment to the commerce of Kingston in one direction, it has, combined with increased mercantile relations with the United States, opened up a traffic which has been gradually telling upon its progress. The great water privileges enjoyed along the course of the Rideau [Canal], the facility of transport of the vast resources of the country lying to the north, and, above all, the fact of its being the nearest and most direct route to the greatest lumber mart at present existing, must secure for it a large proportion of the trade in this particular article. Some idea may be formed of the extent of this growing business done in the neighbourhood of the city alone, by the fact that, during this season, there has been already shipped, from *one* mill two millions of feet of lumber, and that there are one million and a half feet ready for exportation. Nor do the forwarders, as they are technically termed, despair that their peculiar department of business will again revive to a considerable extent, indeed they are now enjoying an earnest of its revival. The experiment of *through* shipment would seem to be failing, in as far as the heavier goods are concerned. – The loss of time and increased expense of navigating the rivers and canals does not pay the owners of sailing vessels; they declare that they can make more by quick and rapid runs between the lake ports. Should this eventually prove to be demonstrable beyond dispute, and should the fleet of steam-propellers, capable of performing the work efficiently, not increase in proportion to the swelling importations yearly exhibited by the Customs' returns, we have no doubt that the expectations of the Kingstonians will be realized.

There is in fact a decided aspect of awakening energy about the place, like a man who has resolutely shaken himself out of a fit of apathy or somnolence, and is now determined to go to work in earnest. We wish we could say as much for the architectural excellence of the buildings as for their substantiality. There is a laboured effort at ornamentation, and a want of due proportion about some of them which is truly painful, and not in keeping with the material employed. In the few instances in which freestone or sandstone has been used for the frontage of buildings the contrast is most marked. The city is admirably drained, and now possesses an abundant supply of excellent water, brought from the lake into every cellar by efficient works.

To the great scandal of the authorities, public auctions are permitted to be held every day in the principal business street. At one corner may be seen a collection of old stoves and decaying furniture, with the auctioneer standing on a three-legged table, shouting out the merits of some antiquated frying-pan; at another, and not very far distant, we catch sight of a piece of red calico flaunting in the breeze, and hear the stentorian lungs of the seller resounding in praise of its colour and texture, and so on along the range of vision. This taking place opposite to the doors of the principal hotel, is little calculated to convey a favourable idea of the business activity of the place – faint but distinct glimmerings come through the mind of Dickens' pictures of Bailiffs' Sales and Rag Fair.

It is somewhat singular that the most prominent object the spectator sees in approaching or entering nearly every city with which we are acquainted is its prison – as if it were a monitor put to warn the visitor against any breach of those laws, under the security of which he was moving about and enjoying himself. So it is with Kingston, on entering the bay from the westward – the Provincial Penitentiary [in the Village of Portsmouth] is the principal object of interest. A large and apparently secure place it is. Horribly dismal to look at, and much more so to think of. In spite of all exertions to render this system of punishment as complete as can be, at considerable expense, statesmen are fast losing confidence in it. It is not found to be productive of that amount of moral reform which was anticipated, and daily experience shews that the confirmed offender gains no good, while the novice in crime runs a great risk of being confirmed in his evil course. In the meantime it is the only effective institution for long-continued personal restraint in the country, and is generally well filled.

There is one advantage which Kingston possesses over Toronto, for which its inhabitants cannot be too grateful. The number of pleasant outlets for recreation which exist. An evening's row up the Cataraqui to Kingston Mills, is a treat in which many a Torontonian would rejoice on a sultry summer's day.

We have said that this is the easiest and quickest point of communication with the neighbouring states. Kingston is five hours nearer New York [City] than any other point of Upper Canada, and an enterprising company is now cutting a canal through one of the Islands [Wolfe], which will reduce the distance between Kingston and Cape Vincent [New York State] from twenty-one to twelve and a-half miles, by this means they will much facilitate the trade between the two countries and forge a link which will bind still more closely the growing bonds of union between them. The inevitable current thus given to the commerce of Western Canada, is truly unfortunate, and would seem to call loudly for some active measures to secure a more speedy and direct communication with the Mother Country. It is a matter of regret, to find individual localities directing all their energies to the furtherance of their individual interests, irrespective of the national prosperity. Until we possess frequent ocean communication with Britain and more complete means of internal intercourse, we must be to a certain extent dependent upon our neighbours for trans-Atlantic commerce.

The society of Kingston is of a very social and pleasant kind; like all military stations it partakes of the polish and freedom resulting from the intercourse of men who have seen much of the world, and who, during the period of their service expatriation, seek to pass life as agreeably as circumstances will permit. This mutual dependence produces the greatest harmony and good feeling. The value of property is rapidly encreasing. The establishment of manufactories of various kinds in addition to those which exist, for which there are great *privileges*, would tend much to promote its welfare.

It is also like most Canadian Towns devoid of a public Library or museum. There is a Mechanics Institute which possesses a tolerable collection of books, and several societies of a social and charitable nature.

HAMILTON

If in the progress and prosperity of those cities of which we have already attempted the delineation, we were able to discover some peculiar local features, striking in themselves and sufficiently indicative of the influence they exercised on the destiny of those places, we shall have less difficulty in recognizing them in this youngest member of the family. Few places can be found, we would rather say no place can be found, to illustrate so completely the mode of growth of this colony as the city of Hamilton. It has sprung up within a very brief space of time, and has, from fortuitous local advantages, become as substantial in appearance, as either of its compeers on the lake. The abundance of excellent stone in its neighborhood, of a colour and composition more nearly approaching those with which the eye is familiar in the old world affords the material and gives the appearance of a British Town to it. There is also in the extent and arrangement of the large wholesale mercantile establishments, an air of solid wealth and enterprize, for which we are utterly unprepared, when told that we are about to visit a place literally little more than twenty years old. If we seek for the reasons of this rapid increase in this place, we shall find them in its geographical position, and the nature of the surrounding country.

It is placed at the western extremity of [Lake] Ontario, and is the natural termination of the lake navigation, although its advantage in this respect is confined to the summer period entirely, and even this has only been effectively secured by the completion of the Burlington Bay canal [1830]. During the winter season the Bay is usually frozen over, which precludes the access of vessels to the port of the city; this is an obstacle, which, however, may be in a great measure obviated by an extension of the railroad to an accessible point on the coast in the immediate neighborhood. The immense extent of territory lying to the westward and southward of the city, and to which it forms the culminating point of traffic, is now only being completely opened up, and a considerable portion of it is in the process of settling. The establishment of the plank and macadamized roads and more recently of the Great Western Railroad, has given a direction to the intercourse and will finally secure a trade, which nothing else could have accomplished.

The site of Hamilton is very good, but it has the disadvantage of lying at the foot of that mountain range which borders the lake from Queenston. On these heights and beyond them are some of the most fertile lands in the Province with a surface of a pleasing character. The absence of prominent buildings on which the eye may rest, is a remarkable feature. On the [west] is Dundurn Castle, the residence of Sir Allan Napier MacNab. The streets are well and regularly laid out. The society of Hamilton is purely a mercantile one, and a considerable portion of its wealthiest members are from the "land o' cakes." The descendents of the loyalists who came over to Canada in large numbers, at the declaration of independence by the United States, compose a large proportion of the inhabitants of the surrounding country, but in the city itself recent immigrants preponderate. There is always a violent demonstration of loyalty upon every admissable occasion, and this neighborhood has always been considered as the stronghold of this feeling. Long may they continue steadfast in it.

Despite the rivalry which appears to be growing up between Hamilton and Toronto, it is not probable that their interests will ever be antagonistic. As the stream of population spreads out more widely over the face of the land, so will the element of their mutual growth multiply and become more distinct. They are far enough apart, to be each the centre of a district more extensive than the largest county in England, and which will, in the course of a very few years, at the same rate of influx, become quite as, if not far more, populous. It were well that this spirit, therefore, should animate them in a laudable manner. There is sufficient room for improvement in many departments of social life, and in the several appliances so essential to the improvement and well-being of communities. It is not alone the worth of property, the largest trading fleet, the wealthiest merchants, the fastest boats, or the greatest number of railroads, which combine to elevate the character of a city. We look in vain for almost the germ of a Public Library, a museum, even a theatre. We may be told that they will be formed in time, that the places are too young yet! The reply to this is simple and evident. In places less wealthy they exist, surely nothing else is wanting for their establishment.

PORT HOPE

Port Hope, in the Township of Hope, is pleasantly situated on Lake Ontario, and commands from the upper part of the town a fine view of the lake and the adjacent country. An inconsiderable, but rapid stream [the Ganaraska] runs through it, forming at its embouchure a natural harbour, which requires only to be cleaned out to be one of the safest and best protected on Ontario, as it is of considerable size and is well sheltered from the east, west, and north. Two piers have been erected near the mouth of the stream, but the continual deposit of alluvial matter brought down, and the wash of the lake have formed a bar which will render it necessary for the citizens to avail themselves of the hitherto neglected advantages of their natural basin, and it is now in contemplation to erect, lakeward, two outer piers which will thus form a commodious harbour.

The town is prettily laid out and is rapidly improving; the business part is principally in a valley sloping gently to the north, while on the east and west the ground rises more abruptly and is studded with the residences of the citizens. On the hill to the right may be distinguished the English Church [St. John's], a plain and unpretending wooden structure.

A great part of the town was destroyed by fire a few years ago, and substantial three story brick buildings are rapidly rising on the site of the former unsightly wooden piles which then lined the principal streets.

Directly in the foreground is the new Town Hall, of red brick, a large and convenient building, with a good market in the lower part of it, and a little to the right are some extensive grist mills, of stone, newly erected and capable of turning out very large quantities of our present staple.

Port Hope can boast of a full proportion of the usual manufactories found in other improving towns in the Province and reckons amongst them, saw-mills, breweries and foundries, distilleries (Port Hope is famous for the spirits produced there,) carding and fulling mills, tanneries, asheries, soap and candle factories, with many other manufactories for various purposes.

The Banks and Insurance Companies are all fully represented, while there are churches for the members of the Episcopalian, Presbyterian, Methodist and Baptist persuasions. The Catholic Church was destroyed a short time ago by fire, but another is in progress of erection. Port Hope, in short, from its pretty situation, its thriving state, the energy of its citizens, and its fine back country, forms a very desirable location for the emigrant. The society is on an easy footing, and a Mechanic's Institute has been formed, which must tend still further to add to the many advantages offered to the intending settler.

The shipping, properly belonging to and owned at Port Hope, is as yet but inconsiderable, but the enterprising citizens have repeatedly avowed their intention, as soon as the new harbour is completed, to increase this branch of business, and place this thriving little town on an equality with any other of similar importance on the lake.

COBOURG

In the township of Hamilton, on the north shore of Lake Ontario, and at the lower end of a fertile and extensive valley, sloping upwards gradually from the water's edge, stands Cobourg, the capital of the United Counties of Northumberland and Durham. Built on a gravelly soil, the town enjoys the advantage of dry, clean streets, which are judiciously laid out, broad, and well planked on either side. Few places present from the Lake a more pleasing ensemble than does Cobourg, and the tourist will be still further gratified at finding, on landing, that this really pretty town requires not distance "to lend enchantment to the view," but that it is clean and well-built, presenting to the most careless observer evidences of daily-increasing and well-deserved prosperity.

Victoria College[4] is built on rising ground, somewhat in the rear of the town, and commands a fine view of the town and lake. It was completed in the year 1836, at a cost of nearly £12,000, raised by the voluntary offerings of the Methodist body in England and Upper Canada.

In addition to Victoria College there are the following educational establishments: – The District Grammer School, Cobourg Church Grammar School, besides a great many other excellent private schools: the Diocesan Theological Institute was for many years in successful operation and produced several of the scholars who now adorn the pulpits of the Anglican Churches throughout the Province, it is, however, now merged into Trinity College, Toronto, where the same results, only on a more extended scale, are becoming visible.

The Court-House is a large and commodious building. Cobourg contains places of worship for members of the English Church, the Church of Scotland, Free Church, Wesleyan Methodist, Episcopal Methodist, Congregational, Bible Christian, and Catholic persuasions. The Banks and Insurance Office Companies all have branches, thriving establishments, and the man of business will find every facility for the conducting of his business. The Jail and Court-House, a handsome stone building, has been built at a short distance from the town, and forms the nucleus of a small village which has sprung up round it since its erection. A dredging machine is in constant operation, cleaning out the basin and forming a safe harbour of refuge, which on a late occasion, during almost a hurricane, afforded perfect shelter to the steamer *Princess Royal*, on her passage from Kingston to the westward.

The extensive cloth factory of Messrs. Mackechnie and Winans is the largest establishment of the kind in the Province, and affords employment to nearly two hundred hands. In addition to this important factory there are numerous grist mills, foundries, tanneries, gypsum mills, saw and planing mills, breweries, etc.

Steamers are daily callers on their passages up, down, and across the lake, while stages run in every direction. The township of Hamilton is generally well settled and contains a large number of excellent well-cultivated farms, on which a large proportion of the fine cattle and sheep that annually carry off the prizes at our agricultural fairs are raised: to the improvement of the breed of sheep, in particular, have the farmers of these counties applied themselves, and the texture of the fabrics manufactured at the Ontario mills afford conclusive evidence of the complete success of their labors.

LONDON

The tourist unacquainted with the rapid growth of our towns in the west, will almost, on leaving Ingersoll, in proceeding westward, come to the conclusion that he has left civilisation behind. In proportion, therefore, will be his astonishment on emerging from a long pine tract, to see at some distance before him a large, well-built, and populous town. Yet London, the capital of the County of Middlesex, may lay claim to all, if not more, than this description. The town is finely situated, where the two branches of the Thames unite; and from its elevated position, is both

[4] Victoria College affiliated with The University of Toronto and moved to Toronto in 1892.

healthy and picturesque. The Church of England [St. Paul's, 1845-6], the handsomest Gothic edifice in Canada West, was designed and erected by Mr. [William] Thomas, architect in Toronto, the [Catholic Church], also, a very fine church has been recently built, and is a commodious and handsome structure. London boasts in all of some thirteen or fourteen churches, and Baptists, Wesleyans, Congregationalists, Presbyterians, whether of the old form, the Free Kirk or Secession, Universalists, and Colored Baptists have built, it would almost seem in a spirit of emulation, comfortable and substantial brick or frame places of worship. The Court House and Jail, [1826-41], is a fine pile of buildings and was erected at a cost of over six thousand pounds. A new Town Hall and Market House, a Mechanic's Institute, and a very large Grammar School have also been recently erected; a common brick schoolhouse has been built by the Corporation, at an expense (says Smith's Canada) of seventeen hundred pounds. The barracks, which are roomy and commodious, are to the north of the town. There are flourishing bank agencies and building societies here, with societies innumerable, while there is no room to complain of the want of grist and saw mills, distilleries, foundries, tanneries or asheries. Labatt's Brewery is too well known to all true lovers of malt to require particular notice; treble, double, or single X, are all to be had, and of a quality that would almost shake one's belief in the exclusive excellence of Hodgson or Bass's pale East India.

London has been singularly unfortunate in respect to fires, and has four times, within the last few years, suffered from the devouring element; on one occasion, the fire of 1845, one hundred and fifty large buildings were destroyed. The result of these repeated purifications has been that it contains fewer mean and shabby looking houses than most towns of similar importance.

Much, doubtless, of the prosperity, everywhere visible, and the rapid increase in the population (nearly six thousand), is to be attributed to London having been so long a military station; but still, it is in the energy of the inhabitants and the productiveness of the adjacent country, that the real cause is to be found. The well-stocked shops and the expeditious yet safe mode of doing business, have long rendered London a place worthy of note in the far west, and speculation is even now rife as to how the railroad will affect the interests of the town. There are always some croakers to be found in every community, and such individuals are at present busy with their prognostications that, as the railroad progresses and the facilities of transportation are multiplied, so will the prosperity of this new thriving town in the same ratio decrease; but the same calculations were made years ago with respect to horses in Great Britain; yet as railroads increased, so did the number of horses increase likewise; and, granting that one class of travellers will cease to stop in London, in the same manner as business increases, so will it be found necessary to have, likewise, an increase of travellers. Besides, the Canadian Cockneys have too much enterprise amongst them not to make a fresh business if the old one diminishes, and we have very little doubt but that, so far from injuring the town, a railroad will only add fresh energy to the already wide-awake Lunnuners.

ST. CATHARINES

The town of St. Catharines, now numbering about 5000 inhabitants, may be said to date its origin from the first carrying out of the project of the Hon. W. H. Merritt in 1824, of uniting the two Lakes, Erie and Ontario, by a ship canal.

So extraordinary, however, of late years has been the rapidity of rise with which the towns and cities of Western Canada have as it were sprung into existance, that our minds, familiarized to the contemplation of the almost magical changes taking place about us upon every side, have been led to regard the more gradual development of St. Catharines as a comparatively slow and tedious operation; but few and short seem the intervening years to those who yet survive to look back upon the time, when the yet unbroken forests waved majestically over this fair portion of our land.

Amongst the many elements of future greatness possessed in a striking degree by St. Catharines, we may mention as one of the first in importance, the unlimited amount of water power, with a fall of about 300 feet in a distance of four miles, furnished by the completion of the Welland Canal.

This gigantic undertaking which now allows of the free transit of ships of 350 tons burthen, between Lakes Erie and Ontario, and whose vast importance as a national work second in its ultimate results to none upon the face of the globe, is only now beginning to be properly appreciated.

St. Catharines and her inhabitants have good cause to be proud of their Canal, nor is their confidence in its amazing resources either exaggerated or misplaced. And their geographical position, which may be considered at the head of the ship navigation of Lake Ontario; the largest vessels navigating those waters being able to ascend to the Town, gives them the possession of all the facilities of trade and export, enjoyed by towns situated upon the sea-board: and with Lake Erie for a "mill-dam" and Lake Ontario and the River St. Lawrence for a "tail-race," they possess within themselves an amount of hydraulic power, applicable at a trifling outlay to every description of machinery, not exceeded if indeed equalled by any other locality in the known world.

Nor are these her only sources of gratification, planted as she is in the midst of a picturesque country, capable of the highest degree of cultivation, and possessed of a genial soil and salubrious climate, eminently adapted to agricultural and horticultural purposes. Nor is the spirit of enterprize with which her inhabitants would seem to be endowed, altogether unworthy of the natural advantages they undoubtedly possess. A company has recently been formed for the purpose of lighting the Canal and the Town of St. Catharines with gas, which is now going into immediate operation. A branch railroad is also about to be constructed, for the purpose of uniting the Town and Port Dalhousie, the lower outlet of the canal, with the Great Western Railway, at a point a mile and a half above the town, intended to run in connexion with a line of first class steamboats to the ports upon the lower lake. A company is also forming to bring the Lake Erie water from the top of the mountain through large pipes, to every part of the town. An extraordinary degree of activity prevails in every branch of business – four vessels forming an aggregate of nearly 1200 tons have already during the present summer been launched in the ship-yard; and another of a large class, is fast hastening to completion. Five large flouring mills, comprehending altogether thirty-one run of stones, make merry music as they go: the saw-mills, two in number, have to work night and day to supply a small portion of the demand; there are five machine shops, and one axe and edge-tool factory; two very large foundries busily employed in the most profitable application of alchemy, yet discovered, for transmuting iron into gold – and various smaller factories of different descriptions, planning-machines, &c., all in busy operation, combined with the activity prevailing in the erection of new buildings, altogether gives the town at the present period a look of prosperity and business capabilities, far in advance of its size and appearance.

One subject more, from amongst the many, which in a short article of the present description must necessarily be omitted, we have reserved unintentionally for the last – we allude to the St. Catharines Salt Springs.

These important and grateful additions to the wealth and comfort of the inhabitants, after having for some years been allowed to fall into a state of total neglect and disrepair, have at length attracted the notice they have long justly merited; and promise to afford in a few months, all the comforts and benefits of saline baths, both hot and cold, to the inhabitants of Canada and the adjacent states, at a distance of upwards of 300 miles from the sea. Salt of the finest quality is here manufactured, though at present only in limited quantities. We confidently predict for these Springs, when their virtue shall have an opportunity of being generally known and appreciated, as great and deserved a reputation, when applied to their legitimate purposes, as any upon this continent.

The Genesis of Ontario Politics in the Province of Canada (1838-1871)

Paul G. Cornell

In 1838 Lord Durham reported on "the peculiar geographical character of the province [Upper Canada] . . . its inhabitants scattered along an extensive frontier, with imperfect means of communication, and a limited and partial commerce, have, apparently no unity of interest or opinion. The Province has no great centre with which all the parts are connected, . . . Instead of this, there are many petty local centres, the sentiments and interests (or at least what are fancied to be so) of which, are distinct, and perhaps opposed". If we accept his analysis without question we are driven to wonder whether the history of this Upper Canada region can be studied as a single social and political entity. In seeking reasons for political disaffection and retarded economic progress Durham gives no credit to his despised Family Compact for the co-ordination and leadership that they had in fact given in the province's first forty-five years of very primitive pioneer development.

Thirty years later Upper Canada had become a self-conscious and viable province of Ontario: with a sense of identity, a metropolitan centre in Toronto, its land fully settled, its commerce prosperous, new industries multiplying, and the whole welded together by a network of railways. All this had happened in the years 1840-1867 while it had been attached to Lower Canada in the united province of Canada. Statesmen of that era were baffled by the extraordinary complex of divergent pressures and tendencies of those years, and later historians continue to share their puzzlement. The facts of geography and economics dictated that Upper Canada establish and maintain intimate connections with Lower Canada, while most pressures in the maturing society urged on the consolidation of regional institutions fulfilling local needs. This study seeks to identify, particularly in the political field, the main foundations of the province of Ontario in the years 1837-1871.

I

Between the dying days of 1837 and September 1841 a perplexed British government had resolved upon a course of action to start the Canadian colonies on a new course of progress, and the policy had been set in motion by twenty-three months of unremitting activity by Lord Sydenham.

The new policy had various ingredients. The economic unity of the St. Lawrence River Valley–Great Lakes region was to be recognized and the French-Canadian "problem" solved by joining Upper Canada and Lower Canada into one province. The stalled economy was to be sparked into new life by a large infusion of new capital for public works and a reform in public administrative procedures. Tensions between groups of Reformers and Tories were considered to be exaggerations of real social and administrative problems, grown out of proportion in an isolated backwoods society. They could be overcome by good effective administration. The rigid confrontation that had brought active rebellion could be thawed by isolating and ignoring the leaders of extreme groups while sponsoring practical men of moderate views. Theoretical ideas, current in the colonies and in Britain about applying the techniques of responsible cabinet government, were inadmissable and wrong-headed. Theoretically they would place the Governor at the mercy of two quite different masters: the British government and colonial public opinion. In practical terms, both Upper and Lower Canada were rent by the contentions of extreme, irresponsible political groups; the present colonial population would not be able to operate with moderation the highly sophisticated conventions of cabinet government.

For Canada West (the new official name of Upper Canada) Lord Sydenham's initiatives left several important legacies. He used his personal experience of British business and political methods with machiavellian shrewdness to get the wheels of government rolling again. A Colonial Office dispatch of October 16, 1839 authorized him to remove and replace members of the colony's Executive Council when public policy dictated. One main citadel of Compact Tory power was thereby immediately undermined. Sydenham used the threat of this power to secure the acquiescence of Upper Canadian Tories in his policies, and then he removed them from office. The governor masterminded the campaign strategy for the 1841 general election, and personally arranged the details. Compact Tories were excluded from a slate of officially favoured candidates, while middle-of-the-road independents and moderate Reformers were sought out and encouraged. These candidates were given every available aid and assistance and the personal attention of the governor. Their opponents were excluded from government patronage and pointedly snubbed. Of the forty-two members returned by Canada West only 6 Compact Tories and 7 ultra-Reformers consistently opposed the governor's policies in the Legislature. Sydenham's methods had reduced Tory representation to only 14%, while his manoeuvering among Reformers had disorganized their sense of party solidarity. For the moment he held the initiative in the political life of Canada West.

The *élan*, and even supercilous contempt, with which Sydenham manipulated his colonial demesne, did not disguise his use of every trick of contemporary British political life to achieve his immediate aims. Perhaps Canadians did not need lessons in the use of influence, patronage and physical violence in political manoeuvre. There remained for a generation, however, the memory that the highest representative of the British government gloried in political expediency.

Finally, it had been a part of British strategy for solving the problems of 1837, that the English-speaking majority in the United Province should in time, effectively assimilate the French Canadian minority. Given the different well-established institutions in the provinces of Upper and Lower Canada, and the solidarity of the French Canadian community, the policy had no hope of success. Yet the formative months of 1840 and 1841 were the time to set the pattern for such changes, if they were to come about. There is no evidence that Sydenham tried to bring the institutions and people of Canada West into active co-operation with the English community of Canada East. On the contrary, he set the pattern of legislating separately for the institutions of the two sections of the province; and in organizing the 1841 general election he recognized two different campaigns, one in each of the late provinces, to be organized separately and dealt with by a different strategy. Tacitly, he recognized the continuation of the old provincial boundary.

II

With Sydenham's removal from the scene the various forces operating upon public life were freed to find their own equilibrium. Most significant in the long run was a new massive wave of immigration from the British Isles, gathering momentum from 1842 onward. The population had doubled before the end of the decade. New capital investment brought the rapid completion of the canals on the St. Lawrence with accompanying employment and increased circulation of money. Meanwhile the consolidation of fiscal and budgetary policy in one provincial government cleared the way for the expansion and articulation of private mercantile organizations throughout the whole area.

From well before 1837 energetic merchants in Niagara, Kingston, York, Hamilton, St. Catharines and London had opened up the commerce and markets of Upper Canada. They were and for years inevitably would remain the up-country agents and tributaries of Montreal wholesalers. Yet residence in Canada West gave insights and impressions about business prospects that differed subtly from the view in Montreal. Upstate New York on Lake Ontario, and Pennsylvania, Ohio and Michigan across Lake Erie all gave prospects of growing markets for Upper Canadian produce, while the Erie Canal opened at Buffalo an alternative route to the Atlantic and markets overseas. People travelling to Britain came and went quite regularly through the United States rather than by way of Montreal. Here was a basis for the gradual evolution of an Upper Canadian economy in the future. Meanwhile the merchant class of Canada West grew in numbers and in influence, and sparked the rapid growth of numerous towns.

These social and economic developments had their influence on political life, while the constitutional arrangements of 1841 presented new problems of their own. From the political battles of the 1830's there were legacies of party loyalties and alignments: particularly the idea of "Tories" opposed by "Reformers". Both these political camps were now transformed – the Tories dethroned from the inner councils of government, the Reformers systematically disorganized by Sydenham, and their radical wing in exile or hiding. Forty-two Lower Canadians had now to be included in all calculations of parliamentary manoeuvering – a new factor that would require new tactics. If a succession of governors general had been prepared to devote themselves to acting as their own chief minister and political agent they might have delayed the reappearance of party politics. Sir Charles Bagot was certain that this was not possible.

From the session of the Legislature in 1842 political party activity was again untrammelled by executive restraints. While the Compact Tories were no longer an official party, their staunchest followers were still at hand. The growing merchant community would want stability in society and a favourable, paternalistic government policy: they might be wooed to support the Tories. Farming populations tend to be conservative unless roused to deal with a collective wrong: they too might be organized by the Tories. There was still a strong "War of 1812 patriotism" in Upper Canada that had been exploited more than once by the Tories, an emotion not very different from the British patriotism alive in many of the new immigrants. All these tendencies seemed to be available if a reinvigorated Tory party could grasp and use them.

For the Reformers too there were hopeful tendencies. Compact Toryism had a repellent exclusive quality, and its Church of England connections grated on the sensibilities of the majority of the people. The popular interpretation of the Mackenzie Rebellion could be turned to portraying a Reform party as the defender of the people, frustrated by aristocratic and corrupt interests entrenched in power. Most important for the Reformers, however, was the absence of their radical wing, and the presence of Robert Baldwin and his fixed idea about Responsible Government. Without the radicals the Reformers could appeal to moderate merchants, traders and farmers as the advocates of good middle class government. Baldwin's idea of Responsible Government was a touchstone that encompassed all others, for if government responded exactly to the will of the people, it would, ideally, legislate for every man his heart's desire.

As the party battle developed, Baldwin and his Reformers held the winning hand, while the Tories could not seem to get organized under William Draper. In 1842 and 1843 Baldwin's Reformers developed a working alliance with LaFontaine's French Canadians to control a majority of the Legislative Assembly, while both leaders entered the Executive Council, and for some months insured the co-ordination of executive actions with the general will of the Assembly. During this happy interval most of Sydenham's "official" moderate members from Canada West moved into support of Baldwin, so that his following numbered at least 25 members in the House. It is interesting that Baldwin was not overly punctilious about insisting on an Upper Canadian majority for all major executive acts at this time. On November 3, 1843, his supporters were in a minority of 14 to 27 (of members from Canada West) on the decision to move the seat of government from Kingston to Montreal. Thirteen days later they were in a minority of one (12 to 13) on the second reading of the Assessment Bill for Upper Canada.

What seemed to be a quite inevitable drift toward the functioning of cabinet government was halted abruptly in late November 1843, when Sir Charles Metcalfe, on orders from Britain, refused the proffered advice of his Executive Council on a matter of government patronage in Canada East. The issue was tried before the electorate in a general election in the summer of 1844 with a verdict in favour of the governor's contention. Baldwin's Reformers shrank in numbers to 12 (with 1 independent) and were faced in the new second parliament by 29 Tories and moderates. In referring the theory of Responsible Government from the confidential discussions of the council table to election propaganda for popular consumption, something of its clear theoretical purity was lost (to be restored later by historians and party politicians bent on establishing some neat pattern of development). For purposes of the election the principal aim of the moment was to secure the return of Baldwin, W. H. Blake, J. H. Price, J. P. Roblin, M. Cameron and other Reformers, rather than W. E. T. Corbett, G. Duggan, W. R. Graham, D. B. Stevenson, Alex. Fraser and other Tories and moderates who supported the governor. Personalities, the control of patronage, and immemorial political feuds in the ridings entered into the public contest.

In the following years from 1844 to 1847 the way was open for the reorganization of a new Tory party, an alternative to the Reformers, that would lead public life calmly and moderately into developing the new Canada West. The possibilities of the moment were understood by W. H. Draper, one of the province's leading barristers, and he rightly identified John A. Macdonald, J. H. Cameron and William Cayley as the nucleus of a new generation of Tories about whom the party might grow. Too many of the old guard, George and Henry Sherwood, W. B. Robinson, Sir Allan MacNab, J. Johnston and their ilk, were present with their long memories of older, better Tory days. They resented Draper and quarrelled among themselves. The crowning problem was one of political strategy: the need for a working alliance with a significant group of Lower Canadian members to control a dependable majority in the Assembly. Three major efforts by Draper to frame an alliance with the French Canadians failed. A new general election at the end of 1847 weighed the accomplishments of the recent Tory administration and found them wanting: 23 Reformers faced 18 Tories and one independent at the beginning of the third parliament.

The British government had come into the hands of the Whig party some months previously and had changed its stand on the question of cabinet government for mature colonies. The new governor general, Lord Elgin, was instructed to preserve absolute neutrality in the political warfare leading up to the general election. Thus Baldwin and his Reformers had a free rein to present the principles of Responsible Government in the election campaign and implement them after their victory. It was the Reformers who had worked out the election-winning formula that appealed to the moderate electors. They now entered upon six years in office.

III

In 1848 and 1849 the Baldwin formula seemed to meet the needs of Canada West exactly. The Reformers had insisted upon the cabinet government principle and were now operating it with the full backing of the British government. A dynamic legislative programme brought moderate, common sense solutions to the need for more representative municipal institutions, the secularizing of university endowments, the revamping of municipal assessment procedure and the streamlining of judicial procedure. A resolution, popular with business people, urged the British government to secure the free importing and exporting of natural products with the United States. While it made no wide popular appeal in Canada West, the Baldwin Reformers maintained an intimate working agreement with LaFontaine and his French Canadian party of Canada East and were thereby assured of a dependable majority in the Assembly.

Almost in the hour of victory, however, the Baldwin Reformers' political position began to be outmoded. For one thing, the achievement of Responsible Government had removed that idea from the field of reforms to be fought for, and opened the question: what new goals lay open for reforming spirits? A spate of new political ideas and controversial religious positions gained currency in Canada West: some stemming from the climate of the 1848 liberal revolutions in Europe and political radicalism in England, the Free Kirk disruption of the Scottish Church, and the Protestant resentment of the new Roman Catholic territorial dioceses in England. The large Irish immigration continued to import Orange-Roman Catholic tensions. All these new currents replenished the ammunition for continuing older controversies. The proclamation of amnesty for the revolutionaries of 1837 brought W. L. Mackenzie, Peter Perry and Caleb Hopkins back into public life, to join with a rising generation of radicals who were involved with the new ideas.

Baldwin's Reformers had never captured the confidence of the upper echelons of the Canadian business world, although he had a loyal following among the ranks of Upper Canadian merchants. It was still not certain in 1849-50 that Francis Hincks, the Reformers' chief financial expert, would be able to build lasting confidence between the Reformers and the business community in general, for its requirements from the government in capital aid, company legislation and tariff adjustments would become ever more importunate. It was perhaps a sign of the times when on July 24, 1850, Holmes (a liberal spokesman for Montreal business interests) seconded by W. B. Richards (a well connected Midland District Reformer) moved the third reading of a general Companies Incorporation Act for manufacturing, mining, mechanical and chemical industries, that it was Baldwin himself, seconded by J. H. Price, who moved a six month's hoist. In the ensuing division, not on party lines, Baldwin and Price were in a minority of 8 to 22 among members from Canada West.

In 1851 it became clear that Baldwin's political organization in Canada West was rent by disunity, caused by the pressing of the new radicals on the left of the party, for more constitutional and legal innovation. The process came to a head on June 26, 1851, when W. L. Mackenzie, seconded by Caleb Hopkins, moved for a special committee to report a bill for the abolition of the Court of Chancery in Upper Canada. The members from Canada West voted 25 to 9 in support of this proposition, which was intended to demolish Baldwin's own work of the previous year in reorganizing this Court. Baldwin resigned immediately, claiming that he had lost the confidence of his constituents.

The Reform ministry was reorganized in the next months with Francis Hincks undertaking the leadership in Canada West. Two principal problems had to be met:

a new accommodation with the radical Reformers to silence their disruptive tendencies, and a new approach to the business community of Canada to meet its growing needs for government aid. In their whole approach to public life the two classes were mutually antagonistic. At the moment Hincks came to power the railway building mania was about to seize the imagination of the province, and Hincks led his government toward aiding and encouraging railway building. Very soon most radicals in the party drew back with distaste from involvement in the large scale capital borrowing that was the price of railways. As the provincial and municipal governments became more and more involved in railway financing the radicals proclaimed conspiracy by financial "interests." Hincks and his government became "corruptionist." In the constituencies and in parliament the Reformers had ceased to be an alliance, and presented a spectrum of political shadings from radical rebels of 1837 to moderate individualists like Sandfield Macdonald.

In the summer of 1854 these divisions among Reformers brought down the Hincks ministry. The proportions of the schism were exactly defined in the general election in August. To fill its 65 seats Canada West had returned 25 Hincksite Reformers, moderates of the centre. In opposition, 25 Conservatives on the right and 14 Reformers on the left together constituted a majority from their section of the province (one riding was vacant). Since the government still held the support of the majority from Canada East, the ministerial crisis was exclusively an Upper Canadian affair, and the 14 ultra-Reformers in opposition were the telling factor.

IV

A new generation of public men was coming into view with the general election of 1854 while the old was making its final appearance. It was, for instance, the last general election for as different people as William Lyon Mackenzie and Sir Allan MacNab. John A. Macdonald was now recognized as heir apparent in the Conservative ranks, and with him were the stalwarts of the next decade: J. H. Cameron (Toronto), W. F. Powell (Carleton), E. Murney (Hastings North), D. B. Stevenson (Prince Edward), G. MacBerth (Elgin West), J. Langton (Peterborough) and others. The ultra-Reformers did not march in step as a homogeneous party. Joseph Hartman (York North), Billa Flint (Hastings South), J. Scatcherd (Middlesex West) and D. McKerlie (Brant East) had urgent reforming instincts; George Brown, in his second parliament, was beginning to find them kindred spirits; while Sandfield Macdonald, for instance, followed his own courses. In the ranks of Reformers that supported Hincks in September 1854, were many good Reform party men who in the following years would find it impossible to preserve a distinct middle way between the emerging political poles of Grittism and Conservatism. Some, like J. Gould (Ontario North), H. Munro (Durham North), R. Bell (Lanark North), H. Bigger (Brant West) drifted within a few months into the Clear Grit ranks, others like Angus and J. C. Morrison (Simcoe North, Niagara), D. Roblin (Lennox and Addington), R. Spence (Wentworth North) and Sydney Smith (Northumberland West) continued to claim to be Reformers, but voted the Conservative party line on most occasions.

Expediency, rather than far-seeing design brought a workable solution to the ministerial crisis of September 1854. It became clear in negotiation that there was much practical common ground between Hincks' moderate Reformers and the Conservatives. A rebuilding of the Upper Canadian wing of the ministry, excluding the ultra-Reformers Malcolm Cameron and John Rolph but including three Conservatives and two Hincksite Reformers, secured the necessary working majority. On the morrow of the cabinet changes on September 11, 1854, only 20 left-wing Reformers were in opposition while 44 Conservatives and moderate Hincksite Reformers supported the government.

Succeeding months and years brought a gradual readjustment in the alignment of individual members, and an evolution in the policies of the various political groups. In parliamentary terms, the ultra-Reformers began to use the name Clear Grit, and finding more and more common ground among themselves, developed a party *esprit de corps* and attracted many moderate Reformers into their ranks. Merchants and business men of stature joining the party further diluted its agrarian radicalism. The Tory party, too, was undergoing a transformation that would see it emerge as a Conservative party. There were visible tensions still between the Tory wing and the new moderate men. Expediency and shared goals brought moderate Reformers into alliance, or into the party's ranks. The exclusion of Sir Allan MacNab from the cabinet and from party leadership in 1856, and the succession of John A. Macdonald to leadership marked the completion of this process.

The division of the Upper Canadian political scene into two camps was evident in the general election of 1857. In most ridings the voters now had a simple choice between two candidates, one a "Ministerialist", usually a Conservative, but occasionally a Hincksite Reformer, and the other a Clear Grit. In retrospect, the arrangements of September 1854 stand out as a great watershed in Upper Canadian politics. Previously the followers of Baldwin and Hincks had really been a party of the centre. Soon after 1854, and for many generations, every little Ontarian born alive was either a Liberal or a Conservative.

V

Although since 1841 Canada West had been joined to Canada East like a Siamese twin, for over a decade its political life had stemmed from issues arising within its own borders. It is conceivable that political developments up to this point would not have been very different if Upper Canada had gone its own way, and not entered into the union. In its different circumstances Nova Scotia's experiences had "won" Responsible Government and evolved a two party system, with Tories transformed into Conservatives and Reformers become Liberals. From 1857 onward, however, many of the motives in the public life of Canada West became inextricably involved in the fact of union with Canada East. With the astonishing growth of population and its accompanying economic developments, the business and financial community of Canada West gained a sense of identity and began to make its own demands on the provincial government. The more effective electioneering propaganda for Canada West involved rivalry with the English-speaking financial interests of Montreal and Lower Canada's French Canadian community. The strategy for building a viable ministry began to depend very much on the political affairs of Canada East.

This change was in large part due to the emergence of the Clear Grit party as the champion of the special attitudes of Canada West. Particularist tendencies had of course been evident in both parts of the province from 1841, but the actual building of a party on these lines in Upper Canada began in 1855. Late in the session of that year a Separate School Bill for Upper Canada was introduced by a French Canadian and pushed through parliament against the votes of a majority of members from Canada West. Here was ammunition for a cry that Canada West was "dominated" by French Canadian Lower Canada. The party machinery of the Clear Grits was lying fallow awaiting the energy of a new cause, and in central and western Upper Canada the Toronto *Globe* was gaining prestige as the most widely circulated liberal paper. The necessary spark to galvanize all into action was provided in 1856 by George Brown, the *Globe's* proprietor, when he introduced the theme: Canada West would only find justice and its optimum development if it was represented in parliament in numbers corresponding to the population, without regard to any dividing line with Canada East. The proposition was soon contracted to the phrase "Rep. by Pop."

The Clear Grit party found unity in this cry, and won the 1857 general election: their 34 members were opposed by only 24 Conservatives and 5 Hincksite Reformers. (Two ridings were vacant.) With a majority of five in their section of the Province they hammered away at the Macdonald-Cartier government from February to late July of the new session, demonstrating beyond doubt that the ministry was kept in power by Lower Canadian votes. The earnest will of the Upper Canadian majority was frustrated by the arrangement of the constitution. However, quick victory was suddenly in sight when the Macdonald-Cartier government was defeated in a division concerning Ottawa as the permanent seat of government, and resigned. George Brown and Upper Canadian liberals, concluded an *ad hoc* arrangement with *Rouge* and liberal members from Canada East and were sworn in as a new ministry. The confidence of parliament was immediately tested on August 2, 1858, and the Brown-Dorion government was defeated. The old government under Georges Etienne Cartier and John A. Macdonald returned to power.

These events of August 1858 clearly demonstrated the essential difficulties of the constitutional situation: the liberal majority of Canada West was powerless to effect legislation for Canada West, and there was apparently no substitute for a ministry formed on the strength of the French Canadian party. The ranks of the Upper Canadian Clear Grit liberals began to fray again, when "Rep. by Pop." was seen to be ineffectual. There was a strong movement in favour of a solution that had been repeatedly urged in earlier years by W. L. Mackenzie: simply dissolve the Union of 1841. To arrest further disintegration, a full scale convention of Clear Grits and liberals was assembled in Toronto in late 1859 to hammer out a new policy. A movement in favour of simple dissolution of the Union was averted. Many of the delegates recognized that the Union had worked out well from an economic point of view and had removed the obstacles to Upper Canadian development that had been so evident in the 1830's. Further, there was fear that outside a union, Upper Canada would be inexorably drawn into annexation to the United States. Again it was George Brown who led the convention's thinking toward resolutions in favour of converting the union with Lower Canada into a federal arrangement. A federal union would preserve the economic unity of the St. Lawrence–Great Lakes area, and provide a strong enough base for the economic penetration of the prairie West. Meanwhile local parliaments for Upper and Lower Canada would allow "Rep. by Pop." full play in dealing with all the cultural and social matters that had brought Upper and Lower Canadians close to blows.

There is an inference in Liberal history writing that John A. Macdonald and his Conservatives were from 1858 onward somehow usurping power, with something less than honour in the process. In retrospect, it is not clear that a Clear Grit government could have taken power in February 1858 and from that date provided Upper Canada with complete self government but for the tie of union with Lower Canada. The gathering of various radical Reformers into a viable party in the period 1855-57, and their election victory in the latter year, depended upon their anti-Lower Canada emotion: a sectional emotion. With this motive removed, it is at least conceivable that moderate opinion would have supported either Hincks or Macdonald, or a coalition of both, to provide long years of government catering to the energetic expansion of the Upper Canadian economy. Given the circumstances of the Union in the late 1850's, the Conservatives and their Hincksite Reformer allies were providing just this sort of practical government.

The record of Upper Canadian politics in the following seventy months, though filled with manoeuvre and experiment, added little to the situation known in August 1858. The general election of 1861 returned Liberals and Conservatives in equal numbers from Canada West, while there was less party solidarity in Canada East. The Cartier-Macdonald government survived for some months but was eventually upset by the defection of many of its Lower Canadian supporters in May, 1862, over a question of defence policy. Curiously, on this vital division the government actually had a majority of six in Upper Canada.

Sandfield Macdonald undertook the formation of a Liberal ministry and again opened experiments seeking an alternative to the Cartier-Macdonald alliance. In theory, his prospects for success should have been very good for though he could depend on the general support of the Clear Grits he had never been one of them, nor had he ever voted in support of "Rep. by Pop." His moderate position might attract many Upper Canadians while of all the Upper Canadian Liberals, he should have had the best prospects for gaining broad support among Lower Canadians. As events worked out he stayed in power till March 1864, but it was an uneasy experience. Down to May 1862 he enjoyed a slim majority of about three in Canada West. When he was defeated in the House by Lower Canadian votes he called a general election for the summer of 1862 and won a resounding victory in Canada West – a majority of 25. From the viewpoint of the United Province, however, the election was a grave disappointment, for his Lower Canadian allies had been reduced to about 18. There was no scope for vigorous government with a majority of only two or three, dependent on the votes of a few independent members. The situation of 1858 had returned with slight variations: now it was a government with a large Upper Canadian contingent and a small Lower Canadian tail, faced with an opposition with a large Lower Canadian representation and a minute Upper Canadian tail. Deadlock was reached in June 1864 when both the Sandfield Macdonald-Dorion alliance and their Liberal-Conservative opponents had attempted to form a lasting ministry, without success.

VI

The final chapter in the political history of the United Province of Canada in the years 1864 to 1867 was prelude to Canadian federation. The political parties led by Cartier (Canada East – *Bleu*), Brown (Canada West – Grit) and John A. Macdonald (Canada West – Conservative), on the initiative of George Brown agreed in June 1864 to join in a drive to solve the political deadlock by introducing the federal principle to the Canadian constitution. This was the Great Coalition that masterminded the Canadian federation of 1867.

As seen from Upper Canada the Great Coalition was a truce between Clear Grit Liberals and Conservatives to achieve a new degree of autonomy for their region. The two parties brought differing approaches to the constitutional problem. Brown and his Liberals would have preferred to concentrate on remodelling the Union of Upper and Lower Canada, restoring to each its own Legislature, and providing a joint authority to administer interests common to the two regions. Hopefully Upper Canada would gain both a new initiative for its self-realization and expansion westward, and still retain the advantages of the economic unity of the Great Lakes–St. Lawrence River region. The operation of the "Rep. by Pop." principle in both the new provincial legislature and the federal joint authority would, it was thought, achieve Upper Canadian goals.

The Conservative approach to the Great Coalition was to concentrate first on seeking a federal union of all the British North American provinces, reverting to the smaller federation only in case of failure with the larger scheme. This insistence on the larger British North American union was at first not necessarily the expression of a new national sentiment, nor was it merely a partisan tactical move to assure the future of the party. It was the only practicable scheme. From 1854 onward the Conservatives had recognized mutual economic advantage in co-operating closely with the *Bleu* party in Lower Canada. The insistence by their Liberal opponents on particularist Upper Canadian attitudes had obviously led into the *cul-de-sac* of political deadlock: the creation of particularist attitudes in Lower Canada that exactly matched their own. The way out of the deadlock must be on the very practical lines of extending to all British North America the habit of co-operation among provinces for mutual economic benefit. It was a recipe that had worked well in Liberal-Conservative hands for 95 of the 117 months since the fall of Hincks' government in 1854.

The division in the Canadian Legislature which passed the Confederation Resolutions on March 11, 1865, recorded 54 members from Canada West in favour and only 8 opposed (7 Clear Grits and 1 Conservative). Soon thereafter activity in party ranks began to prepare for the realities of a federal political system. For the Liberal-Conservative leaders their best tactic was to perpetuate the semblance of a coalition ministry that had conceived the plans for federation and must now, logically, be the best equipped party to implement them. For the Liberals in Upper Canada the practical problem was more difficult, for they must either strike out independently on a new tack of their own, or have their identity lost, absorbed in the coalition ministry.

George Brown withdrew from the cabinet in December 1865; joining the seven anti-federalist Clear Grits, he began to recreate the Liberal party. Many of the party's faithful followers from the battles of the previous decade both in parliament and in the ridings responded to his lead. On the eve of the general elections of 1867 a Liberal party convention in Toronto attracted an enthusiastic attendance, and disowned the few Liberals of former years who continued to work in coalition with John A. Macdonald. Apparently they were prepared to give battle with the Conservatives on the old party lines.

VII

The general elections of 1867 were anticipated as a definitive testing of party alignment under the new constitutional arrangements. The British North America Act respected the principle of "Representation by Population" and assigned 82 seats in the House of Commons to the new province of Ontario, in place of the 65 seats Canada West held in 1866. Where a major party was faced previously with fielding candidates in 65 ridings, it had in 1867 to deal with 82 federal and 82 provincial ridings. Both parties were hard pressed to find sufficient candidates of good calibre, but in the end 157 federal and 164 provincial candidates stood for election. For the only time in history, the federal and provincial elections were held concurrently in each riding. There was no prohibition against a candidate offering himself for both the House of Commons and the Ontario Legislature. On July 1, when the Dominion of Canada was proclaimed, Sir John A. Macdonald and leaders of the Confederation movement were sworn to office in the federal government; Sandfield Macdonald became Premier of Ontario in a six man cabinet, half Conservative and half "Coalition Liberal." It was in these unique circumstances, with administrations already appointed to office at Ottawa and Toronto, that the general elections of 1867 hold unusual interest.

It was apparent that most of the veteran politicians of Canada West viewed the federal House of Commons as the important new political arena; 49 members of the Canadian Legislature in 1866 offered themselves for the Ontario seats in the 1867 federal election, and 36 were returned. By contrast, only seven sitting members ran in the Ontario provincial election and the four who succeeded (E. B. Wood, T. R. Ferguson, Sandfield Macdonald and John Carling) all held federal seats as well. In addition, 22 former members of the Canadian Legislative Assembly stood for election to the House of Commons, nine being successful. Nineteen other political veterans contested Ontario provincial seats, 12 with success. Thus the Ontario contingent to Ottawa in 1867 was much the same sort of group that would have been returned to a ninth parliament of the United Province of Canada, while the Ontario Legislature was largely a new group of men with only a few veterans.

Approximately 48 federal members from Ontario supported the Macdonald government in 1867, including five who had been Liberals or Reformers in the past. The hopes of the Liberal party were frustrated, for there was really no alternative to the appeal of Macdonald's federal policies in that year. Where Liberal members were returned it was from areas of the province which had demonstrated years of loyalty to the Clear Grit party.

Party alignment in the House of Commons was obvious, for it continued the lines of cleavage established in the Canadian Legislative Assembly before 1867. This was not the case, however, in the new Legislature of Ontario. Sandfield Macdonald's provincial government (dubbed the "Patent Combination" by its opponents) was carefully conceived both in membership and policy to appeal to all moderate men and avoid old partisan feuds. Most members were new to public life and had left no clue to their previous political loyalty. The absence of divisions in the House clearly testing confidence in the government increases the difficulty of assigning each member to one party or another. It is clear, however, that about 28 members, led by Edward Blake and Archibald McKellar, constituted themselves a coherent Liberal party in opposition. By actively advocating many of the old Clear Grit principles – an extended franchise, cheaper and simpler legal procedures, amelioration of the condition of debtors, and strict legislative control of appropriations – they developed a sense of party solidarity, in contrast to the uninspired ranks of Conservatives and moderates supporting Sandfield Macdonald. The Liberals defeated Sandfield in the second provincial general election in March and April 1871 and toppled his government soon after.

It is a curious fact, then, that the federal and provincial general elections of 1867, though held concurrently in each riding, produced quite different results. In many ridings there is a close correspondence between the proportions of the votes cast for each party in the federal and the provincial elections. For instance on September 24, Bothwell's returns show in the federal election: David Mills (Liberal) 1333, David Glass (Conservative) 1224; and in the provincial election: Archibald McKellar (Liberal) 1309, Kirby (Conservative) 1238. By contrast, Middlesex East sent a Conservative to Ottawa and a staunch Liberal to Toronto (federal: Crowell Wilson (Conservative) 1896, D. McFie 1756; provincial: James Evans (Liberal) 1821, Taylor 1791.) Three-sided contests, uncontested elections, the ambiguous stand of some moderate independents, all serve to make general conclusions about the political battle meaningless.

When Ontario was inaugurated as a province in 1867 it did not speak with either a decisively Liberal or a Conservative voice. For the moment the Clear Grit or Liberal party had lost both the federal and provincial contests to the Conservatives and their allies, though neither party could feel assured about its future. In the following years both the federal and Ontario governments came under the control of long-lived ministries that followed moderate policies in tune with the needs of economic expansion. It was the Liberal nucleus, first assembled by Blake and McKellar and soon to be led by Oliver Mowat, that controlled the province of Ontario's destinies down to the end of the century. Although not so consistent in their success, the federal Conservatives continued to dispute Ontario ridings with Liberals in support of Sir John A. Macdonald's governments.

BIBLIOGRAPHICAL NOTE

The original sources for this field are the *Journals* of the Legislative Assembly of the Province of Canada (1841-1867) and of the Legislative Assembly of the Province of Ontario (1867-1872), together with the newspapers of the day, especially the Toronto *Globe* and the Toronto *Leader*.

Much of the basic material before 1867 is compiled and interpreted from a general Canadian point of view in P. G. Cornell, *The Alignment of Political Groups in Canada, 1841-1867* (Toronto, 1962).

The excellent biographies of John A. Macdonald by D. G. Creighton and of George Brown by J. M. S. Careless are essential to unravelling the public life of the period after 1854.

Confederation: The Atmosphere of Crisis[1]

C. P. Stacey

The story of Canadian Confederation was complicated and many-sided. Much of it of course was purely political: the breakdown of the Union of 1841 in Canada, and the relations and rivalries of political groups and individual politicians. Perhaps this side of the tale has received rather too much attention – partly as a result of historians' concern with personalities. My colleague Professor Creighton has raised the John A. Macdonald personality cult almost to the status of a major Canadian industry; my other colleague Professor Careless – ably seconded by the Toronto *Globe and Mail* – has contended resolutely for a place in the sun for George Brown. Mr. Careless, indeed, has argued, not merely that George was a major – perhaps *the* major – Father of Confederation, but that Mrs. George was the one and only Mother of Confederation.

Now all this is undeniably important. I should like however to recall another side of the story: the influence of events outside British North America, the violent external forces and pressures that bore upon the Canadian situation, and the Canadian reaction to those pressures. I have no intention of dealing in detail with the military and diplomatic history of those crowded and exciting years; that can be found in books. What I should like to present – and to do so in a few pages is probably beyond my powers – is a sort of essay in historical atmosphere. For I think it is evident that the atmosphere of the eighteen-sixties – an atmosphere dominated by foreign dangers and domestic preparations to meet them – goes far to explain the success of the great Canadian national project whose Centennial we are celebrating in 1967.

The Confederation drama was one play where the offstage noises were a vital part of the action. Those noises were largely echoes from the bloody battlefields of the American Civil War. They often threatened to drown the voices of the Canadian performers, the Macdonalds, the Browns, the Cartiers, as they spoke their dignified lines. Armies greater than Napoleon's were locked in conflict on the soil of North America; and as the statesmen of the British provinces strove to make plans for

[1] This paper is based upon a lecture given at the National Museum of Canada, Ottawa, on February 22, 1967.

their countries' future, the gunfire of Bull Run and Antietam and Fredericksburg rattled the windows of their offices.

Let me, very briefly, set the stage.

In the spring of 1861 the Civil War broke out. The British Government immediately sent large reinforcements of troops to British North America, simply as a precaution in an unpredictable situation. November brought the *Trent* Affair, when an Anglo-American war was closer than it has ever been since 1814. Now 11,000 more British soldiers were hastily ordered to the North American colonies, and many of them came marching up through New Brunswick to Quebec through that winter's snows. There was great excitement and much patriotic activity in Canada; but when the crisis passed off and a bill was brought into parliament to organize a militia force adequate to play an important part in defending Canada against the States, the honourable members voted it down and turned out the government. It seemed impossible to raise an adequate force without conscription; and conscription was already a dirty word in Canada.

That was 1862. The next year things moved on. The tide of war began to turn against thc South. In July the capture of Vicksburg put the Union in control of the whole course of the Mississippi; and the same week General Lee suffered his crucial defeat at Gettysburg. Ever since the *Trent* Affair the New York press had been calling Britain and Canada horrible names, and people began to wonder what would happen when and if the Southern Confederacy collapsed. In 1861 foolish Englishmen and Canadians had made fun of the Northern armies. Now no one was doing that any more. President Lincoln was at the head of the greatest military power on earth. In England the government and the governing class began to take alarm. And in Canada the legislature in the fall of 1863 actually appropriated nearly half a million dollars for the militia. That was peanuts, if you like to use a modern vulgarism; but only eight years earlier the militia had got along with $10,000.

The year 1864 was decisive. That summer, while the armies in the south bled each other white in a succession of appalling battles in front of Richmond, the Great Coalition was formed in Canada, dedicated to the federation of British North America. The Fathers met at Charlottetown in September and Quebec in October; and while they laboured at making a constitution General Sherman was marching from Atlanta to the sea. That march cut what remained of the Confederacy in two, and left a horrible black swath of destruction stretching across Georgia.

> So we made a thoroughfare, for Freedom and her train,
> Sixty miles in latitude, three hundred to the main . . .

Very few Canadians wanted that kind of freedom, or wanted to be introduced to it in that kind of way; and yet at this precise moment things took a turn that suggested the nasty possibility of General Grant or General Sherman cutting the same sort of pathway across Canada.

The Confederate government had conceived the rather crazy idea of using Canada as a base of operations against the Northern States. In September 1864 Confederate soldiers executed a piratical operation on Lake Erie, seizing one steamer, scuttling another, and scaring the cities on the American shore of the lake almost into convulsions. Next month something worse happened. A party of Confederates from Canada attacked the unsuspecting town of St. Albans in Vermont, robbed the banks, killed one citizen, tried to burn the place, and escaped across the border. The Canadian government did its best to perform its international obligations; it managed to arrest most of the raiders and recovered the stolen money. Then in December a stupid Montreal magistrate named Coursol did his country a serious disservice. Not only did he turn the St. Albans prisoners loose on a legal technicality, but he gave them back the $84,000 from the St. Albans banks, and men and money immediately vanished into thin air. It's really not surprising that a howl of rage went up from the United States. Mr. Coursol might have been in quite serious trouble if he hadn't been the Prime Minister's son-in-law. The Canadian taxpayer made the money good, and the Canadian government took action that showed how badly frightened it was. It actually called out 2000 of its own volunteer soldiers to keep order on the frontier; and it organized a detective force to watch the foreign agents who were abusing Canadian hospitality. This force became in due time the Dominion Police, and is really the earliest origin of the R.C.M.P. I wish I had time to tell its story. The mainspring of it was a Scotsman named Gilbert McMicken, who worked closely with John A. Macdonald. McMicken's detectives were an important element in the security of Canada during the troubled years that followed.

I've said enough, perhaps, to establish the fact that December 1864 was one of the darkest moments in Canadian history. The situation created by menaces from abroad was made worse by anxieties at home. The Irish nationalist society called the Fenian Brotherhood was already attracting attention in the United States, and it had branches in Canada. On the night of Guy Fawkes Day 1864 the city of Toronto got a bad scare when organized bodies of armed men appeared marching on its downtown streets. And just at the moment when the release of the St. Albans prisoners brought relations with the United States to their most critical stage, there were ludicrous panics in rural sections of Upper Canada. Frightened Protestants came pouring into Orangeville, reporting that "Several hundred Fenians had, the night previous, attacked and destroyed an Orange Hall and a Presbyterian Church in Mono, and were rapidly marching towards the village, destroying everything in their way, and putting all Protestants to the sword, regardless of age or sex." People wrote to the *Globe* reporting that Catholic church basements were well known to be bulging with arms and ammunition, "to be ready at the appointed time".

Such was the atmosphere in which the Canadian parliament met in January 1865 to consider the Quebec scheme of Confederation. The debates contain plenty of evidence that the members well knew the nature of the crisis that confronted the country. I quote just one long sentence from George Brown's great speech:

> The civil war . . . in the neighbouring republic; the possibility of war between Great Britain and the United States; the threatened repeal of the Reciprocity Treaty; the threatened abolition of the American bonding system for goods in transit to and from these provinces; the unsettled position of the Hudson's Bay Company; and the changed feeling of England as to the relation of great colonies to the parent state; –

> all combine at this moment to arrest earnest attention to the gravity of the situation, and unite us all in one vigorous effort to meet the emergency like men.

In that single sentence there is a good deal of the history of Canadian Confederation.

Before the Canadian debate ended, the electors of New Brunswick struck what might have been a fatal blow at the federation plan, rejecting it and the Tilley government that supported it; while the government in London was dragging its feet on joint arrangements for Canadian defence, and members of both Houses of Parliament there were loudly advertising the opinion that Canada couldn't be defended at all. The provincial government at Quebec refused to be discouraged. It decided to send off to England the strongest delegation it could muster – Macdonald, Cartier, Brown and Galt – to mobilize British support in surmounting the emergency. Before all the delegates were on the ocean, they knew that the event they had feared so long was upon them. General Lee had surrendered, and the Grand Army of the Republic was fully available for a possible job in Canada.

In London the Canadian delegates solemnly told the Colonial Secretary that they now felt "obliged to urge such measures as if war were immediate & certain," and they actually indicated that they might be prepared to spend as much as £9,000,-000 on the defence of the province and related objects. In spite of this, no far-reaching military agreement was made. Nevertheless, something was accomplished. Canada declared herself ready "to devote her whole resources, both in men and money, for the maintenance of her connection with the mother country", and the British government on its side assured her that it "fully acknowledged the reciprocal obligation of defending every portion of the Empire with all the resources at its command". Moreover, the Colonial Office, which had pushed the Quebec scheme from the beginning, now spoke out even more strongly in support of it, and it is clear that its motivation was mainly military. Edward Cardwell, the Colonial Secretary, wrote to the Maritime governors in June 1865,

> Looking to the determination which this country has ever exhibited to regard the defence of the Colonies as a matter of Imperial concern, the Colonies must recognize a right and even acknowledge an obligation incumbent upon the Home Government to urge with earnestness and just authority the measures which they consider to be most expedient on the part of the Colonies with a view to their own defence. Nor can it be doubtful that the Provinces of British North America are incapable, when separated and divided from each other, of making those just and sufficient preparations for national defence, which would be easily undertaken by a Province uniting in itself all the population and all the resources of the whole.

By this time the war clouds were beginning to disperse. The gigantic Union Army, far from marching on Canada, was doing what democratic armies like to do when the jobs they were created to do are finished: it was going home. But as the danger of war with the United States receded, another menace took its place. The American Fenians began to threaten Canada, and the American government saw no powerful reason for restraining them. This is no place to tell the Fenian story. But the spring and summer of 1866 witnessed Fenian enterprises at several points on the border, and the result was thoroughly favourable to Confederation.

In April one Fenian faction made a pass at Campobello Island in New Brunswick, creating great agitation and anxiety just when that province was about to have another general election. The Royal Navy sailed into Passamaquoddy Bay, the regulars arrived, the militia was called out. Tilley and Confederation won the election, and the Fenians clearly deserve part of the credit. In Canada that spring there were fears both of invasion and insurrection. People in Toronto were sure that blood would flow in the city on St. Patrick's Day; and so indeed it might have, had not John A. Macdonald, working through the invaluable McMicken, taken measures to lower the temperature. June brought actual invasion and fighting on the Niagara frontier, and in Upper Canada there was an outburst of patriotic excitement and emotion which I think has no precise parallel in Canadian history. It doubtless played its part in the creation of national spirit. When Toronto buried the volunteers who fell at Ridgeway – who included three undergraduates from its University – the *Globe* wrote grimly, "The autonomy of British America, its independence of all control save that to which its people willingly submit, is cemented by the blood shed in battle on the 2nd of June."

Actual attack by a few hundred filibusters led the Canadian government to take larger military precautions than had been induced by the threat of war with the United States. Six days after Ridgeway the provincial legislature met for the first time at Ottawa, in the great new Gothic buildings that would soon house a national parliament. The raid had shown up the shortcomings of the militia's organization, equipment and training; and in a typical Canadian parliamentary performance the assembly locked the door behind the stolen horse with a real flourish. It appropriated nearly two million dollars for defence out of a budget of seven million. During the next couple of years the Canadian volunteer force was developed into something closer to a fighting army. Numbers of new battalions were created, and a large proportion of the regiments on the militia list today have "1866" as their organization date.

A glance at the military scene in the new capital city will illustrate what was going on all across the province. Ottawa had had volunteer artillery since 1855, when a battery was formed which has had a continuous existence ever since and today is part of the 30th Field Artillery Regiment; and two infantry companies – one English-speaking, one French – came into existence in 1856. In 1861 the sudden threat of war over the *Trent* caused new companies and battalions to be formed spontaneously in cities and hamlets in all parts of Canada. Some of the companies were in the Ottawa area, but it was the Fenian excitement of 1866 that produced major units there, when the local independent companies were consolidated into battalions. In the fall of 1866 two of these battalions were formed simultaneously – the 43rd Carleton Battalion of Infantry (with headquarters at Bell's Corners, just west of Ottawa) and the Provisional Battalion of Ottawa. In 1868 an Ottawa Brigade of Garrison Artillery was organized. All three of these units died when the Fenian troubles were over; but in 1881 a new 43rd was formed, and it is still with us as The Cameron Highlanders of Ottawa. Another infantry unit came to Ottawa from Quebec in 1866 when the provincial civil service moved to the new capital. This was the Civil Service Rifles, which had a regimental headquarters for a time (until it was disbanded in 1868) and then carried on as a company and later two companies. These were absorbed into the Governor General's Foot Guards when that regiment was formed in 1872. But an officer of the Civil Service Rifles is still to be seen on every Ottawa city vehicle, as one of the supporters of the corporation's arms.

While the local militia was growing and flourishing, Ottawa was also becoming once more a British garrison town, which it hadn't been since the 'fifties. The first message sent to England over the new Atlantic cable in August 1866 – or one of the first – was an appeal for regular reinforcements. (The Governor General explained later that he sent it because of a "state of alarm and moral depression *within* the Province", caused by apprehension of new Fenian raids; it was the first of many panics.) Though the British government had been trying for many years to reduce its military commitments in Canada, it sent the troops. Some of them went to Ottawa, and were quartered at Canadian expense in buildings up and down Sussex Street. In 1869-70 the military hospital was in "Earnscliffe", later the home of Sir John A. Macdonald and now the British High Commissioner's residence. For four years up to 500 British soldiers lent a military air to the capital and ornamented its ceremonial occasions. Then in 1870 the British troops were withdrawn and the security of Ottawa – and, very largely, of Canada – was confided to its own militia. It was the end of an era.

. . . . .

As I said in the beginning, I have been trying to evoke an atmosphere – the atmosphere in which the new Dominion of Canada came to birth a hundred years ago. It was an atmosphere of anxiety and danger, dominated by the fear of war with a tremendous neighbour, by constant threats of lawless border aggression, and by the stir of military preparation. It is worth remembering that the Fenian Troubles – as I like to call them – did not consist of one or two isolated incidents. They lasted for seven years. The actual raids were few, but the alarms were many, and the mark on the minds of Canadians was deep.

It is impossible to measure with scientific exactitude the effect of the Civil War crisis and the Fenian Troubles on the Confederation movement and the growth of Canadian nationalism. One can see that there was some specific influence on the Canadian parliamentary debates of 1865 and the New Brunswick election of 1866. The larger and more general effects of these dramatic external pressures are harder to assess. But I think few people would argue that without them Confederation would have happened when it did. Without them Confederation might not have happened at all. These accumulated dangers speeded the course of political events. But they obviously did something more. They helped to form and foster a *national spirit*. They gave a degree of practical reality to that phrase of the orators, "the new nationality". In April 1870, after nearly a decade of bitterness and chronic crisis in Anglo-American and Canadian-American relations, the Toronto *Globe* made a comment whose phrasing sometimes sounds curiously modern. Perhaps it is a good text with which to close:

We have it often thrown in our face by our cousins over the way, that we have no national sentiment, and that so long as we continue in our present Provincial condition we never can have any. . . . We are jeeringly informed that not half-a-dozen people care sixpence for Canada for its own sake; that neither young nor old have any sentiment of loyal living attachment to the land they live in; that five cents more a bushel for their wheat would make nineteen-twentieths of Canadian farmers Annexationists, or anything one might choose; and five per cent more profit on their merchandize render Canadian trafficers ready not only to become Republicans, but to recognize Louis Napoleon or fall down and worship the authority of the Grand Trunk. Were all this as much the case as it is the reverse, our friends are doing their best to disprove the insinuation. Every attempt to starve us by hostile tariffs into whatever terms our neighbours may dictate is giving us more of the feeling of self assertion and independence. . . .

And what tariffs of whatever degree of hostility won't do will not be effected by Fenian Congresses and Fenian raids. . . . Canadians have gained more in national character during the last six years than in any previous twenty; and, if we ask, what has caused this, we shall find that the outrageous proceedings of the Fenians and their abettors have been among the chief agencies. . . . The longer these alarms continue on our borders the more will this feeling of blended indignation and patriotism be awakened, till Canada's diversified people be, through the fire of outward assault, thoroughly and unmistakeably fused into one.

BIBLIOGRAPHICAL NOTE

I have not attempted to document this short paper. If any reader is interested in following the matter up, he will find the documentation in a book and a number of articles which I published a long time ago. The book is *Canada and the British Army, 1846-1871* (rev. ed., Toronto, 1963). The articles most directly related to the subject are "Fenianism and the Rise of National Feeling in Canada at the Time of Confederation," *Canadian Historical Review,* XII (1931), pp. 238-61; "A Fenian Interlude: The Story of Michael Murphy," also in the *Canadian Historical Review,* XV (1934), pp. 133-54; and "The Fenian Troubles and Canadian Military Development, 1865-1871," Canadian Historical Association, *Report,* 1935 (Toronto, 1935), pp. 26-35. I told the story of Gilbert McMicken in a series of C.B.C. broadcasts in 1954; the most important source is the "McMicken Reports" series in the Macdonald Papers in the Public Archives of Canada, Ottawa. The authority for the formation and disbandment of Ottawa militia units is Militia General Orders; in this matter I am grateful for help from the Directorate of History, Canadian Forces Headquarters, and particularly from Mrs. E. A. Sorby, M.B.E.

PART II

The political scene

Democracy and the Ontario Fathers of Confederation

Bruce W. Hodgins

A tendency exists, particularly in this centennial year, to extoll the Fathers of Confederation for viewpoints which they in fact never possessed. They become not only fathers of our federal union, but champions of our so-called democratic way of life. In this connection the centennial euphoria builds on a well-established myth. The traditional Grade XIII history textbook states that George Brown's Grits "demanded democratic reforms such as universal suffrage and short parliaments and the secret ballot." In reality, like all of the Ontario Fathers, Brown opposed what he called "democracy" and argued that universal suffrage was one of the two major defects in the American system.

It was therefore a welcome change when Mr. Mungo James recently wrote perceptively in *Saturday Night*:

> What most middle-income Canadians comfortably forget is that this country of ours was never intended to be a just, or even a democratic society. Those colonial burghers, the Fathers of Confederation, decisively rejected universal franchise at the Quebec Conference in 1864. Many of our early laws were framed in the interest of property owners, and they've proved rigidly resistant to change.

John A. Macdonald, George Brown and the other Ontario Fathers were resourceful men of their age, but they were not democrats.

Analyzing the views of the Upper Canadian Fathers with regard to democracy presents a serious problem in semantics. The Fathers claimed to oppose democracy, but what did they mean by the word? Admittedly they meant something somewhat different from what most Canadians mean by it today. Still, they opposed not only what they understood by democracy but also what we assume in using the term.

We might define general western-style political democracy as a system of government in which the concept of equality of political rights implies the notion that the people through elective machinery determine the complexion of their government. The British and Canadian versions of this democracy imply that despite the monarchical form and the constitutional supremacy of parliament, sovereignty ultimately resides in the people. American, British and Canadian democracy rests on a faith, however qualified, in the good sense of the common man and woman in the mass;

it also rests on the efficacy of the principle of majority rule. In Canada federalism and constitutional guarantees have limited both parliamentary supremacy and majority rule; majority rule is also restrained by the British traditions of fair play and individual rights that predate the achievement of modern democracy. Nevertheless, majority rule has become an organic, popular part of the Ontarian's feeling about democracy. Since Ontario has always been the most populous and wealthy unit in Canada, and since the essence of federalism is apparently not deeply understood by Ontarians, an ambivalence survives as to whether majority rule tends more toward a dominant majority-backed Ontario or toward a dominant Ontarian-led, majority-backed Canada. The attitude of Ontarians both to the province of Quebec and to French Canada, which the Commission on Bilingualism and Biculturalism euphemistically describes as a second majority, constitutes an integral part of this confusion. The ambivalence played a considerable role in the story of Confederation, even though the Ontario Fathers denounced democracy.

In the mid-1860's the province of Canada, which since 1841 had linked Upper and Lower Canada in a unitary constitution, possessed internal self-rule. It operated autonomously with what contemporaries called responsible parliamentary government. The United Province preserved and fostered duality. Canada was not, however, a democracy, and no one called it such. But the working executive was picked from groups which collectively controlled a majority of the members elected to the lower house of the legislature. The Assembly was elected by a minority of the adult males of the province, roughly those heads of households who owned reasonable homes or paid substantial rents. Between the two sections of the province equality of representation rather than representation by population was the rule, and within each section gross discrepancies in the numerical size of constituencies prevailed.

But more important than these statutory divergences from what is considered democratic was the widespread elitist view of the nature of the constitution and of the limited role given to the electorate. Both George Brown and John A. Macdonald agreed that it would be unnecessary and unwise to hold an election before the implementation of Confederation. Yet union of British North America had not been an issue in the previous election, that of 1863. The idea had, however, been vaguely bandied about for several years, and Cartier and Macdonald had in 1858 unenthusiastically accepted it as part of the Conservative platform. The election of 1863 had precariously confirmed the defender of the existing constitution, John Sandfield Macdonald, as Premier of Canada and insecure leader of a temporarily reunited Reform alliance. In Upper Canada John A. Macdonald, who was later to become in the popular mind the chief architect of Confederation, had suffered a humiliating defeat. In 1865 it was left to John Sandfield Macdonald, who was now isolated and temporarily opposed to the Quebec scheme and therefore not a Father, vainly to demand the right for an expression of the popular will on the question of fundamentally changing the constitution.

Imagine the uproar a hundred years later if something similar were perpetrated. For a long time a minority of Canadians have advocated union with the United States. Imagine the Canadian government falling through the defection of a few of its erstwhile supporters. A new coalition government is formed under the titular leadership of an ancient, revered Senator. It is made up of the leadership of the former Opposition and the largest of the three roughly identifiable groups in the former government, but excluding the former Prime Minister and many of his supporters. This government then successfully negotiates union with the United States, and with the help of the party whips, secures parliamentary approval for the plan. Without an election Canadians become Americans. It would be legal but unthinkable. It would be undemocratic.

George Brown, as leader of the Grit Reformers, the largest single Upper Canadian political bloc, has often been portrayed as a democrat. Was not this British-inspired liberal the champion of representation by population, the critic of sectarian and sectional privilege, and the opponent of slavery and primogeniture? In 1865 Brown was much more moderate than he had been in the fifties, yet in 1857 he wrote in his *Globe* that "democratic theories" were inadequate "to the wants of a mixed society," and that the broader the suffrage "the more we add to the dangerous element." The extension of the franchise, he argued, had to await the "diffusion of education" and "what a mass of ignorance is still to be encountered in every constituency!" One hundred and ten years later public opinion polls and television sampling would hardly substantiate an opinion that this ignorance has been eliminated, yet we have political democracy. Long a critic of American republicanism, Brown argued that because of democracy, the American political parties had to eschew before the public all questions of high policy in favour of cant phrases and vituperative attacks. "The balance of power," he argued, "is held by the ignorant unreasoning mass; to swing them is the grand aim of the contest and as truth, character, statesmanship, honest policy, and fair argument would be thrown away upon them, both parties by consent – nay by necessity – resort to other expedients."

For Brown, the liberal-monarchist, democracy was too closely identified with American democratic republicanism. To him it involved universal suffrage, the inordinately wide use of the elective principle, a lack of respect for authority, and a tendency for government under popular impulses to go carelessly to extremes. He saw democracy as illiberal, as a threat to individualism and free institutions, as promoting the tyranny of the unreasoning majority. Yet he saw no illiberalism either in his vehement Free Kirk opposition to separate schools for the Roman Catholic minority of Upper Canada, who regarded the religiously-centred classroom as vital to its view of life, or in his own demand for province-wide representation by population without substantial safeguards for the French Canadians of Lower Canada. His acceptance in 1858 of the idea of some internal federation for the province of Canada was partial recognition that at least for political expediency some such protection was necessary to persuade even a minority of French Canadians that representation by population could be operated with justice to all. In 1850 he violently opposed, as revolutionary and republican, the radical program of the original Clear Grits; these agrarian democrats advocated the use of "elective institutions from the head of the government downward," including elective judges and justices of the peace, universal suffrage, and fixed dates for biennial parliamentary elections. Yet at the Quebec

Conference in 1864, at a time when he envisioned imminent Upper Canadian and Grit dominance of a united British America, this future champion of Ontario provincial rights urged that in the provinces centrally-appointed lieutenant governors ought normally to have the right of vetoing legislation without advice; he also argued that there ought to be a fixed term of three years for the provincial legislatures and that departmental ministers ought to be directly elected and, holding office for the three years or during pleasure, not be voting members of the legislature. Like many other mid-Victorian British liberals enamoured with the idea of laissez-faire and like that great American liberal-cum-conservative Thomas Jefferson, Brown believed in the general superiority and value of the propertied man. Like Jefferson he feared the rootless urban worker. Unlike the American aristocratic democrat and more like Alexander Hamilton, Jefferson's anti-democratic city rival, Brown saw society and politics led by the aggressive urban entrepreneur. A devotee of the dominance of the lower house of parliament through a liberal evolution of the British parliamentary system, Brown effectively argued in favour of an appointed upper house for the new union so that such a chamber might be weak. He approved of not having an upper house at all for Ontario. No democrat, either as he defined the word or as it is now envisioned, Brown still accepted much of the individualistic and egalitarian spirit of nineteenth century North America.

Two of Brown's lieutenants were also Fathers, William McDougall and Oliver Mowat. Wandering Willie McDougall, as one of the founders of the original Clear Grits and in the early 'fifties editor of the *North American*, had once been a democrat. He certainly was one no longer. From 1856 almost until Confederation, McDougall partly echoed the views of Brown. Yet in 1862, McDougall showed himself less devoted than Brown to representation by population when he entered the cabinet of Sandfield Macdonald. This regime regarded representation by population as politically and ethically undesirable at the time and claimed to be devoted to the double majority, the political dualism which was anathema to Brown. Yet McDougall remained a devotee of an elected upper house and occasionally flirted with political continentalism. Brown never fully forgave McDougall for his abandonment of principle in May, 1862 – though Brown himself seems partly to have shelved representation by population in 1859 and 1860 in favour of internal provincial federation. When McDougall declined to follow him out of the Confederation Coalition, Brown in 1867 had both McDougall and his cohort William Howland read out of the Reform party.

From 1862 to 1864 Oliver Mowat gradually replaced McDougall as Brown's chief lieutenant. Yet Mowat was appointed to the bench in late 1864 and was thus out of political circulation until he became Premier of Ontario in 1872. Mowat was later to become the very personification of Ontario provincial rights, of so-called "Grit democracy", yet his role as a Father was not crucial. Like McDougall he had favoured an elective upper house, but unlike McDougall he remained dedicated to representation by population. By conviction a Liberal, he was by temperament a conservative. Certainly during the period before Confederation he was no democrat.

During the Confederation negotiations and afterwards, John A. Macdonald was the great centralist and the great progressive and pragmatic conservative. As early as 1844 he had declared that he did not favour "fruitless discussion on abstract and theoretical questions of government." Still it fell to him to frame many of the clauses of what became the British North America Act, and he did possess underlying philosophical concepts. Like all Conservative Fathers, he rejected both the word democracy and many of those attributes now considered essential for it. He rejected political equality, favoured privilege for the propertied and the well-off, and seemed more concerned about protecting the rights of the minority than providing for majority rule. He championed the autonomy of a monarchical British Canada and the supremacy of parliament, but he rejected the necessary logic of representation by mere numbers and the need and wisdom of popular appeals on matters as vital as Confederation. Such an appeal, he argued, would be the device of a tyrant, would "subvert the principles of the British Constitution," and would be an "obvious absurdity."

Perhaps the clearest expression of his views on popular government came in his speech to the Quebec Conference. Advancing his centralist arguments against the principles of divided sovereignty enshrined in the bloodily divided United States, Macdonald argued that the provinces should only have such powers as are absolutely necessary "for local purposes," to enable them to legislate for "sectional prejudices and interests." "Thus we shall have," he asserted, "a strong and lasting government under which we can work out constitutional liberty as opposed to democracy, and be able to protect the minority by having a powerful central government." The national authority would therefore be more concerned with protecting minority rights than with providing for Grittish majority rule. The sovereign and her governor general, advised by a responsible ministry, would represent the whole nation rather than the mere ephemeral majority as did the American president. But although the provinces were not the primary protectors of minority rights, the central authority ought to use its power with caution so as not to alarm the people of any section.

Here was the essence of the anti-continentalist Macdonaldian constitution. The relationship between the centre and the provinces was more an imperial than a federal one. Macdonald did not mean it to be democratic, but it could easily and logically have evolved into political democracy.

Instead, as Professor W. L. Morton has indicated, the system was overthrown before 1900 through gross deficiencies in national sentiment and through the triumph of the very ambivalent classical federalism which Macdonald and in 1864 Brown opposed. Ironically, as Canada became more politically democratic, it also, alas, became more decentralized and divided. In this reversal the Mowat-led Ontario Grits played decisive roles. Describing the 1890's, Professor Lovell Clark has pointed out how the Orangemen of Ontario inadvertently assisted their Grit political rivals. Classical federalism and continued sectionalism, coupled with the traditional parliamentary system, later helped promote the development of the broad, amorphous majority party which emphasized national unity rather than policy. Professors John Porter and Gad Horowitz have shown how this system of brokerage politics worked against political creativity and advances toward a more democratic society.

Like Brown, Macdonald favoured an appointive upper house. But though secondary to the lower house and though based on equal representation for each section (not province), it was to play a more significant role than Brown envisioned. It was to be an appropriate North American version of the House of Lords. With a materially restrictive qualification for membership, it would represent the principle of property. "The rights of the minority ought to be protected," he argued, "and the rich are always fewer in number than the poor." Such an upper house would provide "a sober second thought," even though in North America its members would necessarily be persons "springing from the people."

During the Confederation debates Macdonald argued that no one at the Quebec Conference had favoured universal suffrage, "that classes and property should be represented as well as numbers." As late as 1889, when alarmed by surging democracy and American ideas, he urged greater influence for the "monarchical idea . . . accompanied by some gradation of classes." During the election campaign of 1861, he wrote to a sympathetic Dr. Egerton Ryerson, who shared many of Macdonald's views including his distrust of Brown, that the outcome might decide whether Canada was to be "a limited Constitutional Monarchy or a Yankee Democracy." Confederation for Macdonald and others was certainly not directed against Britain. The Quebec scheme involved a deliberate attempt to establish a union with a constitution similar in principle to that of Great Britain. It involved an attempt by British American leaders to create a viable, legitimate nation apart and different from the revolutionary, republican and aggressively democratic nation to the south. In the United States democracy had allegedly resulted in a lack of moral force, in a weakening of the sense of authority and responsibility, and in government by faction. Macdonald thus disagreed most emphatically with Goldwin Smith, then of Oxford University, who in 1863 wrote: "It would seem that if Canadian monarchy differs from American democracy as painted by its worst enemies, it is only as the Irishman's ride in a sedan chair with the bottom out differed from common walking." To Macdonald democracy was unconservative, illiberal, republican and dangerous; in a phrase, it was un-British and hence un-Canadian.

Alexander Galt and T. D. McGee of Lower Canada were both more important as spokesmen for the English-Canadian Liberal Conservatives than was the other Upper Canadian Conservative, Councillor Alexander Campbell. Both Galt and McGee shared Macdonald's distrust of democracy, but Galt was considerably less anti-American and McGee was more poetic in his Canadian nationalism. During the Confederation debates, Campbell emphasized that Confederation would save a monarchical Canada from undesirable republicanism. For Campbell an appointive upper house, "conservative, calm, considerate and watchful," would check democratic tendencies not calculated "to advance the common weal."

Were there then no democrats in Upper Canada a hundred years ago? A few existed, but they had little voice in parliament. John Sandfield Macdonald of Cornwall, the titular Leader of the Opposition during the Confederation negotiations, was somewhat nearer to democracy and more North American than George Brown, his rival and fellow Reformer. A liberal or nominal Catholic who, unlike his more famous namesake or Brown, was a native Upper Canadian, Sandfield came from the undifferentiated rural masses. Although he became a most wealthy real estate lawyer and frequent backer of the promotional schemes of his entrepreneurial brothers, he never lost or ceased to use his identification with the humble folk. He has often been called a "moderate Reformer" or a "conservative Reformer" because of his opposition to Brown's Upper Canadian intransigence and because of his many French Canadian friendships. Sandfield was "moderate" in the sense that more than Brown he advocated institutional tolerance, respect for French Canadian culture, and the preservation of the organic unity of the province of Canada. He called himself a "Baldwinite" or a "Baldwin Reformer" and opposed the dogmatism and sectionalism of the Grits. Although he favoured a broad, more pragmatic Reform party, he stood to the left of Brown on most political and social matters. His advocacy of the double majority, though probably as impractical as the Southerner J. C. Calhoun's contemporary advocacy of concurrent majorities, was a faulty attempt to preserve the unity of the whole and recognize the duality of Canadian culture.

He saw in Confederation the shattering of the unity of the St. Lawrence and the Ottawa valleys, the deflection of what became eastern Ontario from its natural entrepot of Montreal in favour of the Grit and Orange-dominated west. He saw Confederation as the antithesis of retrenchment and as an unfair British device to persuade Canadians to assume a "larger burden for the defence of this country than was justified," when already it was overspending and when the now declining American threat to it stemmed primarily from its membership in the British Empire. Confederation's implementation violated the sacred rights of the people. He hailed the first New Brunswick election and its results, arguing that if its people were then "bribed" into submission, they would be unworthy of association and of being "of the race of British freeman." Although he did not always practise what he preached, he argued that in Canada the electors and not the members of parliament were supreme. Members represented their constituents, not themselves, and they had no right on their own to petition the British authorities "to destroy the constitution." Still his career hardly qualifies him as a democrat.

The radical Clear Grit movement of 1850 had had a democratic platform, an amalgam of North American agrarian democratic ideas, English chartist democracy and the old fulminations of W. L. Mackenzie. Although the sentiments survived, the movement had after 1854 been captured by Brownite metropolitan liberalism. The Clear Grit viewpoint found temporary expression in the popular utterances of the phlegmatic and demagogic George Sheppard, in the *Globe* in early 1859 and at the Great Reform Convention in late 1859 where he probably expressed the attitude of a vast majority of the Grits. During the Confederation debates, it was largely without a significant spokesman. In the Assembly Joseph Rymal and in the Council James Currie and David Reesor probably represented the old viewpoint. Relatively unknown, they opposed Confederation. Yet urbanized and made more respectable and less American, this viewpoint would in future under Mowat promote Grit democracy and Ontario provincial rights. It was surely more than coincidental that Mathew Crooks Cameron, the only Ontario Conservative assemblyman to oppose Confederation, a man who vehemently denounced Brown though he favoured representation by population, a man of bitter Orange prejudices, expressed similar sentiments to those of the old Clear Grits.

The largest, most articulate and intellectual group of "democrats" in the Canadian provincial parliament were not Ontarians. They were the anti-clerical *Rouge* oppositionists from the Montreal area led by A. A. Dorion. Although decentralist and sometimes narrowly nationalistic, their criticism of Cartier and the scheme of union was often most perceptive. On the road to transformation or oblivion, in the face of increasing attacks from an increasingly ultramontane and anti-liberal and powerful Church, the *Rouges* were largely dismissed. When decades later they achieved respectability under the Gladstonian Laurier much of their constructive uniqueness, but not their decentralism, would have disappeared. Cleansed of free thought and of social democracy, they would prove fitting allies of Mowat's Grits, and unwitting supporters of Ontario Orangemen in the destruction of the Macdonaldian constitution.

Of all the colonial and British architects of Confederation, the Ontarians were most significant in establishing the governmental framework of our country. The five Ontarians were worthy Fathers of Confederation. They were not fathers of Canadian democracy.

BIBLIOGRAPHICAL NOTE

The chief primary sources for this study are the personal papers of the Fathers of Confederation and their correspondents, found mainly in the Public Archives of Canada, and also in the crucial Upper Canadian newspapers of the day. In this connection the Macdonald Papers, the Brown Papers, the Alexander Mackenzie Papers and the Toronto *Globe* are central. Also useful are the John Sandfield Macdonald Papers. The study could not be undertaken without a careful reading of the *Parliamentary Debates on the Confederation of the British North American Provinces* (Quebec, 1865; Ottawa, 1951) in the Canadian Legislature in February and March, 1865.

What follows is a short list of some of the principal secondary sources:

Careless, J. M. S., *Brown of the "Globe"* (2 vols., Toronto, 1959-63).

Cornell, P. G., *The Alignment of Political Groups in Canada, 1841-1867* (Toronto, 1962).

———, *The Great Coalition: June 1864*, Canadian Historical Association, Historical Booklets, no. 19 (Ottawa, 1966).

Creighton, D. G., *John A. Macdonald: The Young Politician* (Toronto, 1955).

Hodgins, Bruce W., "Attitudes Toward Democracy during the Pre-Confederation Decade," unpublished Master's thesis, Queen's University, 1955.

———, "John Sandfield Macdonald and the Crisis of 1863," Canadian Historical Association, *Report*, 1965 (Toronto, 1965), pp. 30-45.

———, "The Political Career of John Sandfield Macdonald to the Fall of His Administration in March, 1864: A Study in Canadian Politics," unpublished Ph.D. dissertation, Duke University, Durham, N.C., 1964.

———, and Jones, E. H., "A Letter on the Reform Party, 1860: Sandfield Macdonald and the *London Free Press*," *Ontario History*, LVII (1965), pp. 39-46.

Lower, A. R. M., "The Origins of Democracy in Canada," Canadian Historical Association, *Report*, 1930 (Ottawa, 1930), pp. 65-70.

Morton, W. L., "The Conservative Principle in Confederation," *Queen's Quarterly*, LXXI (1964), pp. 528-46.
Pope, Joseph, ed., *Confederation: Being a Series of Hitherto Unpublished Documents Bearing on the British North America Act* (Toronto, 1895).
Waite, P. B., *The Charlottetown Conference*, Canadian Historical Association, Historical Booklets, no. 15 (Ottawa, 1963).
———, *The Life and Times of Confederation: 1864-1867: Politics, Newspapers, and the Union of British North America* (Toronto, 1962).
Walker, Franklin A., *Catholic Education and Politics in Upper Canada: A Study of the Documentation Relative to the Origin of Catholic Elementary Schools in the Ontario School System* (Toronto, 1955).
Wise, S. F. and Brown, R. C., *Canada Views the United States: 19th Century Political Attitudes* (Seattle, 1967).

Edward Blake: A Portrait of His Childhood

Catherine Hume Blake

Edited, and with an introduction, by Margaret A. Banks

In his closing remarks on Edward Blake in *Our Living Tradition* (Toronto, 1957) Professor Frank Underhill stated: "By the time of his death in 1912 his name was largely forgotten in Canada." A reviewer in the *Globe and Mail*, commenting on the article, added: "True enough; and what is the point of digging him up now?" Yet, as we celebrate Canada's centennial in 1967, this forgotten man is considered worthy of inclusion in a volume dealing with the history of Ontario.

Everyone familiar with Canadian history in the years immediately following Confederation knows that Edward Blake was regarded by friend and foe alike as one of the outstanding men of his day. His ability as a lawyer was unquestioned, and it was assumed by many that he would be equally successful in politics, some day becoming Prime Minister of Canada. But although he served for a few months as Premier of Ontario, subsequently became a federal cabinet minister, and then led the Liberal party of Canada for seven years, he never attained the office of Prime Minister nor the fame expected of him in his youth. His career in later life as an Irish nationalist member of the British House of Commons followed much the same pattern; he did useful and important work for the Irish party, but did not rise to such prominence as many of his admirers had considered likely.

It is generally agreed by Canadian historians that one of the reasons for Blake's failure in politics lay in his personality. Blake himself often spoke of his unsuitability for positions of leadership, declaring that he was "by temperament averse to rule." He was too sensitive to the criticism for which all public men must be prepared; his repeated threats of resignation were a constant trial to his colleagues. His shyness and aloofness of manner were also against him; it was only with his intimate friends that he was at ease. Part of his aloofness was, in fact, the result of poor eyesight; he sometimes did not recognize people whom he knew only slightly. This was a source of embarrassment to him and annoyance to others who thought they were being snubbed.

Blake's letters to his friends show that he was not so stern and devoid of humour as is sometimes supposed. Yet, even his personal and family correspondence tells very little of his private life. There has, however, been preserved among the Blake family papers in the Ontario Department of Public Records and Archives a short account of his childhood written by his mother. Rather than repeating here what has been said many times about Blake's career and personality, it seems appropriate to publish his mother's recollections, as they give an insight into his character which is not available elsewhere.[1]

Catherine Blake's account of her elder son's childhood is undated, but internal evidence indicates that it was compiled in 1872, soon after Edward Blake became Premier of Ontario. It was written in the form of a letter to a relative or friend, who apparently had asked for the information. Whether he ever received it is not certain, for the version in the Blake papers is an unfinished draft. The identity of "My dear James," to whom the letter was written, is also a mystery. The context suggests that he was a writer who wanted to compose a chatty article on the life of the new Premier of Ontario, but the mode of address, in an age of greater formality than the present, would seem to indicate that he was a relative or an intimate friend of the Blake family. Catherine Blake's great-grandson thinks it most unlikely that she would have written so personal a sketch to a journalist for publication in a newspaper.

Perhaps a word or two should be said about the author of this short account of Blake's childhood. Catherine Hume was a member of a distinguished Irish family. In 1832, she married her cousin, William Hume Blake, and emigrated with him to Canada. She was undoubtedly a woman of education and culture, though quite unlike the helpless upper class young lady depicted in nineteenth century English literature. We are inclined to think of the working wife who helps support her family while her husband becomes established in his profession as a twentieth century innovation; yet, Catherine Blake was doing it in the eighteen thirties. Her husband had failed to complete his studies in either theology or medicine before coming to Canada and, after concluding that farming was not in his line either, he decided to turn to law. By then his elder son, Edward, had been born and the family left their farm in the western part of the province and settled in Toronto. It was then that Catherine Blake opened a girls' school. She enjoyed the work so much that she continued with it for some time after the financial need had ceased.

The sketch of her son's childhood is not the only writing of historical interest that Catherine Blake has left to posterity. In 1847, her husband was elected to represent East York in the Legislative Assembly of the province of Canada, and the following year he became Solicitor-General West in the second Baldwin-LaFontaine administration. It happened, therefore, that Catherine Blake was in Montreal with her husband in the exciting days at the end of April 1849 when riots followed the passage of the controversial Rebellion Losses Bill. Her graphic account of the events of April 26th-29th, 1849, preserved among the Blake family papers, was published in 1934 in the *Canadian Historical Review*, XV, pp. 283-8.

[1] For providing me with some details concerning Blake family history that have been helpful in editing this sketch, I am grateful to Catherine Blake's great-grandson, Mr. Verschoyle B. Blake, of Toronto.

Her sketch of Edward Blake's childhood follows:

My dear James, in compliance with yr. wish, I will jot down some particulars about Edward in a *rambling, gossippy* way, from wh. you can cull *anything you think proper*. He was born Oct. 13, 1833 at Bear Creek, near the village now called Katesville, his Uncle the Revd. D. E. Blake being appointed Rector of Adelaide was the inducement to our settling in this out of the way place. When he was about a year old we moved to Toronto – a change however good in some respects was not favorable to our child's physique, whose rosy cheeks & chubby face soon became pale & thin, & before he was 3 years old, his chest being attacked, his dear Father brought him over to Ireland for change of air, wh. so restored him as to enable us on his return to commence his education. I dont remember that he learned to read particularly quickly, but when once he had mastered the art, his passion for books became so intense that constant using of his young eyes strained them, & the Doctor forbad him to open a book. He then used to hide himself under the table, or in summer among the bushes, devouring everything he cd. lay hold on – if possible a story – – if not history – at worst a newspaper.

His dear Father disliking schools Edd. recd. a desultory sort of education for some years – & in the morning while dressing gave him his Latin lesson himself, wh. consisted of some lines of Virgil to be read off fluently in English & written out neatly by the evening. For the grammar we had a Tutor, & the English branches devolved on me. [From the first his dear Father took infinite pains with his recitation, & as his week-day hours were all filled up, he devoted a portion of Sunday Evening to reading aloud the Psalms – Isaiah – Milton – Young – & any sacred poetry he thought suitable, requiring Edward during the week to prepare a certain portion for recitations the following Sunday. And what delight his beloved Father used to express at perceiving his little son's capacity & intelligence. I remember one day our being puzzled at a line in the "Night thoughts," when this little mite of a boy whom we thought was not attending, said very simply "I think a comma is left out there" – & so it was, the comma replaced, restored the sense of the passage. At this time we remarked also if a page of any book were read once aloud, he could recite it with scarcely a mistake, & yet his manner was generally so dreamy & listless, that strangers thought his intellect below the average.]

On leaving Woodlawn[2] & returning to town, his dear Father engaged Messrs Wedd & Brown (now masters in the College)[3] as private tutors for Edward & Samuel[4] and those gentlemen were indefatigable in their efforts to advance their pupils in classics & science. [But Edward never liked regular studies, & after a time our kind friend

[2] "Woodlawn" was a house occupied by the Blake family from about 1840 to 1844. It was situated on the west side of Yonge Street just south of the present Woodlawn Avenue West; part of the house, much altered, still stands. The land on which "Woodlawn" was erected was purchased by William Hume Blake in 1838, and building was probably commenced in that year. The whole property was sold by William Hume Blake and his wife, Catherine, in 1844. In the eighteen forties "Woodlawn" was, of course, outside the boundaries of Toronto; hence the reference to "leaving Woodlawn, & returning to town."

[3] Upper Canada College.

[4] Samuel Hume Blake, born August 31, 1835, younger brother of Edward.

Mr. Wedd informed us he thought Edward required the stimulus of a public school, & acting on this suggestion we sent him to college, Mr. Wedd still taking charge of the preparation of lessons in the evening.]

When about 13 years of age Edward accompanied us to Europe, his dear Father being obliged to travel for his health. We discovered for the first time in London his short sightedness, & on consulting an Optician he said he had seldom or ever seen a boy of his age so terribly near sighted. He was his dear Father's constant companion in visiting the law Courts, & also the booksellers in whose shops he took great delight, greedily devouring everything he cd. lay hold on & even then he read with astonishing rapidity.

We crossed over to Bruges to spend the Xmas with some relatives staying there. The father of the family being absent attending Parliament, only arrived the day before X-day, & immediately requested a list of the curiosities of the place, & every information concerning them from his eldest daughter who had been residing there for some time. The young lady not being equal to the occasion, "little Edward" rose to the rescue from his quiet corner, & surprised us all by the accuracy of his details concerning churches & ruins &c. wh. he had never visited, but the statistics of wh. he had gathered from an old guide-book wh. happened to be the only English book within reach. Sir Denham's[5] stinging remark, "I see Louisa[6] the difference between *brains, & no brains*," was forcibly brought to my mind by a congratulatory letter of my cousin's just recd. in wh. she says it is "hard to think of the Premier of Ontario being the quiet little studious boy of Bruges"[7] – as Edward was short for his age & very shy, he appeared even younger than he really was.

[When at Paris in 1848 he greatly enjoyed being present at the sacking of the Tuilleries, & all the stirring events of this period. On returning from their daily walk in the Bois de Boulogne his dear Father & he came across the émeute in the Champs Elysées, & following the living stream were soon in the very midst of the works of destruction going forward in the palace of the Tuilleries. They did not return until late in the evening when Edward radiant with excitement handed me an epaulette he had picked up in the melée as a trophy, a poor soldier being shot close beside him for making free with some article from the palace. For the succeeding three days they perambulated Paris with the greatest interest, but as my taste lay in a different direction I was delighted on the fourth to find ourselves en route for London.] On returning to Canada he resumed his studies at College, but seemed no fonder of regular task-work than before, nor did he seriously apply himself to study, until the last year, when he formed a determination to gain if possible the Gov. Genl's. prize, with this object in view, he began to work in good earnest, & succeeding, had the

[5] Sir Charles Denham Orlando Jephson Norreys, Bt., member of the British House of Commons for Mallow, Ireland. The connection with the Blake family appears to have been through Sir Denham's wife, Catherine Cecilia Jane, daughter of William Franks, Esq., of Carrig, County Cork, Ireland.

[6] Sir Denham's elder daughter, Catharine Louisa.

[7] The congratulatory letter "just recd." dated Jan. 16, 1872, is preserved among Catherine Blake's papers. Written from "The Castle, Mallow," the seat of the Norreys Baronets, it expresses delight at "Edward's high position" and speaks of him as "the little quiet studious boy at Bruges." The writer, M. [or M. G.] Franks, was presumably a relative of Sir Denham's wife.

pleasure but a few weeks ago, of shewing his name inscribed in the College-hall to his own little boy. Although his general manner was quiet & rather reserved he threw himself with great gusto into any amusement of which he partook, at one time being very fond of riding on horse-back, at another he relished going to evening-parties, & often amused us by the energy & perseverance with which he threw himself into the mazes of the dance. But his chief delight was in yachting, & when his dear Father gave him one, he spent much of his time on the water, and often carried off the regatta prizes. How often have I watched him from my window in the early summer-morning, trudging along merrily with pail, mop & broom to polish up with his own hands his beloved "Storm-Queen".

The Mowat Era, 1872-1896: Stability and Progress[1]

A. Margaret Evans

Oliver Mowat, short, stocky, and near-sighted, lacked the forcefulness of George Brown and the eloquence of Edward Blake. He did not catch the public imagination as did John A. Macdonald or Wilfrid Laurier. Yet, after succeeding Blake as provincial Liberal leader in 1872, he presided over the Golden Age of Liberalism in Ontario and remained her Premier for twenty-four years – a record surpassing that of Pitt the Younger, W. L. Mackenzie King, or Macdonald.

Mowat's supporters attributed his long career to his sterling character: he was the "Christian statesman," the embodiment of Victorian virtues. The Conservative opposition remembered him rather as the artful politician who won elections by gerrymandering and the massive creation of "fee-fed" officials. There was truth in both views. Mowat was pious and respectable, and had a strong Presbyterian morality. He did utilize freely the weapons of patronage common in his generation. "Everything else being equal," he said, "no administration was in the habit of preferring their opponents to their friends in making appointments." He had other qualities, however, which contributed more to his political success and the growth of the province under him.

Partly from his Scottish canniness, partly from his professional experience as lawyer and judge, Mowat was accustomed to studying every question thoroughly before committing himself. After his death in 1903, the Conservative *Mail and Empire* of Toronto summed him up as a "solid and safe man, free from extreme tendencies, and exceedingly cautious." Mowat's characteristic moderation appealed to the reason and common sense of Ontarians throughout the divisive issues of the late nineteenth century, the most critical of which was religion. Sectarian antagonism mounted from the 1870's when the Orange order sought incorporation under a special act, through the 1880's when the *Mail* attacked separate schools and the French-speaking schools of eastern Ontario, to reach a climax in the election of 1894 when the Protestant Protective Association attempted to win the "solid Protestant vote." The political press and campaign pamphlets breathed religious and racial venom. Mowat, however, kept the confidence of the majority of both Protestants and Roman Catholics in his

[1] Research for this article was made possible through the assistance of a Canada Council grant.

fairness "to men of all creeds," and made the Ontario Liberals a unifying force in the province, a party in which Protestant and Catholic, English and French, could work side by side.

But if Mowat was in no way an extremist, he was progressive. His legislation revealed his eclecticism as he selected what appeared most suited to Ontario's needs from the practice of the other provinces, England, the American states and the sister dominions. Gladstonian Liberalism was reflected particularly in Mowat's great judicial reform – the institution of a unified system of superior courts for the province, concerning which the *Canadian Law Times* remarked:

> Though as an old equity lawyer it must have been somewhat of a wrench to do away with the Court of Chancery as a separate tribunal, yet in that, as in other things, he loyally followed the lead of the mother country.

Mowat incorporated as well many recommendations from the Royal Commissions appointed by his government. To the Conservative complaint that commissions were "costly luxuries," Mowat replied that a commission was "a regular, a constitutional and an eminently British means for securing information." In a lighter moment, he admitted taking over ideas from the opposition also: "It had been his practice always to accept a good suggestion, no matter from what source it came."

Perhaps the greatest genius of the man was that he could tell with radar-like accuracy when the innately conservative Ontarians were ready for another instalment of advanced legislation. W. R. Meredith, opposition leader from 1878 to 1894, tried to win popular support by the plank of electoral reform; but, clever and well-liked though he was, he failed because he was too far to the left with a Disraeli-like democracy or to the right in completely opposing votes for women. Mowat, meanwhile, steered skilfully in mid-stream, with the current of public opinion which was gradually developing in favour of vote by ballot and elimination of the property franchise. By the end of his premiership, the secret ballot was used in both municipal and provincial elections; it was optional for election of school boards. The franchise was democratized to the extent of full male suffrage in elections for the Legislative Assembly and the inclusion of widows and unmarried women in the municipal electorate. He had achieved these changes by the proper move at the proper moment, so that he neither alarmed the conservatives nor disappointed the radicals. In the 1890's, the "suffragette" agitation built up. Mowat, although personally not opposed to political equality for women, knew that the time was not yet ripe and warily avoided this final step to universal franchise.

Similarly, in setting a course regarding the liquor traffic, he demonstrated that he was the equal of Macdonald and Mackenzie King, the Canadian masters of delaying tactics. Mowat's problem was similar to that of the present day, but in reverse. The Frost and Robarts governments have met a growing feeling for liberalizing the liquor laws; Mowat faced a rising desire for their stiffening, even to the point of prohibiting sale of alcoholic beverages. An abstainer himself, he sympathized with the temperance forces, but in dealing with such a contentious subject, it was well that he had the habit, as one of his followers said, of "nearly always making two bites of a cherry." The policy he adopted was a tightening of provincial restraints on the liquor trade by degrees as public approval of further restrictions evolved. Mowat did not believe, however, that sentiment was strong enough in most parts of Ontario to make adequate enforcement of prohibition possible. He therefore adroitly sidestepped by arranging a provincial plebiscite on prohibition and seeking a court decision on Ontario's prohibitory power.

The question of jurisdiction between Dominion and province in liquor licensing occasioned one of Mowat's several legal disputes in the 1880's with John A. Macdonald, the Canadian Prime Minister. These have been the most famous part of his premiership, because the Judicial Committee of the British Privy Council consistently upheld his Jeffersonian interpretation of the constitution against the Hamiltonian version of Macdonald, as in *Hodge* v. *The Queen*, 1883:

> When the British North America Act enacted that there should be a legislature for Ontario, and that its legislative assembly should have exclusive authority to make laws for the Province and for provincial purposes in relation to the matters enumerated in sect. 92, it conferred powers not in any sense to be exercised by delegation. . . . Within these limits of subjects and area the local legislature is supreme. . . .

If the age had abounded in flags then as now, Mowat's victories for "provincial rights" would have been splendid occasions for waving an Ontario flag, most of all when the favourable settlement of the northwest boundary doubled the size of the province. Mowat was dubbed by the exasperated Macdonald the "little tyrant". To his own people he was the "plucky premier" defending their cause against the centralizing government at Ottawa.

More important, however, if not so dramatic, is the almost neglected story of Mowat's substantial service to the internal development of his province. Here are to be found the real dimensions of the Premier and of his ministers. There was no rapid procession of men in and out of Mowat's cabinets. For twenty years C. F. Fraser, a fiery debater, directed Public Works. The capable A. S. Hardy worked with Mowat for nineteen years in the Provincial Secretaryship and then in Crown Lands, succeeding him as Premier in 1896 when Mowat resigned to become Minister of Justice under Laurier. Cool-headed T. B. Pardee administered Crown Lands until ill-health forced his retirement after sixteen years. G. W. Ross, enthusiastic and fluent, was Minister of Education for thirteen years under Mowat; and scholarly Adam Crooks served eleven years as Treasurer and first Ontario Minister of Education. Those with relatively "short" terms of six to eight years included S. C. Wood, a lucid speaker; meticulous A. M. Ross; J. M. Gibson of many interests; energetic John Dryden; and reflective Richard Harcourt. Macdonald scoffed at Mowat's little ministries of "Mr. Hardy, Mr. Pardee, Mr. Dardy, and Mr. Lardy." The Toronto journalist Goldwin Smith worried about the calibre of persons who would choose provincial politics over federal. The truth was that Mowat's colleagues, if not so brilliant as some of the Canadian ministers, were good business men, competent in their departments and in the Assembly. Their long experience in the affairs of government made for stable administration.

The *Mail* believed that one of the main reasons for Mowat's reelections was his care for the material interests of the province. Mowat always emphasized that agriculture was the "substratum" of Ontario's prosperity. Accordingly, agricultural societies and Farmers' Institutes received grants; numerous acts were aimed at control of weeds and animal and plant diseases; the Ontario Bureau of Industries was organized to publish agricultural statistics annually and so help the farmers to better business management. The Department of Agriculture, which was added to the government in 1888, promoted mixed farming – fruit-growing, stock and poultry-raising, dairying – in order that farmers would not be in so vulnerable a position as they had been in old Ontario when they depended almost entirely on wheat. The Agricultural College and Experimental Farm which Mowat founded at Guelph provided leadership and scientific information. Although the government inevitably made mistakes in management in this first venture into agricultural education in Canada, both College and Farm had a world-wide reputation by the end of the Mowat regime. It was the opinion of the *Farmer's Advocate* of London, which at first had doubted the value of the College, that "all young men who intend to be farmers should take a course here." Furthermore, when the Agricultural Commission Report (1881) drew attention to the slow progress of drainage, Mowat stepped up the practice begun by John Sandfield Macdonald, Ontario's first Premier after Confederation, of advancing public money for major ditches to drain extensive low-lying areas such as those in Essex, Kent and Lambton counties. Mowat also authorized municipalities to borrow from the province in order to lend to individual farmers for tile drains. Witnesses before the Royal Commission on Drainage in 1893 testified that thousands of acres had been "brought from a useless condition to good and first class lands" by these drainage schemes.

The Patrons of Industry, who formed a third party based on agrarianism, endangered Mowat's ascendancy in the elections of 1894, but only momentarily. Because of the Liberal party's record of special interest in agriculture, and the Premier's finesse in handling the sixteen Patrons who were elected to the legislature, they were soon absorbed into his party, much as the third-party Progressives lost their identity in the House of Commons in the 1920's. One of the useful functions of a political party is to counteract the dividing thrust not only of race and religion, but also of class and calling. It was beneficial for Ontario that the heterogeneous party built up by Mowat overcame so quickly the threat of Patronism which represented one class only.

Although at the census of 1891, two-thirds of the population of Ontario was still rural, the province was leading the rest of Canada in urban and industrial growth. This was hastened by the busy decade of railway building in the 1870's, which resulted from municipal initiative with supplementary provincial aid. Toronto, Hamilton and London became important railway cities. Towns along eastern Lake Ontario and the St. Lawrence river were ambitious to be railway centres too. They obtained assistance from Mowat for constructing parts of the lines between Whitby and Port Perry, Port Hope and Midland, Cobourg and Marmora, Belleville and Peterborough, Kingston and Pembroke, Brockville and Ottawa. After the advent of other means of transportation, many of the railways built through the liberality of the Mowat government would be lopped off. In his time, however, they played their part by raising the value of farm property in southern Ontario, giving employment, and stimulating production and trade.

In Mowat's mind, the optimum development of the south, both agriculturally and industrially, rested on opening the Precambrian hinterland. One of Agriculture Minister Dryden's most interesting projects was the establishment of a Pioneer Farm at Lake Wabigoon in Western Algoma, midway between Port Arthur and Winnipeg, in order to prove that this region was adapted to agriculture. The government's pioneering efforts were an immediate success. A "town" sprang up, which the president of the Canadian Pacific Railway named after the Minister, and settlers filled the nearby townships. But generally it was not easy to sell land in the outlying areas of the Muskoka, Parry Sound, Nipissing, Algoma and Rainy River Districts and even in some of the eastern counties. Mowat therefore used the twin lures of free grants and improved transportation by colonization railways, largely subsidized by the province, and colonization wagon roads and bridges to give access to the railways. He followed the pattern of Sandfield Macdonald in granting free public lands only to *bona fide* settlers who fulfilled certain conditions of clearance, cultivation and residence. In order that settlement would proceed in an orderly way, grants were withheld until areas were surveyed. By 1896, one hundred and seven townships had been set apart for free grants.

Expansion of settlement meant immigration if southern Ontario was not to be depopulated. Mowat directed a fairly vigorous immigration propaganda at the people of the British Isles in an effort to draw the two classes most needed by the provincial economy – female domestic servants and experienced farm help. Artisans, clerks and professional people were not welcomed; but people with capital were considered very desirable, and some manufacturers did transfer their enterprise to Ontario. The immigrants intensified the English complexion of the society of the province, and they helped to offset the numbers who were leaving in the hope of bettering themselves in Manitoba, which was having its first wheat boom, or in the United States, which from a distance looked to be much more prosperous than Canada. Between the census of 1871 and that of 1891, Ontario's population rose only some half a million, which was about equal to the number of immigrants during the same period. Disappointing as this was, it was still the highest rate of increase for these years in the old provinces. Without the immigrants, the population would have stood still as in the Maritimes. Actually, the free grant districts competed very successfully with the rich lands of the prairies in attracting settlers. Between 1871 and 1881, the population of Manitoba increased 247%, but that of Muskoka and Parry Sound 392%. In the light of later emergence of rural slums in some of the free grant townships, Mowat appears to have been too eager in encouraging immigrants to settle on lands unsuited to farming. On the other hand, if agriculture was often marginal in the Shield regions, it introduced homesteaders who exposed mineral deposits and helped supply labour and goods for near-by lumber camps.

Mowat proceeded circumspectly in the new field of legislating for a mining industry just at the threshold of its great discoveries. It was not until the Mining Commission appointed by the government reported in 1890 that the public was really aware of the extent and value of Ontario's minerals. The policy was then established of providing government encouragement to mineral development at the same time as ensuring that it furnish a public revenue by royalties or other moderate charges on ores. Mowat avoided the spectacular forms of assistance such as grants to costly smelters, although he created an Iron Mining Fund to spur on the opening of rich iron tracts and purchased a diamond drill for testing mineral deposits. In general, the aid given by his government took the form of improving education for miners and prospectors so that they might more successfully carry on mining operations. A new Bureau of Mines made authoritative information available; the facilities for training in mining engineering and metallurgy at the Toronto School of Practical Science were enlarged; and provincial moneys went to summer schools in northern centres and to a new School of Mines in Kingston. Moreover, the health and safety of workers in mines were protected by extensive regulations borrowed from the experience of Australia and other mining countries. These positive accomplishments were far from the "funeral procession progress" depicted by the Conservatives.

The opposition was on stronger ground when it criticized Mowat's administration of Crown timber. The Premier represented the exploitative age in which Ontario's great forest estate was regarded as an asset to be realized from time to time by favourable sales, without thought to making it a perpetual asset by renewing what had been depleted through cutting or fire. Fortunately for the future, the sale of timber berths, as Mowat and his Treasurers frequently pointed out, meant only the sale of the right to cut timber, and the land remained in the Crown. The Conservatives, however, who urged that forest resources ought to be restored because they were not inexhaustible were much more constructive than the Liberal government. To the twentieth century mind, Crown Lands Commissioner Hardy was surprisingly callous in his remark that there was timber enough for a century to come, and what would happen after a century was "outside the realm of present politics."

Mowat, though guilty of failure to undertake reforestation and of removing standing timber from non-arable land which should not have been cleared, did act to conserve the forests in the sense of preventing their destruction by fire. He instituted the office of Clerk of Forestry and appointed to it Mr. R. W. Phipps, the ablest forestry propagandist in Ontario. Phipps' principle for the forests was simple: "Spend more money in their preservation, and be less eager to make money by cutting them down." As a result of his activities, the province in 1885 acquired the first forest fire rangers in America, and began to be educated as to the harmful effects of cutting trees upon climate, rainfall, soil fertility and flood control. The Mowat government demonstrated further that it was not concerned with contemporary utility alone, when it reserved three of Ontario's now famous parks. Queen Victoria Park at Niagara Falls was primarily for aesthetic and pleasure purposes; Algonquin in Nipissing was preceded in Canada only by Banff National Park as a forest and game reserve; Rondeau in the peninsula jutting from Kent county into Lake Erie was intended for recreation and a wild bird shelter.

Mowat, then, had a kind of "National Policy" for Ontario, which benefited every section of the economy and made it much more diversified than it had been in 1872. Despite the general world depression prevailing through most of his premiership, and the numerous developmental programmes of his government, he augmented the comfortable provincial surplus of four million dollars left by Sandfield Macdonald to five million dollars in 1896. In contrast, Quebec, which had the same advantages as Ontario – a generous settlement under Confederation, control of her own natural resources, and municipal institutions that could share in financing local improvements – amassed a public debt of thirty-two million dollars. Even the Conservative press commended Mowat's financial management.

It was fitting that the second century of legislation in Ontario – the first Upper Canadian Assembly met in 1792 – should begin in the dignified Parliament buildings which were completed in the Queen's Park, Toronto, early in 1893. Ontarians, always desirous of being both economical and progressive, rejoiced that Fraser, Public Works Commissioner, had kept the cost to one and a quarter million dollars, or one-half as much per cubic foot as the public buildings of Connecticut and one-third as much as those of Illinois. The Toronto *Evening News* recalled with amusement the wager of Conservative G. F. Marter that he would buy a new hat for every lady in Draper and Ryde townships in Muskoka if the buildings cost "one cent less than two million." The *News* estimated that Mr. Marter would have to give away eight hundred and forty-seven ladies' hats! For political friend and foe alike, the new Parliament buildings were a source of pride, a symbol of the material advance of the province and her confidence in the future.

As Ontario society, along with the economy, became more complex in the latter nineteenth century, the demand increased for legislation in the interest of industrial workers, for more humane methods of caring for the afflicted and reforming the criminal, and for better ways of saving and educating children. Mowat was typically deliberate and pragmatic in his social enactments. Nevertheless, by the end of his term in office, Ontario's feet were firmly planted on the path not only toward the economic "empire" of the twentieth century, but also toward the broad social services of the modern era. The Fathers of Confederation who had thought of provinces as merely large municipalities would be amazed at the widening functions assumed by the Mowat government.

Departing from the laissez-faire individualism of the mid-Victorian Liberals, Mowat accepted the view of the trade unions that the state has a responsibility in relations between employers and employees. A series of acts, beginning in 1884 and being extended in stages, laid down the main lines along which regulations for factories and shops would develop in Ontario – minimum ages for employment; maximum hours of work, particularly of women and children; rules for sanitation and safety; and government inspection for enforcement. Another set of measures strengthened the lien law for the protection of the right of labour to receive the wages earned. The landmark in legislation to protect employees from risk of injuries at work was the Workmen's Compensation for Injuries Act, 1886, which is usually said to have placed Ontario first among Canadian provinces in the field of employers' liability.

Although there was yet no provision for minimum wages, and the onus of proving negligence against the employer still rested with the injured workman, these acts were advanced for the age. As the Toronto *Globe* said, few acknowledged that the state should "dictate the wages an employer should pay"; and the idea had not been conceived of standardized workmen's benefits paid after an injury without the necessity of bringing an action. Machinery for arbitration in disputes involving industries with at least ten workmen was set up by the Ontario Trade Disputes Conciliation and Arbitration Act of 1894, similar to legislation in British Columbia. Its weakness was that it rested on the consent of the disputing parties, but neither employers nor employees were then agreed in favouring compulsory arbitration or binding awards.

Health took a central place in the public responsibilities under Mowat, as it has in other modern states. A provincial Board of Health, begun in 1882, rapidly took leadership in inquiring into the causes of disease, educating the people in its prevention, and supervising the work of local health boards and the building of municipal water and sewage systems. Excellent effects in suppressing smallpox, typhoid fever and diphtheria were reported. In place of the objectionable "grab-game" by which hospitals and charities had acquired provincial grants, Mowat devised an equitable system under which the amount given to each institution depended on the work done and contributions received from other sources. Government inspection helped to maintain higher standards in buildings and nursing. In the treatment of particular diseases, the province was most active in aiding the mentally disordered. The asylums at Toronto and London were enlarged, and others were added at Hamilton, Mimico, Brockville and Kingston. An asylum for idiots was opened at Orillia, in connection with which a training school for feeble-minded children, the first in Canada, was formed in 1888. Many superstitions still existed concerning the insane, but more and more the province regarded them as ill persons for whom restorative treatment must be supplied. Asylums began to be curative institutions, not just places of confinement.

In tune with changing ideas about persons who had to be committed for crime, the Mowat government put more emphasis than ever before in Ontario history on the reforming and educational work of the provincial penal institutions. The boys' reformatory at Penetanguishene was remodelled to take on the atmosphere of a school rather than of a prison; and the boys were taught trades, though in a limited way. In 1880 the Andrew Mercer women's reformatory and an industrial refuge for girls were erected at Toronto, the latter for the purpose of bringing into an environment of discipline and training girls under the age of fourteen who were in various circumstances tending to an "idle and dissolute life." In the Toronto Central Prison, too, the government attempted to give the men industrial training through productive employment, such as broom or twine-making, which would not compete with the free workingman – a point on which labour organizations insisted.

The new humanitarianism was seen particularly in legislation for children, for example, to protect them from specific harmful influences as in the act prohibiting the sale of tobacco to boys under eighteen. There were objections that this was intrusion into the domain of the family – "a switch hung up behind the door would do far more." But Mowat sponsored the bill himself in a speech that could have been made in 1967, reinforced by doctors' statements on the ill effects of the use of tobacco. The biggest innovation came after the *Report* of the Royal Commission on Prisons (1891) stressed the need to remove the roots of crime. Provincial Secretary Gibson, who introduced the Children's Act of 1893, declared:

> Remove the young from schools of crime, and place them under virtuous and benign influences, and almost in the same proportion do we cut off what, later on, will form a part of our criminal population.

His measure created a social guardianship, the Children's Aid Society, for the child who was neglected or ill-treated by his parents so that he was in a state of vagrancy or in peril of health or morality. Ontario had come a long way in acceptance of the principles of public welfare when this form of state intervention between parents and children met general approval.

It would have been strange if Mowat, who brought so many social problems within the closer purview of government, had left education outside. In 1876 he placed the educational system for the first time in the hands of a Minister. Crooks and Ross, the two Education Ministers under Mowat, consolidated the work of Dr. Egerton Ryerson, Superintendent of Ontario schools since 1844, and Ross in particular modernized the system. Concepts discussed at educational conventions today were favourites with Ross – articulated education, technical education, adult education. "The system is a unit from the kindergarten to the university," he stated after bringing in the idea of kindergartens from the United States, and providing for the affiliation of other universities with the strong provincial university in Toronto. Although there was talk of "over-education" spoiling the masses for practical work, extensions of the franchise made an educated citizenry essential. Amid lingering pioneer prejudices against public education for the "classes," Ross had the courage to affirm that the state's duty was not discharged when elementary education was given, and that the young should be encouraged to push on into high school and university. Ross was concerned as well about diversity in education to meet Ontario's changing conditions. He added commercial subjects in the high schools; and even defended the private school, Upper Canada College, because it was "an effective safeguard against the tendency toward a dead level, a defect common to all systems of Government education." He provided continuing education for artisans and mechanics at schools of art and design, and in evening classes at the School of Practical Science and at the old Mechanics' Institutes which now passed under the Department of Education.

The enlightenment of the Mowat government's educational policies was neutralized by the continuing low qualifications of teachers and irregular attendance of pupils. Many sections, suspicious of Ross's "frills and furbelows," paid a "beggarly pittance" to teachers and expected them to handle classrooms of over fifty pupils. Opposition to compulsory attendance as interfering with parents' authority was not sufficiently overcome until 1891 for Ross to deem it prudent to enforce attendance of children up to fourteen years of age. In spite of these defects, Ontario, in competition with American and European states at the Chicago Exposition of 1893, won a special award:

For a system of Public Instruction almost ideal in the perfection of its details, and the unity which binds together in one great whole all the schools from the Kindergarten to the University.

The public library as a means of popular education in Canada came into being in 1882 with Mowat's Free Libraries Act, which authorized municipalities to establish libraries with the ratepayers' assent and levy a tax for their maintenance. The province would match, up to certain maxima, what the local board spent on books and periodicals. Mowat's library legislation was typical of his expansion of areas of co-operation between provincial and local governments. The criticism sometimes made that he interfered with municipal independence ignores the fact that under the British North America Act municipalities in their own right have no independent authority. Mowat actually contributed to the devolution of self-government in asking localities to undertake enlarged responsibilities in many fields – libraries, education, public health.

Charles Clarke, the old Reformer of Elora, called the Mowat period the time when "Ontario recommenced its growth." Politically, the Mowat era fixed the tradition that responsible government would work provincially as nationally through the party system. His far-reaching legislation was carried with a shrewd eye to political advantage, but it was also good for Ontario. The Liberal party and the province developed concomitantly. Under Mowat's careful but forward-looking guidance, Ontario moved steadily and prosperously toward her maturity in the twentieth century, when his type of leadership, with the same success, passed to the Conservative party.

BIBLIOGRAPHICAL NOTE

Publications specifically on Mowat are few:

Biggar, C. R. W., *Sir Oliver Mowat: A Biographical Sketch* (2 vols., Toronto, 1905).

Evans, A. Margaret, "The Ontario Press on Oliver Mowat's First Six Weeks as Premier," *Ontario History*, LVI (1964), pp. 125-41.

Kerr, Janet B., "Sir Oliver Mowat and the Campaign of 1894," *Ontario History*, LV (1963), pp. 1-13.

Morrison, J. C., "Oliver Mowat and the Development of Provincial Rights in Ontario: A Study in Dominion-Provincial Relations, 1867-1896," *Three History Theses* (Toronto, 1961).

Several works by contemporaries of Mowat are helpful:

Clarke, Charles, *Sixty Years in Upper Canada* (Toronto, 1908).

Ross, Sir George W., *Getting into Parliament and after* (Toronto, 1913).

Willison, Sir John S., *Reminiscences, Political and Personal* (Toronto, 1919).

Manuscript sources of value are the Edward Blake Papers and James P. Whitney Papers in the Ontario Department of Public Records and Archives, Toronto.

Abundant material is contained in the official record: the *Journals* and *Sessional Papers* of the Legislative Assembly of Ontario and the *Statutes of Ontario*; and public opinion is found copiously in the party newspapers, independent journals, and numerous pamphlets.

The Ontario Boundary Question

Morris Zaslow

Where were the northerly and westerly limits of the newly-established Province of Ontario? The British North America Act, the founding instrument of the province as well as of the Dominion of Canada, did not spell these out with any certainty. Article 6 merely assigned to the province the same territorial limits as the former Upper Canada or Canada West, whatever those may have been. Contemporary maps, notably the famous Arrowsmith map of 1857, showed the limits of the Province of Canada as being the height of land separating the Great Lakes and St. Lawrence drainage basin from that of the rivers flowing into Hudson and James Bays. Beyond lay the lands claimed by the Hudson's Bay Company by virtue of King Charles II's celebrated charter of 1670.

Within Canada West, the future Ontario, a population of 1,600,000 was engaged in settling the land and developing its resources. For twenty-five years miners, surveyors, lumbermen and fishermen had been moving forward along the shores of the upper Great Lakes, carrying Canadian settlement to the old fur trading centre of Fort William and the newer village of Prince Arthur's Landing at the head of Lake Superior. In 1850 the Canadian government had signed the Robinson Treaty with the Indians of the Georgian Bay and Lake Superior districts. By 1867 land and road surveys had been conducted in the lakehead district, some 35,000 acres of land had been granted to claimants, and the province had organized seven townships and established municipal institutions for the village of Prince Arthur's Landing. The discovery of a rich silver deposit on Silver Islet in Thunder Bay, almost coincident with Confederation, accounted for a notable increase in interest and travel to and from the lakehead.

Nor was this the farthest extent of the province of Canada's interests in this quarter. For a decade before Confederation Canadians had been eyeing the broad, fertile, empty acres of Red River. Hence the lakehead was the starting point of a trail and water route to that Promised Land known as the Dawson Route, upon which work had already begun. Only in this region did Canadian authority and occupancy actually attain and pass beyond the limit of the Great Lakes drainage basin; and only along the upper Ottawa, where logging operations were under way in the vicinity of Lake Temiskaming, did Canadian interests even remotely approach the northern limit of the St. Lawrence basin. For the rest, the height of land boundary claimed by the Hudson's Bay Company remained untouched, scores and hundreds of miles past the last Canadian lumber camp or farmstead.

But was that height of land the true limit and full extent of the province of Ontario or its predecessor, the United Province of Canada? Before Confederation the officers of the Canadian government had vigorously challenged this interpretation. In 1857 the able Commissioner of Crown Lands, Joseph Cauchon, began assembling an impressive array of documents and arguments to contest the claims of the Hudson's Bay Company to possess all the lands drained by the rivers flowing into Hudson Bay and Strait. Among the grounds raised against the Company were the arguments that Canada had inherited the claims of the French Crown based on the discoveries of explorers like La Vérendrye or the establishment of posts at places like Abitibi; that the Company's charter did not automatically extend its territorial bounds as British sovereignty in America was enlarged through the fortunes of war or diplomacy, but only through its own endeavours at occupying and settling territory; and that numerous acts of the British parliament and of the Crown subsequent to 1760 had extended and recognized the authority of Canada beyond the height of land. But the United Province was not prepared to test its contentions in the courts. Instead, Canadian expansionists put their faith in a political solution, relying upon the desire of the British government to see the northwest placed under an effective government. They asserted that it was the responsibility of the British government to determine the validity of Charles II's charter, and, in the event that it was valid, to terminate the Hudson's Bay Company's monopolistic, anachronistic rule. In the end the Colonial Secretary forced the two parties reluctantly to a settlement (£300,000 in cash plus certain lands) under which on December 1, 1869 (altered to July 15, 1870 because of the troubles at Red River) the Dominion of Canada entered upon the still undefined patrimony of the Company of Merchant Adventurers.

The impending transfer made the question of the western and northern limits of Ontario a timely one for the government of the new province. The Speech from the Throne of November 3, 1869, in the Ontario legislature mentioned the desirability of defining Ontario's boundary in view of the Dominion's forthcoming succession to the Hudson's Bay Company's estate. On July 14, 1871, Premier J. S. Macdonald appealed for action, alleging that "the thoroughfare over which numbers of emigrants and others are making their way from Thunder Bay towards Red River requires that they should be protected *en route,* and the jurisdiction to which the authority of this Government extends ought to be clearly defined in view of that end." The following September, when the Dominion appointed Eugene E. Taché, and the province William McDougall, as their boundary commissioners, the radically-differing views of the two governments immediately became apparent. The Dominion's representative asserted that the northern boundary of the province was the height of land of the St. Lawrence-Great Lakes drainage basin, and its western limit a line due north from the junction of the Ohio and Mississippi Rivers (89° 9′ 30″ West Longitude). As this would have removed the lakehead centres of Fort William and Prince Arthur's Landing, over which the sovereignty of the old province of Canada and of the new province of Ontario had never been challenged, this was clearly unacceptable to Ontario. McDougall, for his part, contended that Ontario's western boundary should lie 275 miles further west, at the Northwest Angle of Lake of the Woods (95° 13′ 48″ West Longitude), while on the north the province extended beyond the height of land, the true boundary of the Hudson's Bay Company's territory being somewhere north of that location. It was no surprise, therefore, that the province suspended negotiations in May 1872.

Meanwhile, settlement continued to enter the region west of Lake Superior as the Dominion government proceeded to develop the Dawson Route into a regular system of wagon roads and steamboat communications, while the activities of survey parties for the Pacific railway foreshadowed early construction of a railway across the district. Following the succession to office in Ottawa of a Liberal administration headed by Alexander Mackenzie, which was sympathetic to the Ontario contention, a temporary accommodation was reached between the two governments. Ontario and the Dominion agreed in 1874 to appoint a three-man commission to adjudicate the boundary; and in the meantime both governments would accept a temporary or conventional boundary to delimit their respective jurisdictions. This line would extend north from the eastern tip of "Hunter's Island" (the territory enclosed by two chains of lakes and rivers now comprising the southeastern part of Quetico Provincial Park), or approximately 91° West Longitude, northward to the 51st parallel of latitude, and then eastward along that parallel to the eastern boundary of the province, due north of Lake Temiskaming. Land north and west of this line would fall under the sway of the Dominion, while Ontario would exercise jurisdiction over the territory south and east of the line. Each government agreed in advance to ratify all claims to land issued by the other party in any portion of the territory that might change hands as a result of the arbitration.

The agreement continued for four years until the three arbiters (none of whom had been designated to the original panel) met for three days in Ottawa, August 1-3, 1878, and issued their decision, unaccompanied by supporting reasoning or explanations. The award was wholly in the province's favour. On the west it gave Ontario the line of the Northwest Angle; and on the north the English and Albany Rivers, the coast of James Bay east to the meridian of Lake Temiskaming, thence south to that point and along the Ottawa River. Ontario thus stood to receive an increment of approximately 110,000 square miles (a tract roughly 650 miles long by 180 miles wide) over and above the Dominion's original contention in 1871.

Gleefully the province proceeded to proclaim its authority over the new territories while it awaited reciprocal federal government legislation. But the Conservatives had returned to power as a result of the Dominion general election of October 17, 1878, and Sir John A. Macdonald refused to ratify the award. The Dominion went its way as before, while Ontario took steps to establish its authority over the entire territory of the award. Two stipendiary magistrates were appointed, E. B. Borron to superintend the northern portion (the District of Nipissing), and W. D. Lyon the western section (the District of Thunder Bay).

Mr. Borron's task was relatively peaceful and uneventful, since his district continued, little altered, as the domain of Indians, Hudson's Bay Company traders, and

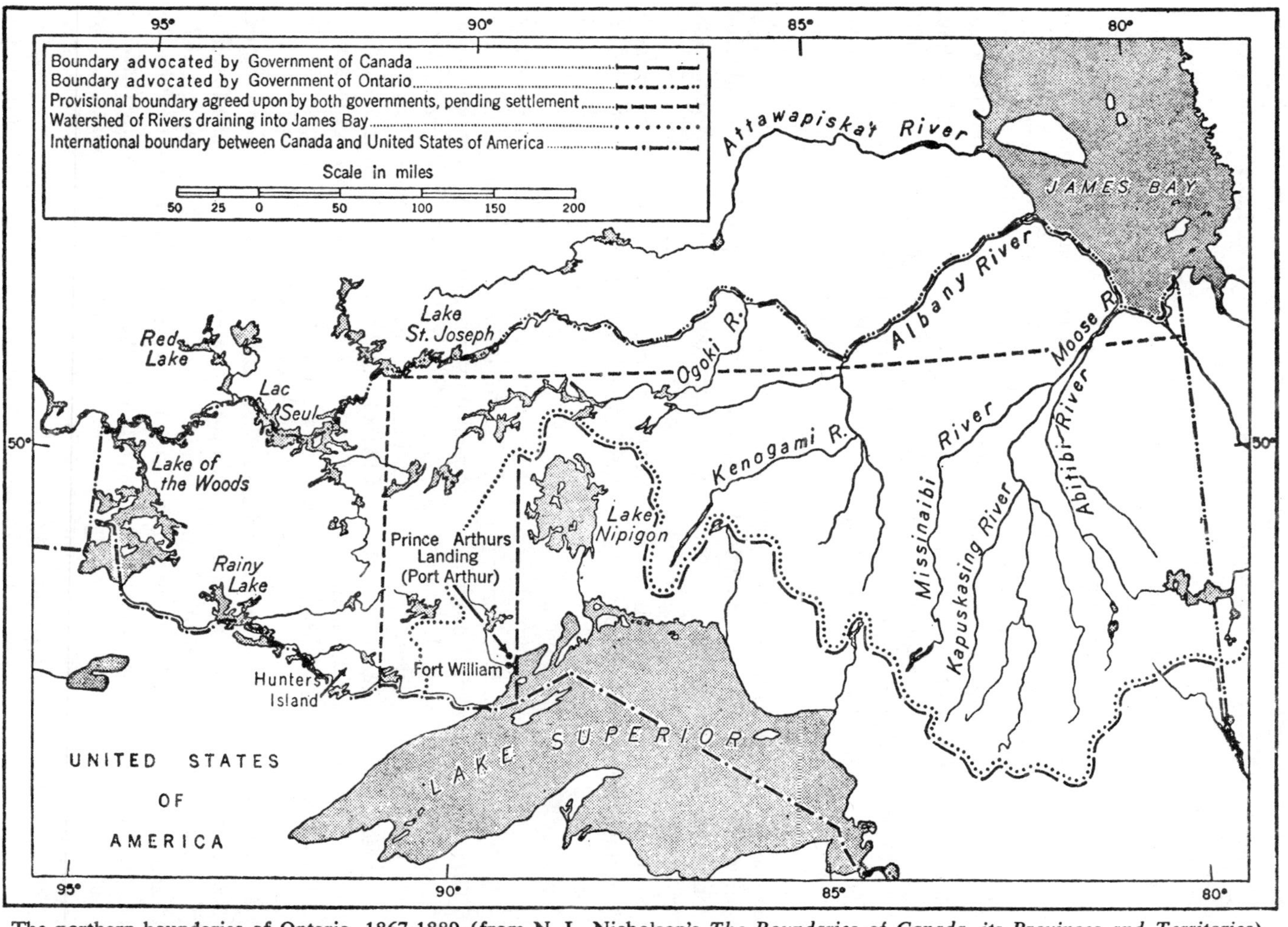

The northern boundaries of Ontario, 1867-1889 (from N. L. Nicholson's *The Boundaries of Canada, its Provinces and Territories*)

missionaries. Arriving at its 'capital', Moose Factory, after his first descent by river upon James Bay, the magistrate found himself treated as an intruder, completely at the mercy of the traders and without a vestige of authority. He speedily became convinced that the path of wisdom and of discretion was not to contest their rule, since it appeared to suffice for the needs of the country. His advice to the province was not to interfere "until we are in a position to provide a really sufficient substitute," and in the meantime to secure the co-operation of the company officers by commissioning them as provincial justices of the peace. During his annual forays to Moose Factory Borron gradually gained the confidence of the traders, while his trips, by as many different routes as possible, enlarged the government's knowledge of the region and its economic potentialities. He called for pressure upon the Dominion government to make it fulfil its obligations towards the Indians, to cease scandalously neglecting their interests, and to give the people some service in return for the taxes it drew from them. Gradually he began to suggest a more active provincial role in the territory – a public school, hospital and jail for Moose Factory; a constable; legislation to licence traders, protect native hunting and fishing rights; and strict enforcement of liquor prohibition. Thus, as the traditional order began to deteriorate the province began gradually to assert its authority.

In the west, a far more difficult situation faced Magistrate W. D. Lyon. The District of Thunder Bay already possessed a considerable population which was augmented by potentially dangerous elements attracted by railway construction, lumbering operations, prospecting for gold, wide-open frontier towns, and the other opportunities afforded by a developing region. Here the province and the Dominion were brought most directly in conflict. In addition to continuing to administer the section west of the provisional line of 1874, the Dominion claimed authority over a Pacific railway belt (which included the right to take timber for railway purposes from a distance of twenty miles on either side of the railway) in the territory under provincial jurisdiction east of the line. Since both governments granted timber berths and mineral claims in the same area and the laws of each in fields like liquor control differed widely, the chances of conflict were innumerable. Mr. Lyon complained that railway contractors and trespassers were stripping the country of vast quantities of timber, and that Dominion licensees were being allowed to acquire large areas of timber land at extremely low prices and under arrangements that permitted them to pick off the good timber while ignoring less likely-looking intervening sections of forest. By 1881 Lyon was reporting that

> The people of the locality are suffering in many ways from the unsettled condition of affairs. There is no civil court to collect debts, no land agent to locate settlers, no registry office to record deeds, no timber agent to protect the forest. There are timber limits to be had, but there is no security for the expense of exploring and surveying them. All is uncertainty and confusion. The mineral lands will become so mixed up before long that men who own locations will not be able to recognize their own property.

He also claimed that the Dominion's rule was ineffectual – that bootleggers were operating in league with government detectives; prostitution was widespread and open; and the village of Rat Portage, now Kenora, was filled with desperadoes who "put the officers of the law at defiance" and in true Wild West fashion, walked about "with knives and revolvers exposed in their belts." In May 1881 when Lyon held his first court session there, his authority was defied by a railway contractor and his bailiff was arrested and jailed by Dominion agents.

To compound the difficulty, in the spring of 1881 parliament extended Manitoba's boundaries east and north to a junction with those of Ontario, thereby injecting that province into the controversy as the successor to the Dominion's contest with Ontario. The federal government's action was not altogether altruistic. Since the Dominion controlled the natural resources of Manitoba, it could continue to exercise control over the resources of any part of the Disputed Territory which might be awarded to Manitoba. For that province, the prize was the opportunity of administering mineral and timber lands important to its prosperity and of securing control of ports of its own on Lake Superior. Ontario began to assert its authority in earnest in the western sector in 1883. A police force was organized, and violations of Ontario timber regulations were punished by seizures and fines. A magistrate's court was set up at Rat Portage, a municipal government was organized for the town, and preparations were made to hold the Ontario provincial election of 1883 in the area. As Manitoba had taken similar steps the previous year and was also holding its own provincial election of 1883 for the same region, the dangers of collision were obvious. Both elections passed without violence, but shortly afterwards trouble broke out over liquor licenses. Each government began to act against the other's licensees, touching off a series of retaliatory arrests that persuaded both of the wisdom of referring the boundary question to the highest tribunal of the Empire, the Judicial Committee of the Privy Council.

Here once again Ontario emerged triumphant. To the amazement and consternation of the Dominion, the Judicial Committee reiterated the decision of the 1878 arbiters in its own judgment of July 22, 1884. The location of the western boundary revolved upon the interpretation of a phrase in the Quebec Act (1774), which described the southwestern limit of that colony as running "along the bank of the [Ohio] river westward to the banks of the Mississippi, and northward to the southern boundary of the territory granted to the Merchants Adventurers of England trading in Hudson's Bay." Manitoba's contention was that the word "northward" meant due north from the junction of the Ohio and Mississippi Rivers (i.e. the line claimed by the Dominion in 1871), while Ontario claimed that "northward" meant north along the eastern bank of the Mississippi River to its source in Lake Itasca, then due north to the Hudson's Bay Company's territory. The Ontario interpretation was borne out by other contemporary legislation such as Carleton's Commission, and it had already been accepted in the Treaty of Versailles (1783) in which Britain conceded the Mississippi River as the western boundary of the United States. Later, in fact, that boundary had been extended north to the Northwest Angle of Lake of the Woods by an international commission which afterwards carried the boundary westward along the 49th parallel to the Rocky Mountains. So the ruling of the Judicial Committee on this point, like that of the earlier arbitration, was understandable enough. Perhaps, as the article on boundary questions in *Canada and its Provinces* suggests, the Dominion had been most unwise in pursuing the objective of depriving Ontario of the lakehead ports. This indefensible claim had aggravated and alarmed the province, and it discredited the Manitoba and Dominion case. But would Manitoba have been satisfied merely to pursue the lesser goal of the height of land west of Lake Superior? And would this change of stance, in effect amalgamating the question of the western boundary with that of the northern boundary, have improved the case of Manitoba before the Privy Council?

For the Lords Justices also rejected the other Manitoba-Dominion contention that the northern boundary was the height of land between the St. Lawrence and Hudson Bay drainage basins. Instead, they confirmed the earlier verdict of the arbiters that the northern boundary was the line of the English and Albany Rivers and James Bay, some one hundred miles beyond the height of land. They accepted the arguments of Ontario that the Hudson's Bay Company's claims had been limited by its acceptance of narrower boundaries of the Albany and Eastmain Rivers in a submission to the British government in 1700 and 1701, and that wider territories gained by British arms and diplomacy in 1713 and 1763 were not afterwards regranted to the Company but were open to all British subjects. They also followed Ontario's argument that the charter of 1670 was not sacrosanct but had been curtailed by subsequent acts of legislation, proclamations and commissions, which, correspondingly, had extended Canada's jurisdiction. The northern boundary of Upper Canada was proclaimed in 1791 and later instruments as ascending the Ottawa River "into Lake Temiscaming, and from the head of the said lake by a line drawn due north until it strikes the boundary line of Hudson's Bay"; and the commissions issued to governors after 1828 actually read: "the line drawn due north from the head of the said lake until it strikes the shore of Hudson's Bay."

In the case before the Judicial Committee of the Privy Council, Manitoba and the Dominion employed the claims the Dominion had been bequeathed by the Hudson's Bay Company, while Ontario, ironically, availed itself of the arguments that had been developed by the former province of Canada in its dispute with the Company. Thus the claims of the Hudson's Bay Company under its charter of 1670 were finally put to the legal test only after the Company ceased to be concerned with them; and in this testing they were decisively rejected by the highest court in the British Empire. In fact, so far from the Company possessing beyond challenge all the lands drained by the utmost reaches of rivers emptying into Hudson Bay, its claims now were judged insufficient even to assure it unfettered possession of an important stretch of the coast itself. The surprising result has been attributed to the superior presentation and argumentative skill of Ontario's attorneys, notably Premier Oliver Mowat who was closely questioned for two days by the justices, as well as to the long years of preparation that had gone into the Ontario argument as compared with the unpreparedness of the Manitoba and Dominion cases. James White also suggested that the Ontario spokesmen had used maps that exaggerated the extent of French occupation before 1760, but this would not appear to have been the major factor in their success.

But the wily Sir John A. Macdonald still was in no mood to yield, and despite the urgings of Ontario, the Dominion delayed taking steps to have the Judicial Committee's decision implemented. In the House of Commons he gave as a reason for delay the desirability of settling the boundaries of Quebec and Manitoba as well as Ontario, so that all three might be incorporated into one imperial statute. More important, however, he continued to assert the Dominion's claim to the natural resources of part of the territory awarded to Ontario. "Even if all the territory Mr. Mowat asks for were awarded to Ontario, there is not one stick of timber, one acre of land or one lump of lead, iron or gold that does not belong to the Dominion or to the people who have purchased from the Dominion government," he had stated publicly in 1882. Macdonald based this claim to the resources on the fact that the Dominion government in 1873 had secured the cession of the land between the height of land west of Lake Superior and Lake of the Woods from its Indian inhabitants by the Northwest Angle Treaty of 1873. This new contention occasioned further delays until in 1888 a test case had worked its way through the courts to arrive before the Judicial Committee of the Privy Council. In this St. Catharines Milling Company Case (or Indian Title Case) the court ruled once more in favour of Ontario. By this time, too, the Dominion and Quebec were approaching agreement upon a comparable northward extension of that province, though action was delayed pending the completion of surveys of the territory in question. So, finally, the Dominion took the necessary steps and Ontario's territorial rights received the sanction of an imperial statute, The Canada (Ontario Boundary) Act, 1889. After a twenty-year campaign, Ontario had finally emerged victorious, with its limits extended west to the Lake of the Woods and north to James Bay.

By entering upon this vast new territorial heritage Ontario secured an unshakeable position within the Canadian federation. The whole of the Great Lakes system in Canada was enclosed within the province and Manitoba's ambition of gaining an outlet of its own on Lake Superior was frustrated. With Ontario lapping the edge of the prairies, and in control of that region's most convenient water outlet, its commercial and social hegemony over the Canadian West was assured. Thanks to the integration of the economies of western and central Canada, Ontario's manufacturing and financial sectors were able to attain heights unequalled within the Dominion. The northern outlet on James Bay, secured in 1889, has proved of much lesser significance. Despite the construction of a railway to link the Bay with southern Ontario and frequent projects to ship iron ore and other mineral resources of the Hudson Bay basin to markets in central Canada and the United States by this route, the northern port of Moosonee remains a dead-end rather than an important port of entry to the Arctic.

The enlargement of Ontario added immense natural wealth in pulpwood, metallic minerals and waterpower to the province which was further augmented by the Dominion government's cession of the remaining portions of the Northwest Territories south of the 60th parallel to the provinces of Ontario, Quebec and Manitoba in 1912. With the securing of this territory (to which Ontario gave the name District of Patricia), the province attained its present extent, more than triple the limited area the Dominion had sought to assign it after Confederation, a veritable empire stretching 1,000 miles in either direction. Today these added territories, containing over 315,000 inhabitants, approximately 5% of Ontario's total, still stand on the threshold of development. They are criss-crossed by more than 2,600 miles of railway: 590 miles of the C.P.R.'s main line, 1,515 miles of C.N.R. track (including both the former National Transcontinental and Canadian Northern main lines), as well as portions of the Algoma Central and Ontario Northland roads.

As the natural wealth came under development and the integration of northern and southern Ontario proceeded, the provincial economy began to expand in important new directions. Ontario became a major producer of copper, iron, silver and gold, and a leading source of lumber, pulpwood, and newsprint. Today communities like Timmins and Atikokan, Geraldton and Red Lake mark the principal mining districts of the region; while towns like Kenora and Dryden, Kapuskasing and Fort Frances are the most prominent centres of forestry industries that extend over virtually the entire region. In the prosperous cities of Fort William and Port Arthur the north includes manufacturing and transportation centres of vital significance for the economy of Ontario and of Canada. The waterpower of the region has become an important source of electrical energy, helping to drive the busy engines of an increasingly mechanized, industrialized and urbanized Ontario, and serving mines, pulp and paper plants and communities within the region itself. Today sites on the English, Rainy, Kamanistikwia, Albany, Mattagami and Abitibi Rivers have been harnessed for power generation. But in the long run, perhaps, the greatest future of the northern regions may lie in their scenic and recreational values which draw visitors to Quetico Park, Minaki, Moosonee, or to the countless secluded spots that lie just beyond the railways, highways or float-plane landing sites.

Developing this wealth for the benefit of the people of Ontario has added greatly to the burdens of successive provincial governments. The announcement in 1878 of the award was greeted both with rejoicing at winning "a vast and magnificent territory" and with the chastening thought of new responsibilities "to preserve peace and order, to administer justice, to maintain civil rights, to encourage settlement, to improve existing means of communication, to promote education." Since then, the province has had to accept responsibility for resource development, social organization, and human welfare in the northland. To provide for the orderly development of the region, administrations have instituted appropriate systems of leases and claims for mineral lands, timber limits, pulpwood concessions and forest management licenses, reserved the waterpower for a provincially-owned system, established parks and reserves, managed fish and game resources, and the like. To encourage the occupation of arable sections, the province conducted explorations and surveys of suitable areas, opened them to homestead settlement, and provided schools and roads, the last-named being the particular responsibility for a time of a Department of Northern Development. Foremost among the provincial works was the construction of a provincially-owned railway system from Lake Nipissing northward to James Bay which has developed into the Ontario Northland Railway. For a time, in fact, provision was even made for an Ontario railway (or railways) to proceed to Fort Nelson or Churchill on Hudson Bay across a right-of-way reserved through the territory awarded to Manitoba in 1912. More recently, faced by the economic troubles of the depression and by the severe social and cultural upheavals of the postwar decades, Ontario governments have grown increasingly attentive to the region's human needs for the resettlement of families, the reorganization of communities, the provision of more adequate educational and vocational opportunities for the people, and the acceptance of a proper share of the responsibility for the well-being of the deprived, underprivileged Indian population. Periodically, northern and northwestern communities complain that their needs are misunderstood or ignored by southern-dominated Ontario legislatures. But it is doubtful that these northern areas could have been developed so rapidly, or to such heights, without continuing oversight and expenditures by successive provincial governments, backed by the financial strength and the tax resources of the wealthiest section of Canada.

Ontario has evolved into a very different political and geographic entity from that created in 1867 thanks to her subsequent extensions – into a province whose destiny to a considerable extent is wrapped up with the settlement and development of its forested, lake-studded, rock-girt northern regions. A new dimension was added to the older agricultural colony, a vast region incredibly rich in resources of wood, mineral and water. The older section of Ontario transmitted its technical skills, institutions, labour force and accumulated capital to help develop this virgin territory. In turn, as the north advanced, it became a source of essential raw materials for southern industries and an important customer for the products, services and facilities of the older Ontario, representing a highly successful intra-provincial economic integration. Thanks to the northland, Ontario has become a leading exporter of raw materials and of semi-manufactured products; and thanks to the south, a major industrial and financial centre. Ontario thus is a nearly self-sufficient province, balancing protectionist and low tariff attitudes and interests. The north to a considerable extent has become the cultural dependant of the more mature south; but it has also imparted something of its vigorous, rugged nature, its mosaic of peoples and societies, and its continuing sense of purpose to the older section. Oliver Mowat's successful stand before the Judicial Committee of the Privy Council must surely rate as one of the most momentous events in the province of Ontario's first hundred years.

BIBLIOGRAPHICAL NOTE

Biggar, C. R. W., *Sir Oliver Mowat: A Biographical Sketch* (2 vols., Toronto, 1905).

Jones, R. L., "The Ontario-Manitoba Boundary Dispute," unpublished Master's thesis, Queen's University, 1928.

Morrison, J. C., "Oliver Mowat and the Development of Provincial Rights in Ontario: A Study in Dominion-Provincial Relations, 1867-1896," *Three History Theses* (Toronto, 1961).

Nicholson, Norman L., *The Boundaries of Canada, its Provinces and Territories*, Canada, Department of Mines and Technical Surveys, Geographical Branch, Memoir, no. 2 (Ottawa, 1954).

Ontario, Legislative Assembly, *Sessional Papers*, 1882, no. 69 (Toronto, 1882), "Correspondence, Papers and Documents of Dates from 1856 to 1882 Inclusive, Relating to the Northerly and Westerly Boundaries of the Province of Ontario."

———, 1889, no. 60 (Toronto, 1889), "The Proceedings before the Judicial Committee of Her Majesty's Imperial Privy Council on the Special Case Respecting the Westerly Boundary of Ontario."

Poole, A. F. N., "The Boundaries of Ontario," *Canadian Bar Review*, vol. 42, no. 1 (1964), pp. 100-139.

White, James, "Boundary Disputes and Treaties," A Shortt and A. G. Doughty, eds., *Canada and Its Provinces* (23 vols., Toronto, 1914-17), vol. 8, pp. 878-907.

James P. Whitney and the University of Toronto

Charles W. Humphries

James P. Whitney, Ontario Conservative leader since 1896, finally succeeded in overturning the Liberals under George W. Ross in January of 1905, by winning 69 seats to the Liberals' 29. Whitney came to the Premier's office unburdened either by heavy pledges or confining ties. Nevertheless, the new government did face several pressing problems which demanded solutions, among them unravelling of the tangled affairs of the University of Toronto.

When the Conservatives came to power James Loudon had been the sincere but unconciliatory president of the University of Toronto for a dozen trouble-filled years. The educator had continually been at odds with William Mulock, the vice-chancellor, and Edward Blake, the chancellor, until they had retired from the academic scene in 1900. The departure of the latter had created a vacancy to be filled by W. R. Meredith who had been Whitney's onetime leader in the provincial Legislature. The president had faced student rebellion in 1895 and harsh, unfounded undergraduate criticism in 1904. In the first case the government had had to appoint a commission to investigate the troubles and, in the second, a select committee of the university's Senate had examined the state of affairs. And more than once he had come into conflict with the university's Board of Trustees. Unhappily, as W. Stewart Wallace says in his *History of the University of Toronto* (Toronto, 1927), Loudon seems to have been a man who carried his own black cloud with him.

Nevertheless, the difficulties of Loudon's presidency were symptomatic of deeper, enduring root problems which were not of his creation. During his time in office, the University of Toronto was constantly under the shadow of the provincial parliament buildings, located just to the east. The legislature had hamstrung the institution financially and troubled it administratively. W. R. Meredith described one aspect of this unfortunate situation to Whitney:

> ... I want to tell you of a very bad practice which prevailed under the last administration [George Ross's] and which I hope will not be followed by yours [sic]. I refer to the practice of members of the staff [of the University of Toronto] urging upon [cabinet] ministers appointments to the staff[,] promotions and increases of salary for themselves & others. I venture to suggest that this is all wrong and that all com-

> munications should come through the President [of the University of Toronto] or the Principal of the University College according as they relate to the University or University College.

Loudon was not the man to stand up to Ross in the face of intervention by politicians and, as Dr. Wallace has noted, "appointments were made to the staff without consulting the wishes of the president, and even against his express recommendation."

On the financial side, the attitude of the Liberals under Ross has been described as "niggardly and cheese-paring." It is true that in 1901 the province had undertaken the financial maintenance of the departments of chemistry, physics and mineralogy and geology, but the deficits of the university had continued to mount thereafter until Whitney estimated that the 1905 shortage would amount to over forty-five thousand dollars. The institution obviously was in need of generous financial assistance if it was to rise above a cap-in-hand existence.

Whitney was quite conscious of all these aspects of the university problem when he assumed office. In 1895, before he had become party leader, he had attacked the Liberal government of that day about the causes of the student strike and, thereafter, he had been quite prepared to debate the Liberal attitude toward the institution. In 1901, he had begun to formulate the Conservative policy. The Tories, he had said, would grant more assistance to the university; they would not permit it "to remain suspended between heaven and earth, like the coffin of Mohammed . . ." "We must take a forward position on the university question," he had told the Legislature, "or else consent to be left hopelessly in the rear with disastrous results, one of which will inevitably be that our young men will go elsewhere for higher education." He had wanted the finances of the institution "put on a sound, stable, and permanent footing" by means of an annual payment of an amount sufficient to meet its requirements; this, he had suggested, should come out of the provincial succession duties. Beyond this important consideration, he had argued for a relaxation of governmental control over the university so that "the governing body of the university" would have the chief powers in matters of policy and appointments. Lastly, Whitney had asked for a sliding scale of fees so that poverty would not be a barrier to the higher education of either men or women. More than three years before its electoral triumph, the Conservative party possessed a clearly enunciated policy for the University of Toronto.

The Liberal administration had mustered some aid for the University of Toronto in 1901 but had refused to be moved by Whitney's arguments for greater assistance and academic freedom. George Ross had privately taken the view that his government had been as generous as it dared to be on a matter which would gain little widespread support and might possibly create hostility. "I think the University question is the most dangerous one we have taken up this Session," he had written to a cabinet colleague in 1901. "Although our followers will stand by us, I am quite uneasy as to the effect upon the country." And the premier had thought that Whitney was using the luxury of opposition to engage in an irresponsible game. "I fear very much we cannot give more aid to the University," he had written to J. S. Willison, editor of the Liberal *Globe*.

It was with some difficulty I prevailed upon my supporters to go as far as is proposed by our present Bill. I also doubt very much if Mr. Whitney will move an amendment granting further aid. Of course he is very much under Meredith's influence, and may possibly be induced to endeavor to outbid us for the support of the Alumni of Toronto University. The effect at the ballot-box, however, will be of no consequence to him if he does. I was sorry to see you give him so much credit for his present course. He was really playing hide and seek until he saw the game was up; then he thought to recover himself by bidding higher for what he thought was popular support than we dared go. I hope to be just to my opponents, but in this case he has got infinitely more credit than he deserved.

Once in office, Whitney soon revealed that he had not been just "bidding higher" "for the support of the Alumni." In the Legislature in mid-May, 1905, the Conservative Premier unveiled the first portion of his remedies for the University of Toronto. His primary concern was to give the institution greater strength and independence through adequate funds. There would be government money to aid in the construction of men's residences, a new physics building, a science building addition, Convocation Hall and a new hospital (to be used jointly by the city of Toronto and the university medical faculty); and a thirty-year grant of thirty thousand dollars per annum for building purposes. "The total proposed expenditures dealt with by the Bill," he told the Legislature, "would be $1,600,000 and of this sum the direct grants by the Government would amount to $465,000. While this was a large sum, it would at once put the University beyond the danger of embarrassment."

There was little for the Liberal opposition to say. The former Minister of Education, Richard Harcourt, had the temerity to suggest that the Conservatives were following lines laid down by the former administration; Ross urged a similar argument and also stated "that residences were not an essential feature of University life." Outside of the legislature, among those concerned for the welfare of the institution, there was wide acceptance of the government's action. One longtime Liberal, Sam Blake (a brother of Edward), was ecstatic:

The first letter that I write this morning must be one to you thanking you most heartily and congratulating you on your splendid work for the University. In your first Session you have done more than has been done at least in ten years past by the former Government. We have received pauper doles and promises, depending upon political exigencies, and our University has been almost run to the ground. You have now given us splendid aid, and you will arouse largely the sympathy of the whole country in favour of our Provincial University. . . . It was humiliating to read the pitiful utterance of the Leader of the Opposition. Those who have been applying to the Government and using efforts in and out of season to bring them to time, will know how utterly misleading are his statements. He might well have closed his twaddle by repeating to the House "how Bill Adams won the Battle of Waterloo" – he being Bill Adams!! May you long be spared in strength to build up on true and honest lines our Province, which has run so much to seed during the past twenty years.

With such generous legislation, the Conservative administration began the work of providing the University of Toronto with a new, substantial foundation.

This measure, however, left the administrative side of the university untouched and that also demanded attention. The report of a Senate committee (headed by

Meredith) investigating charges of favouritism by Loudon in the awarding of fellowships strongly recommended that the over-burdened president be relieved of his lesser responsibilities while being strengthened by a clearer definition of his powers. In June of 1905, a committee of the Alumni Association suggested greater centralization of university government and increased freedom from political interference. The latter proposal was in line with the pleadings of the *Globe* which also had continually preached the need for higher salaries and stronger administration.

Throughout the summer of 1905 Whitney must have given thought to the composition of a commission that would thoroughly investigate the University of Toronto. He certainly was in touch with that aging academic, Goldwin Smith, and there is evidence to indicate that Meredith never permitted the Conservative leader to forget the subject. By late September, the Premier had reached some conclusions; "I have delayed a little about the composition of the University Commission," he wrote to Meredith.

> After a good deal of fussing on my part, because nobody has interfered with me, I have decided tentatively on the names. Perhaps I might have done better, but at all events, if I finally decide on those I am about to mention, I will have the satisfaction of knowing that they were chosen by myself. The names are Goldwin Smith, Yourself, [J. W.] Flavelle [Chairman], [B. E.] Walker [general manager of the Canadian Bank of Commerce], Rev. Canon Cody, Rev. D. B. McDonald [sic] and [A. H. U.] Colquhoun, the latter also being Secretary.
>
> I do not expect to please everybody, but it has been a very difficult task to work out these names.

These men remained Whitney's choices for the commission and the public announcement was made on October 2.

The terms defining the scope of the inquiry were broad; the commission was directed to report on:

(a) A scheme for the management and government of the University of Toronto in the room and stead of the one under which the said University is now managed and governed.

(b) A scheme for the management and government of University College including its relation to and connection with the said University of Toronto.

(c) The advisability of the incorporation of the School of Practical Science with the University of Toronto.

(d) Such changes as in the opinion of the Commissioners should be brought about in the relations between the said University of Toronto and the several Colleges affiliated or federated therewith, having regard to the provisions of the Federation Act.

(e) Such suggestions and recommendations in connection or arising out of any of the subjects thus indicated as in the opinion of the said Commissioners may be desirable.

Although there was wide approval of the Tory leader's course of action on this question, there were words of criticism. President Loudon, unaware of the Premier's intentions, had informed him just hours before the public announcement of the creation of the commission that the time seemed "opportune for the re-organization of the University." The president suggested "a small committee" properly equipped to examine the problem and make proposals; he wanted the group to consist of Meredith, Smith and himself. But now Loudon was cut out of any position of influence.

One critic suggested that the commission might have been strengthened on the academic side by the addition of educational experts from Harvard or Cambridge and that the two graduates named to the group – Cody and Macdonald – left something to be desired. Whitney was explicit in his reply to this two-pronged attack:

> . . . The object [of the commission] is not to investigate the University, but premising that the present state of affairs, and the present system of management have become intollerable [sic], the Commission is instructed to enquire into the merits of other systems and report a new system, having regard to the conditions that prevail here. In doing this the Commission will necessarily avail itself of the knowledge of various gentlemen such as those whose names you mention. But I am bound to say it would never occur to me to suggest that men from Oxford, or Cambridge, or perhaps even from Harvard, should lay down a scheme for the management of our University. So far from agreeing with you I am afraid I should consider their presence on the Commission a decided weakness.
>
> I am not so much surprised at the objection made to the two gentlemen who are supposed to represent the graduates. Considering the present atmosphere which surrounds University matters I apprehend any choice made by even an angel from Heaven, for instance, would not be considered suitable by many graduates, but in my opinion there are few if any graduates of our University better equipped in ability, industry, love for the University and honesty of purpose than the two gentlemen I have chosen.

The Premier was convinced that Ontarians must shape their provincial university; no transplanted Harvard or hybrid Oxford-Cambridge for him.

Given the personal idiosyncracies, the professional politicking and the intellectual attitudes of a host of academics, the commission had difficult work before it but, starting in November of 1905, it attacked the problem and its report was presented to the Ontario Legislature in April of 1906. "The labours of the Commission," the document explained,

> . . . have been directed not to the severing of the connection between the University and the State . . . but to submit such changes of administrative machinery as may tend to harmonize and unify its somewhat disjointed parts and lend new vitality to the whole system. A method has been sought by which the Province might adapt from the experience of other State institutions. . . . We have been mindful of the fact that the University of Toronto, although faulty in its scheme of government, has a history and traditions peculiarly its own. . . .
>
> Nor should it be overlooked that the future expansion of the University, not less than its present needs is a consideration of vital moment. We have a right to assume that in the years to come the University of Toronto will more and more assert its influence in the national life of Canada. . . . A scheme of government created today must keep in view the gradual but certain enlargement of half a century hence.

After an examination of the history of the institution and a review of its present circumstances, the report advanced the recommendations of the commissioners. They concluded that "the powers of the Crown in respect to the control and management of the University should be vested in a Board of Governors, chosen by the Lieutenant-Governor-in-Council"; "the Senate . . . based upon the principle of representation of the federated and affiliated institutions and the faculties and graduates, should direct the academic interest of the University"; "the School of Practical Science should be united with the University as its Faculty of Applied Science and Engineering, and the same . . . connection should, as far as practicable, apply to the relations of the Faculty of Medicine to the University"; "University College should continue . . . as constituted, with a Principal, Faculty Council and Registrar of its own"; "there should be created, a Council of the Faculty of Arts composed of the Faculties of all the Arts Colleges and representatives of the federated Colleges, and a Council for each Faculty"; "there should be created a Caput or advisory committee, having authority in certain matters of University discipline"; "the office of Vice-Chancillor should no longer exist"; and "the office of President should be clothed with additional powers." Other suggestions were made, including recommendations for the creation of law, forestry, art and music schools. Security of tenure for full professors and higher salaries for all teaching staff were also proposed.

The report did not ignore the necessity of financing the operation of the institution and, after projecting what demands would be made of the provincial legislature over the next three years, the commissioners thought that a percentage of the succession duties, based on the average receipts of the previous three years, should be set aside for the use of the university. Since the revenue from these duties had risen steadily in recent years with the exception of 1902, the commission obviously had an increasing yearly grant of money in mind. It suggested two hundred and seventy-five thousand dollars as the amount of the initial annual grant.

Within a month, the government had its legislation – almost completely based upon the report – ready for presentation to the legislature. It was Whitney – not the Minister of Education, R. A. Pyne – who introduced the measure which incorporated all the major recommendations of the commission, save the proposal for an endowment of a million acres of northern Ontario lands. The Premier cut the amount of the initial grant to two hundred and fifty thousand dollars, to be taken from succession duties, and he indicated that his figure would be constant for a time and not tied to a percentage of the average income from these duties. He emphasized that political interference would be impossible under the new arrangement and then indicated that Loudon would be replaced as president. There was little for the opposition to say, and so it muttered about state benevolence drying up private assistance and defended the Liberal treatment of the institution; but it voted with the government at every major step.

One outstanding problem remained connected to the university question: the selection of a new president. Faced by the sweeping legislation of 1906 and a broad hint from the Premier that he was on his way out, Loudon definitely resigned from the presidency in July, refusing to stay on until a successor was found and accepting a pension equivalent to full pay. Principal Maurice Hutton of University College was named acting president and the search for a new chief administrator was begun.

The Premier was in receipt of suggested names for the office almost as soon as the university legislation was law. Howard Ferguson – a young legislator from eastern Ontario – was one of these correspondents, and he offered the name of Canon Cody. Whitney penned a reply in which he outlined the type of man for whom he was looking. "My idea of the man who should be President," he told the Kemptville lawyer,

> is that he be fairly well educated, very level-headed, a man who understands human nature thoroughly and knows something of Collegiate management. In addition, he should be a man of great force of Will, not hasty in his decisions, but firm as a rock when he has come to a decision. In fact, the man whom I think is necessary might fairly be called an intellectual tyrant. If you take away any offensive meaning of the word "tyrant" you will have my exact view.

Probably without realizing it, Whitney had largely described himself. And, when Ferguson mistakenly thought that the Premier meant a "tyrannical" attitude toward the students, the Conservative chief replied: "I had in view his dealings with the nineteen Governors.... I mean that the President shall be a man of force of character enough to meet the opposition or antagonism of the Governors when necessary."[1]

The Board of Governors pursued the hunt for a new president throughout the balance of 1906. Goldwin Smith grew annoyed because of the delay in finding a man and the barriers in the way: "There is an objection to a stranger, an objection to a clergyman, an objection to one of the present staff on account of connection with cliques and quarrels. What is left?" In April of 1907, all finally agreed on Robert Falconer, a clergyman, a stranger and Principal of Pine Hill Presbyterian College in Halifax.

The legislation for the University of Toronto has to be ranked as one of the major achievements of Whitney's entire period as Premier of Ontario. It provided the institution with a foundation for growth in the twentieth century and it represented a complete break with almost every aspect of Liberal policy towards the University of Toronto. By accepting almost every recommendation of an exceptional group of commissioners, Whitney may well have been the greatest friend the institution has ever had. And he took this action when it counted for little in terms of popular support, although a number of prominent Liberals discovered that their usual harsh words about Conservatives were severely tempered by the Premier's legislation. As the praise for his action came in, Whitney showed honest pride in his accomplishment:

> I shall always feel that nothing can come to me in the future which will equal my satisfaction, and, indeed, I may say my thankfulness, in having been permitted to put upon the Statute book very important legislation intended to make permanent the position of our University and to secure its usefulness.

[1] In addition to W. R. Meredith and Sam Blake, the new Board of Governors contained some powerful personalities; among them were W. T. White, J. A. Macdonald, E. B. Osler, Chester Massey, E. C. Whitney, J. W. Flavelle, John Hoskin, Goldwin Smith and B. E. Walker. Whitney alone drafted the list of persons to serve on the first Board of Governors.

BIBLIOGRAPHICAL NOTE

This paper is mainly based on primary sources. Chief among them are the J. P. Whitney Papers located in the Ontario Department of Public Records and Archives; they were of critical importance in detailing matters related to the University of Toronto. A small collection of Whitney Papers, in the author's possession, was also consulted.

The Wilfrid Laurier and J. S. Willison Papers, deposited in the Public Archives of Canada, were used to a lesser extent. The chief newspaper examined was the *Mail and Empire*; and the volumes of *The Canadian Annual Review* for the years covered by this paper were extensively read. Of minor importance to this essay were the G. M. Wrong Papers at the University of Toronto and the G. M. Grant Papers at the Public Archives of Canada.

The Evolution of a Victorian Liberal: N. W. Rowell

Margaret Prang

The career of Newton Wesley Rowell both reflected and influenced the social changes accompanying Ontario's transition from a rural to a dominantly urban society. His concerns as politician and churchman illuminate the growing pains of nineteenth century Ontario Liberalism and of Methodism as they endeavoured to find new directions in the twentieth-century industrial world. Many of Rowell's interests and activities were expressions of those dynamic and expansionist forces which were the prime movers in the creation of a trans-continental nation, forces whose aggressive thrust in these past one hundred years has often cast Ontario, in the view of Canadians in all the other provinces, in the role of "the imperial province."

The new Dominion of Canada was but four months old when Newton Rowell was born on a farm in London township, Middlesex county. His father had migrated to the district from the north of England twenty-five years earlier and was now a moderately prosperous farmer, a respected member of the local British Wesleyan congregation, and an active temperance organizer and speaker. On his maternal side, Rowell was deeply rooted in the Upper Canadian community. His mother was the daughter of Edward Wilkins Green, who migrated to Canada in 1818 as a boy from the north of Ireland, and of Mary Coyne, whose father, Henry Coyne, was well established in the Talbot settlement. Henry Coyne's inn south of London had been a rallying point for resistance to the autocratic "Lake Erie Baron," Colonel Thomas Talbot. Newton Rowell grew up on family tales of attempts to outwit the inflexible and tyrannical "old Colonel," of the civil disabilities suffered by the early Methodists in Upper Canada, and of the Reformers' struggle against the Family Compact. There was never any doubt that the family version of Upper Canadian politics flowed from the constitutional reformism of Robert Baldwin; it was a tradition of moderation, one in which there was no countenance for the rebellion of William Lyon Mackenzie.

After a public school education in the village of Arva, Newton Rowell left the family farm to take a six months' commercial course in London to fit himself for clerical work in his uncle's drygoods and millinery business. His spare time study for the high school matriculation examinations was enhanced by his successful completion of a three year Chautauqua home reading course. At the same time he was active in the Methodist Church, doing the reading preparatory to his designation as a lay preacher, and organizing one of the first Epworth Leagues in Canada, shortly after that movement was launched in the United States as the official Methodist young people's organization. His decision to study law was implemented in 1886 when he was articled as a student in a leading London law firm and began to prepare for the examinations of the Law Society of Upper Canada. Occasionally, Rowell spent an evening in the club rooms of the Young Liberals where the hanging of Louis Riel, the tariff, the merits of the new federal Liberal leader, Wilfrid Laurier, Ontario's factory legislation, and other lively topics of the day were debated.

In the autumn of 1890 Rowell's firm sent him on a trip through western Canada to collect the debts of two bankrupt distributors of farm machinery. His duties kept him in Winnipeg and southern Manitoba for six weeks and for an equal time in the Northwest Territories. Working his way westward via the C.P.R. and travelling by buckboard cart to farms north and south of the railway line, he acquired an impressive education in extensive grain farming of a type quite different from the agriculture practiced in western Ontario. Everywhere he heard complaints about the slow progress toward full responsible government in the Territories, and concluded that the local leaders, most of whom were Ontario men, would prove perfectly capable of running their own affairs. In every town of any size the Methodist church was already established, visible evidence of the success of the home mission endeavour on the prairies about which he already knew so much. By the time he got to the Pacific coast Rowell was as convinced of the unlimited possibilities of the West as the most enthusiastic local resident. Henceforth the tasks of building a Canadian and Christian society on the prairies, and Canada's role as a Pacific nation occupied a large part in his imagination and his thinking about his country's future.

When Rowell took up the practice of law in Toronto in 1891 many of the hopes of the first post-Confederation generation of Canadians were still unrealized. Yet Toronto had an air of quiet confidence in her position as the capital of the most populous province and as a metropolis preparing for the day when it would fully exploit its hinterland north and west. The city's population had doubled in the past ten years to 180,000, and a steadily expanding vision of greater things was reflected in the nineties in the slow rise of the new City Hall and in the equal solidity of other Romanesque buildings like the Union Station, the library of the University of Toronto, the armouries on University Avenue, and the massive red sandstone Legislative Buildings in Queen's Park. Robert Simpson's new department store at Queen and Yonge, across the street from the flourishing Eaton's, testified to the healthy increase in the demand for consumer goods of all kinds. Jarvis Street, boasting the first long stretch of pavement in the city, was an impressive thoroughfare for the fancy carriages that went to and from the street's large mansions, built and furnished in the full ornateness of late Victorian style and providing visible proof of the amenities available to the most affluent members of the community.

In this society there was never any shortage of work for a good lawyer, especially in property and corporation law. Rowell's advancement in his profession was rapid and before the turn of the century he was well established as one of the leading younger members of the Toronto bar. Toronto offered much more than a good living. As the centre of the political and religious endeavours to which Rowell was already committed it also abounded in opportunities for leadership in the creation of the good life.

Rowell was a frequent participant in the lively debates of the Toronto Young Liberals on subjects ranging from commercial union with the United States, to which he was strongly opposed, to methods for the control of electoral corruption, a subject that remained a life-long concern. Among the club's members he acquired friends he would keep to the end: the editor of the *Globe*, J. S. Willison, and a future editor of the same paper, Stewart Lyon, then a member of the editorial staff; W. E. Rundle, barely embarked on the course that was to take him to the presidency of the National Trust; A. E. Ames, who was able to purchase a seat on the Toronto Stock Exchange before he was thirty; Joseph Atkinson, a *Globe* reporter who already had dreams of his own Liberal newspaper, soon to take form in the Toronto *Star*; and J. J. Warren, at the beginning of his success as corporation lawyer and entrepreneur. Most of the young men of Rowell's acquaintance had grown up in rural Ontario in circumstances very like his own and had found Toronto a highly satisfactory arena for the exercise of their native talent and their devotion to hard work. A few had studied at the University of Toronto, but most had attended small town high schools or were as largely self-educated as Rowell himself.

Increasingly, Rowell was called upon to speak on political platforms, as a delegate to the first national political convention ever held in Canada – the Liberal Convention of 1893 – as a speaker in by-election campaigns, in the provincial general elections of 1894 and 1898, and in the federal contest of 1896 which brought the Liberals to power in Ottawa after eighteen years of opposition and made Wilfrid Laurier Prime Minister. Rowell's speeches in defence of Liberal policies were distinguished for careful organization, the effective use of statistics, and a concluding emotional peroration that testified to his Methodist credentials and evoked a warm response in audiences attuned to pulpit oratory. In content his political addresses were strictly orthodox: on provincial platforms he lauded the honesty and efficiency of Mowat's long administration, which had brought prosperity, the affirmation of provincial rights, steadily expanding educational opportunities, and increased care for the aged and the infirm – all with regular budget surpluses. In the federal general election of 1896 he had a great deal to say about Conservative corruption; even more frequently, like every Liberal campaigner, he dissected the National Policy to display its inadequacies and argued for freer trade, although not enough to disturb the Ontario manufacturers who had been persuaded that they had nothing to fear from the tariff policies of a Liberal government. A secondary theme in 1896 was the wisdom of Laurier's rejection of the Conservative remedial legislation to re-establish separate schools in Manitoba, and the merit of the Liberal policy of compromise. Like many strongly Protestant Ontario Liberals, Rowell did not willingly dwell at length on the school issue, although he could defend the Liberal position. Privately, he felt some anxiety about Laurier's proposed compromise and would have preferred to see the party take its stand on a straightforward adherence to the principle of provincial rights; as it was, he found reassurance in the evident determination of the majority in Manitoba to refuse any settlement that went very far toward the reinstitution of a separate school system.

In the federal election of 1900 Rowell had his first experience as a candidate. Largely at the urging of J. S. Willison, he agreed to contest the riding of East York, a riding which included part of the city of Toronto as well as the towns of Markham and Unionville and the adjacent prosperous farming districts. Rowell planned to make the marked prosperity of Laurier's first term in office, and especially the role of the new imperial preference tariff in the expanding economy, the chief thrust of his campaign. Unfortunately, the Conservatives made Canada's participation in the Boer War the major battleground, and nowhere more sharply than in East York. The sitting Conservative member, W. F. Maclean, publisher of the Toronto *World*, commanded the best of facilities for convincing the voters that Laurier's policy on the Boer War was "too little and too late" and that "a vote for Rowell is a vote for Israel Tarte" and domination by French hostility to the Empire. It was all rather ironic: a year earlier Rowell had been one of the leading orators of the day when Ontario's Minister of Education, G. W. Ross, instituted "Empire Day," a celebration which soon spread across the nation and throughout the Empire, and he yielded to no one in his devotion to the Empire or in his vision of its responsibilities as bearer of "the white man's burden." His natural inclination in the campaign of 1900 was to declare that Canadian assistance to Britain in South Africa "must become a precedent," but he refrained from doing so: a candidate running under Laurier's banner could scarcely come out against his leader's assurance to Canadians that the sending of troops to fight the Boers would not be a precedent.

Whatever the voters of East York thought of the primary issues, they rejected Rowell as their representative. The traditionally Liberal voters in the rural sections of the riding, so long held by Alexander Mackenzie, remained faithful, and it was the city voters who swung the balance against Rowell. In the province as a whole the Liberals lost eight seats, although they had slightly more of the popular vote than had the Conservatives. Ontarians had contributed 34 members to the government ranks and were thus still an important element of strength behind Laurier's second ministry.

In the following decade Rowell gave much thought to imperial issues. He followed with general approval Laurier's rejection of all forms of imperial centralization, was an early and consistent advocate of a distinctive Canadian navy, and looked forward to the day when Canada would be an equal partner in a great Britannic commonwealth of nations. His impassioned public addresses on the past grandeur and future glory of the British Empire led many to stamp him as an imperialist. Yet he was not an imperialist in any of the styles exhibited by the various brands of imperial federationists; his brand of imperialism was a common one in Ontario: its basis was a strong Dominion nationalism which looked upon the Pax Britannica as the framework within which Canadian autonomy could develop and as the guarantor of Canadian opportunity to play an increasing part in the providential, civilizing mission of the Anglo-Saxon peoples. Unlike many of his Liberal friends in Toronto, he saw no threat to the Empire in Laurier's reciprocity agreement of 1911 with the United States, and charged the Conservatives, in their jingoistic campaign against the agreement, with giving the world the impression that "the loyalty of Canadians is a purchasable quantity and depends on trade advantage." After the Liberal defeat of 1911 Rowell encouraged the non-partisan movement that developed in Ontario in favour of a positive naval policy and supported Borden's Naval Aid Bill, although he believed that Canada should both maintain and man the dreadnoughts Borden proposed to purchase for the British navy. This was only one of many issues on which he proved to be less than the perfect "party politician." Such flexibility won him respect in some quarters, but produced suspicion among the machine politicians in his own party.

. . . . .

Although publicly Rowell presented the conservative social philosophy of the Liberal party, privately he was developing more advanced points of view. In this process the decisive influence was Methodism. Soon after his arrival in Toronto Rowell joined the congregation of Metropolitan Church, and also began to work in the Fred Victor Mission, a downtown settlement sponsored by the congregation and financed chiefly by the Massey family. He continued to take an active part in the promotion of the Epworth League and was in constant demand throughout the province as a lay preacher. On the whole, he found the educational approach of the Epworth League's reading courses more efficacious than either the ambulance work of the recently popular settlement house or calls to the old-time penitent's bench. In 1892, at the age of twenty-five, Rowell was elected as a delegate from the Metropolitan congregation to the Toronto Conference of the Methodist Church, and two years later he attended the church's General Conference, the youngest man in the history of Canadian Methodism to sit in either of these assemblies. A feature of the latter gathering was the discussion of the report of the church's first Committee on Sociological Questions. Canadian Methodists were still agreed on the proscription of the well-known evils: drinking, gambling, dancing, most forms of theatrical entertainment, and Sunday street cars. A few had begun to add to this list of individual sins, such social evils as slums, low wages and long hours, and poor working conditions. In 1894 Canadian Methodists took no radical stand on these questions, but went only as far as to suggest that it was a Christian duty to be concerned with them.

Rowell's thinking about social issues was greatly stimulated by two visits to England in the 1890's and another in 1901 when he was a delegate to the Third Ecumenical Methodist Conference. The social and political influence of the nonconformist conscience was then at its height in England. Thanks to the more advanced industrialism of their country, British Methodists were further involved in the debate on Christian responsibility for the collective evils of society than were their Canadian brethren. Some contended that Gladstonian Liberalism, which most of them had supported, had provided all the social amelioration that was wise. Others were embarked on the path which led to the Liberal reform programme of 1906, while still others favoured the more radical approach of a distinctive Labour Party. Rowell's endeavours to understand the diverse views of British Methodists and Liberals were given added urgency by the shock of seeing the slums of the larger British cities. Unfortunately, Canada already had the beginnings of such slums, but he was convinced that with proper social legislation there was yet time for Canada to prevent their growth.

The good life must not be confined within the present bounds of Christendom. When the Protestant missionary movement of the Anglo-Saxon world was at its peak just after the turn of the century one of its major expressions was the interdenominational Laymen's Missionary Movement. Rowell was largely responsible for introducing the movement into Canada, travelled across the country in its interests, and took a leading part in organizing the National Laymen's Missionary Congress that brought 4,000 Canadian laymen to Toronto's Massey Hall in the spring of 1909. There Rowell gave to the movement's rallying cry – "The evangelization of the world in this generation" – his own nationalistic emphasis, calling on the Christian men of Canada to play a unique part in history by leading the world in the evangelization of mankind.

Rowell was fearful lest the will of Canadian laymen to undertake this formidable task be weakened by the theological controversy that was then raging within his own denomination. The question as to whether the Rev. George Jackson was a suitable occupant of the chair of English Bible in Victoria College was front page news from Halifax to Victoria and excited great interest among Canadian Protestants of all denominations. Jackson, a British Wesleyan Methodist, came to Canada as the pastor of Sherbourne Street Methodist Church in Toronto, the wealthiest Methodist congregation in Canada and one that included among its members such prominent citizens as J. W. Flavelle, H. H. Fudger, Senator G. A. Cox, and S. R. Parsons. "Higher criticism" was not introduced into Canadian Methodism by Jackson; since at least the 1880's the professors of theology at Victoria had been training their students in the historical methods of the German scholar Harnach and his continental and British disciples. But the new approach to the Bible was not always explicit in the sermons preached from most Methodist pulpits; when it was spelled out by a skilful preacher like Jackson, many Methodists, including most of the Sherbourne Street congregation, had little difficulty in accepting it. Often, the new liberal theology was a welcome relief, for it provided a means of reconciling religious faith with a growing awareness of scientific and historical methods of interpreting human life. But many Methodists felt profoundly threatened by a point of view which accepted evolution as the means God had used to create the universe, and taught that both the Old and New Testaments could best be understood against the background of the historical events that had produced them.

When Jackson agreed to leave the Sherbourne Street pulpit to go to Victoria College a resistance movement developed. The exponents of conservative views of the Bible found their champion in the highest officer of the church, Dr. Albert Carman, the General Superintendent of the Methodist Church and chairman of Victoria's Board of Regents. He chose to launch and then to pursue his attack on Jackson in a rather unorthodox manner, through the pages of the Toronto *Globe*, apparently hoping thus to align the rank and file of Methodist laymen on his side. In the ensuing controversy in the church, especially in the Toronto Conference, and a year later in the General Conference, it was evident that Carman had indeed aroused a good deal of support, particularly in the small towns and rural areas of Ontario. Jackson's defenders were most numerous among the occupants of city pulpits, who tended to be the better-educated clergy, and their congregations.

As one of the laymen who had shared responsibility for bringing Jackson to Canada in the belief that the church needed his intellectual sophistication, and as a member of the Victoria College Board of Regents, Rowell had a very close interest in the Jackson controversy. Behind the scenes, and in due course on the floor of the General Conference, he was the chief lay spokesman for the more liberal element. He had the satisfaction of seeing Jackson upheld and freedom of teaching at Victoria reaffirmed by the highest court of the church. For Rowell, as for many other Canadian Methodists, the Jackson controversy was no crisis of faith. In their willingness to accommodate themselves to changing Biblical scholarship they were well within the main stream of Methodism: the essence of faith lay in personal experience, which could only be confirmed by the Bible; the Bible itself need not necessarily be understood literally and was thus relatively invulnerable to changing theories about its origins.

Although Rowell argued the issues on theological grounds, there was a strong practical emphasis in his approach to the battle over higher criticism. He feared that "a barren theological controversy" would weaken missionary zeal, delay the achievement of church union in Canada, and limit the ability of Protestantism to meet the opportunities presented by the rapid settlement of the West, largely by peoples whose ways were not the ways of Ontario. His anxiety was well-founded, as was his realization that an issue of this kind could not be fully settled by any formal agreement and that the more conservative views of the Bible would have a long life. The Protestant churches of Canada confronted two enormous challenges at one and the same time: the need to face the impact of natural science and historical criticism on religion, and the task of holding or winning the thousands of new settlers in the West. They met these challenges only partially; their failures do much to explain why the West never truly became "new Ontario."

. . . . .

When Rowell assumed the leadership of the Ontario Liberal party in the autumn of 1911 he was under no illusion about the extreme difficulties of the task he had undertaken. The long Liberal regime that stretched back almost to Confederation had ended in 1905 with the crushing defeat of the administration of G. W. Ross in the midst of electoral scandals that prevented any Liberal from continuing to believe in his party as "the pure party." Then, while the Liberals marked time in confusion over leadership and policy, the Conservative government of J. P. Whitney directed the affairs of the province with a firm hand, and in a number of areas, notably in the extension of the publicly-owned hydro system, expanded measures that had been more timidly initiated by the Liberals. Rowell was brought to the leadership of the Liberal party by elements in it who were confident that the new leader was beyond corrupting, and on the understanding that the party would now commit itself to a more vigorous temperance policy and to other measures of social reform that would recognize the problems of an increasingly urban society. Since a provincial election was held six weeks after Rowell accepted the leadership and hard on the heels of the disastrous federal campaign of 1911, there was little time or money to prepare for the contest. A minimal platform was agreed upon, which was mainly a repetition of earlier policies; in many ridings the party organization was negligible, with the result that the Conservatives won sixteen seats by acclamation. The Liberal party simply hoped to hold its own and to elect the new leader in the safe seat of North Oxford. This was accomplished and a little more, with an increase of two seats; but Liberals were still outnumbered by Conservatives in the Legislature by almost four to one.

Now plans were made for the renewal of the party; new organizers who had no association with the earlier days of electoral corruption were placed in the field, and badly needed secretarial services and a headquarters staff were secured. In this Rowell enjoyed the advice and the considerable financial means of a group which included the financiers A. E. Ames, E. R. Wood, J. H. Gundy, W. E. Rundle, and F. H. Deacon, and J. E. Atkinson, publisher of the Toronto *Star*, and J. F. Mackay, business manager of the *Globe*. With the exception of the Presbyterian Mackay, all these men were active Methodists.

In working out a new party platform temperance was the most controversial question. Rowell and his keenest supporters had taken part in many plebiscites on prohibition, including the provincial vote of 1894 and the Dominion plebiscite of 1897, both of which had been won by the "dries." But both the Mowat government and the Laurier administration had found reasons for refusing to act on these verdicts. Laurier had taken the view that the majority in favour of prohibition was too slight; as every Ontario prohibitionist knew it was slight because Quebec, alone of the provinces, had voted overwhelmingly against progress. What the Dominion Alliance for the Supression of the Liquor Traffic wanted was a firm adherence to prohibition by one of the political parties, so that the issue could be transferred to the realm of political action. In Rowell the temperance forces had at last found a party leader who was prepared to go that far; by the end of his first session in the Legislature the Liberal party of Ontario was committed to contend for the abolition of the bar at the next election. Against the charge that the closing of workingmen's bars was class legislation if the licenses of the businessmen's clubs and sale in shops for consumption at home were left untouched, Rowell made it clear that as far as he was concerned the long term objective was a completely dry Ontario. At the same session Rowell declared his support for women's suffrage, but it did not become party policy until 1916. Although he looked on the granting to women of the right to vote as a reform that could be justified on several grounds, he shared the belief of many advocates of the measure that a majority of women voters would use their new power to further the temperance cause, and thereafter to support other forms of social legislation that would have an equally beneficial effect on the homes of Ontario.

In setting out to develop a party that would be more aware of the problems of an industrial society Rowell faced formidable difficulties. Not a single predominantly urban riding had returned a Liberal; the core of his following was from the traditionally Grit areas of rural, western Ontario. This group would commit itself to prohibition, which had long enjoyed greater support in the small towns and farming communities of the province than in the larger centres, but it was unlikely to give single-minded support to social legislation beneficial mainly to city dwellers. Thus in speeches outside the Legislature Rowell advocated a programme of new social legislation, especially a scheme of social insurance covering old age, sickness, and unemployment, but this never became official party policy during his period of leadership. These ideas, however, did gain some acceptance among Liberals in rural constituencies who could readily understand that if their party were ever to come to power again it would have to gain much greater support from urban voters. At the same time, many of the urban working men to whom Rowell hoped to appeal were unwilling to give up the pleasures of the bar on the strength of promises of workmen's compensation, shorter working hours, better health services, social insurance, and other perhaps distant amenities.

Rowell faced even greater difficulties than those arising from the contradictions between the present structure of his party in the Legislature and the direction in which he and his friends wished to advance. The dominant political fact of the hour was that the Whitney government had seized the initiative on many of the major problems of the province in a manner that left little for the Liberals to do but to criticize the details of government policy or to call for more of the same. This was true of workmen's compensation legislation, of the regulation of conditions and hours of work, public health measures, hydro policy, and the development of northern Ontario. All this scarcely created an heroic role for the opposition or its leader, although it contributed to the education of the Liberal party and perhaps did something to strengthen the hand of the reforming elements among the Conservatives.

On another issue – bilingual schools – there was little significant difference between Ontario Liberals and Conservatives. The Whitney government's Regulation 17 of 1912, restricting the use of French as a language of instruction to the first two years of schooling, reflected the almost unanimous conviction of Ontarians that everyone in the province must learn English. Agreement that Ontario was an *English*, not a dual culture, created a strange alliance of opinion ranging from the officers of the Orange Order to the Irish Roman Catholic bishops. The chief political controversy arising from Regulation 17 was not within Ontario itself but inside the federal Liberal party. In a long and painful dialogue between Rowell and Laurier both men appealed to "the Mowat tradition" in education. Laurier, contending that the heart of that tradition lay in toleration of minority rights, pleaded that Ontario Liberals should do battle for a more generous attitude toward French, while still acknowledging the primacy of English for all children in Ontario. Rowell was just as insistent that Mowat had stood first and foremost for provincial rights, and that the minority in the province must depend on the goodwill of the majority. Although he had no desire to deprive Franco-Ontarians of opportunities to study their mother tongue in school as an additional subject, Rowell never publicly criticized Regulation 17 either in principle or in detail. For any political leader in Ontario to do that, he told Laurier, would be "political suicide." But neither Rowell nor his advisers, nor his followers in the Legislature, save the handful of representatives from strongly French ridings, had any desire to question the basic assumptions and purpose of the government's policy. Long before the beginning of the world war Laurier and Rowell, and the federal and provincial Liberal parties, were in serious disagreement over a matter involving the fundamental structure of the Canadian Confederation, a disagreement which contributed to the growing disunity of the nation as the war progressed.

By the time of the general election of 1914 the Liberals were markedly more spirited and better organized than they had been three years before. Rowell made the liquor question the key issue of the campaign and "Abolish-the-Bar" became the major Liberal slogan. The official church courts and papers of the Methodist, Presbyterian, and Baptist churches, and numerous clergymen of those denominations, and even the occasional Anglican, declared the abolition of the bar to be a moral issue which should cut across party lines and urged their flocks to vote for prohibition candidates; in most constituencies that meant support for Liberal candidates. On this question, as on the lesser issues of the contest, the Whitney government stood on its record, pointing to the substantial reduction in liquor licenses and in convictions for drunkenness under the policy of local option maintained by the Conservatives. In the result, it seemed that the large body of "temperance Conservatives," whom the Liberals had hoped to swing behind them, were prepared to follow only a Conservative route to prohibition. With a slight decrease in percentage of the popular vote cast for the Liberals, the distribution of seats in the Legislature remained substantially unchanged.

Within a few months the outbreak of war gave temperance advocates new arguments for their position. Prohibition could now be urged as an economy measure that would save grain for more vital purposes, and as a reform that would ensure a sober population capable of prosecuting the war effort with maximum efficiency. Now the Liberal party formally committed itself to the closing of clubs and shops as well as bars for the duration of the war. There was encouragement for the prohibitionists in the advent to the premiership of W. H. Hearst, who was known to be a "temperance man" and was believed to favour stricter control of the sale of liquor than many members of the Conservative party. The prohibitionists now formed "The Committee of One Hundred" with the aim of taking the liquor question out of politics once and for all and pressing the fight to a victorious conclusion. Although the Committee's programme was in effect the Liberal policy and most of its moving spirits were Liberals, it was officially non-partisan; Rowell was careful to promote this image of the Committee by taking care not to publicize these connections.

So successful was the campaign of the Committee of One Hundred that before the opening of the 1916 session of the Legislature a parade of 10,000 persons marched through Queen's Park to present the government with a petition favouring total prohibition signed by more than 852,000 Ontarians, men and women over the age of eighteen; according to the committee, the signatures from eligible voters represented 73% of those who had voted at the previous election and 48% of all those on the voter's list. The anti-prohibitionists, supported by most of the labour organizations, the commercial travellers, the hotel keepers, and of course, the brewers and distillers, also had their voice in the Personal Liberty League. In the circumstances of the time, their arguments that prohibition was anti-democratic, bad for provincial tax revenues, and generally detrimental to the economy, received a poor hearing in quarters where they would have been acceptable in peace-time. Premier Hearst asked the Legislature: "Is this a time to talk of personal liberty, to think of our pleasures, our appetites, our enjoyments, when the civilization of the world is hanging in the balance and the very foundations of liberty are tottering and dependent upon the strength of Great Britain and her allies in the field and on the high seas?" Every member of the House answered "no" and voted for the Ontario Temperance Act. Ontario was dry by the unanimous vote of the elected representatives of the people.

The war also changed government policy on women's franchise. It was becoming increasingly difficult for politicians to laud the contributions of women to the war effort while continuing to deny them a primary right of citizenship. After years of resistance to the idea, the Conservative party in 1917 introduced a bill to give the franchise to women; again there was not a single negative. But the government took the position that the revolution thus begun had gone far enough, and rejected Rowell's proposal to allow women to sit in the Legislature themselves.

Although this turn of events deprived Rowell of the position he had once thought to hold in the history of these developments, he could find some satisfaction in having helped to create the climate that had forced the government to change its earlier policies. With the adoption of prohibition and the extension of the franchise to women the way seemed to be open for a great post-war era of further social reforms.

BIBLIOGRAPHICAL NOTE

The most important sources for the aspects of Rowell's career discussed here are the small collection of Rowell Papers relating to these years, the Laurier Papers, and the Willison Papers, all in the Public Archives of Canada. There is also some material in the Carman Papers in the Archives of the United Church of Canada, Victoria University, Toronto. Indispensable sources are the Toronto *Globe*, the Toronto *Star*, and *The Christian Guardian*.

That Tory Hepburn

Neil McKenty

Get this fact. We are in this thing because of the little fellow, the workman who isn't working any more, the farmer who is struggling against unbelievable odds. I've seen these people, talked to them, you can't credit their situation. We're in this thing because of them. There is going to be a new deal in this province.

It was the last week of June, 1934, and for the first time in nearly thirty years a Liberal premier of Ontario was speaking. Mitchell F. Hepburn, the 37 year old farmer from near St. Thomas in Elgin County, had ousted George Henry's Conservative Government on June 19 to become the youngest premier in the province's history. Before he resigned from office a little more than eight years later on October 21, 1942, Mitch Hepburn would lead the Liberals to another overwhelming victory in 1937, virtually destroy the provincial party because of his destructive feud with the federal leader, Mackenzie King and, according to many, change from a genuine reformer advocating "a new deal" for "the little fellow" into a narrow conservative whose chief pre-occupation was furthering the interests of big business. The main evidence adduced to illustrate Hepburn's turn to the right was his policy during the strike at the Oshawa plant of General Motors in April, 1937. Instead of supporting the workers whom he had extolled in previous years, Hepburn came down solidly on the side of management.

The genesis of Mitchell Hepburn's "turn to the right" deserves closer examination. During his first campaign for the premiership, Hepburn made no statement that received more publicity than his remark, "I swing well to the left where even some Liberals will not follow me." These words, spoken during a provincial by-election in York West in May, 1932, constituted an open bid for the substantial labour vote in that riding. In the minds of men like Conservative Premier George Henry, the words also labelled Hepburn as a radical if not a Red. One prescient observer noted at the time, however, that Mitch Hepburn had not really staked out his claim in the vast untracked country of radical reform. He did not stake it out then or ever.

In the earliest years of his political career in Elgin County, at the beginning of the 1920's, Mitch Hepburn belonged to the United Farmers of Ontario, an organization that could be considered radical only to the extent it advocated political gimmicks such as the direct referendum, recall of judges and, in some quarters, class government. If the UFO was politically radical in this narrow sense, most of the farmers who belonged to it were socially conservative. Mitch Hepburn himself, busy running a large farm and a cooperative dairy, was always more interested in the marketing features of the UFO program than he was in its political planks. Moreover, between hoisting milk cans, the young farmer had time to talk to the people along Elgin's back concessions, to imbibe their "populism," their bias against the big-wigs and entrenched power, time to develop those fundamental rural characteristics of business acumen and thrift which had made many of them reasonably prosperous and which would not basically disturb the *status quo*.

While federal member for Elgin West (1926-1934), Hepburn showed himself to be a traditional *laissez-faire* liberal coated with an emotional antagonism toward big business. He demonstrated the first by his consistent fight for freer trade and the second by his sustained assault on the financial policies of the Sun Life Assurance Company. If his attacks on Sun Life were a bit irresponsible, neither position was particularly radical and it is interesting that during his eight years as a federal member, Hepburn had practically nothing to say about social and economic reform.

When he became provincial Liberal leader in December, 1930, Hepburn was faced with the worsening depression. His remedy for the faltering economy was not to introduce innovations in the economic and social order such as the newly formed CCF advocated. His rhetoric was radical; his policies were not. What Hepburn emphasized in his successful campaign of 1934 was not radical reform but the elimination of corruption at Queen's Park, drastic economies in the administration of government, no increase in the provincial debt, and the crowning benefit of all this, a balanced budget. One of Hepburn's first statements after winning the premiership revealed his priorities and his basically conservative approach: "The first job is to overhaul the machinery of government. That means two things as I see it. First, eliminate inefficiency – rip out deadwood, political appointees, hangers-on, those who draw big salaries for doing little. Second, cut out unnecessary functions of government – those that have outlived their usefulness or are too paternal."

This was basically a conservative program, in so far as it was an attempt to restore conditions that were associated with prosperity before the depression. That the Hepburn program in 1934 was substantially conservative was noted in an editorial in the *Canadian Forum* shortly after the election: "It is at least evident that the electors did not declare themselves in favour of an alternative and positive policy of reform in their general 'swing to the left'." Consequently, continued the *Forum*, the result of the 1934 Hepburn sweep was "negative."

This analysis was correct. What gave the 1934 campaign its air of excitement and challenge was not commitment to reform (except on the part of men like Arthur Roebuck and David Croll), but Hepburn's radical rhetoric, his evangelical fervour, his promise not of reform but of revival. He was on the side of the little man (where most of the voters were) against the tycoons, and it was in this essentially negative role that Mitch Hepburn considered himself a "reformer." At a meeting in Elgin shortly after the election of 1934, Hepburn himself put this succinctly: "I'm an out-and-out reformer and I'll fight against the protected interests to the end." So a reputation for reform was built up on rhetoric, on fighting the Sun Life, attacking the Quebec power barons who were allegedly over-charging Ontario for electricity and on selling the limousines of Tory cabinet ministers at Varsity stadium (an action that was colourful and flamboyant, certainly, but whose purpose was basically conservative, to help balance the budget). In November, 1934, a few months after the Liberal sweep, there was no incongruity in the *Canadian Forum's* entitling an article, "That Tory Hepburn."

That is not to say that Mitch Hepburn did not combine a liberal humanitarian instinct with his traditional rural conservatism. His untiring work for war veterans and his support of old-age pensions during his years as a federal Member illustrate this. But his humanitarianism was a matter of the heart rather than the head, a feeling for the underdog rather than a positive commitment to ameliorate the social order. The less government interference with the social and economic fabric the better was a principle Hepburn had expressed in the House of Commons long before he came to Queen's Park and started flying around the country with wealthy friends like Sir James Dunn of Algoma Steel, J. P. Bickell, the mining magnate, and Sell 'Em Ben Smith, the American financier. His government's intervention to pay a subsidy to aid Algoma Steel production seems to run counter to Hepburn's principle of minimal governmental interference. In fact, he rationalized it quite easily as merely the Government's attempt to put one of the primary, free-enterprise industries back into profitable production, an aim supported by most conservatives.

Nowhere does the tension between Mitch Hepburn's liberal humanitarian instincts and his social conservative traditions emerge more clearly than in his attitude toward labour. Hepburn's practical experience with labour was limited to his Bannockburn farms, four miles south of St. Thomas. There, at times, he employed upward of thirty men (some of whom he had gone to great trouble to bring out from Europe). Often he went out of his way to display kindness to these men and to their families. He was much closer to his able farm manager, William Tapsell, and his hired help than he was to the corporate tycoons who tried to reduce the price paid for his tobacco. But a workman should know his place, Bannockburn was being run to show a profit, and a man who did not do an honest day's work received short shrift from Mitch Hepburn. He was a fair, honest employer; there was no labour trouble but at Bannockburn, Mitch Hepburn was on the side of management.

That was about the extent of Hepburn's practical experience with labour before he became the Ontario provincial Liberal leader. During his campaign for Queen's Park he came down solidly on the side of the workers when George Henry's Conservative government sent in soldiers and tanks to break up a strike of furniture employees at Stratford in September, 1933. "My sympathy lies with those people who are the victims of circumstances beyond their control," Hepburn stated, "and not with the manufacturers who are increasing prices and cutting wages at the same time." It was significant, however, that when Senator A. C. Hardy, one of Hepburn's closest backers and advisers, remonstrated with him for speaking out on the strike which "is pretty close to Communistic," Hepburn replied that his major concern was the government's use of force and not (by inference) the rights of the workers.

As Premier, Hepburn's first contacts with labour were friendly. When the Conservative mayor of Toronto, William Stewart, announced in July, 1934, that he would not receive the large group of "hunger marchers" converging on the city, the Premier and Attorney General Roebuck (at the time also Minister of Labour) arranged to meet them at Queen's Park. "These marchers," Hepburn announced, "are entitled to every courtesy. If they are down and out, they are to be regarded as unfortunate and it is the purpose of this government to help them on their way back to recovery."

Of more help than kindly words to the "down and out" was the labour legislation introduced by the Hepburn government during its first session in 1935. The Industrial Standards Act, piloted through the House by Arthur Roebuck, was one of the most advanced pieces of labour legislation ever placed on the statute books. The Act provided that where workers and employers representing a preponderant group in any industry agreed upon minimum standards of wages and hours in the presence of a government representative, these rates and hours were to be imposed on the rest of the industry in the province or in a designated area. The purpose of the Act was to equalize wage rates and raise them to a level where a decent standard of living could be maintained for factory employees. It was aimed at cleaning up the sweat shop conditions which had prevailed in the province.

Many, including labour leaders, hailed the Industrial Standards Act as enlightened legislation, and Mitchell Hepburn, as head of the government that introduced it, must be given full credit. At the same time, it is interesting that the man primarily responsible for the Industrial Standards Act, Arthur Roebuck, was not at all comfortable in the government during most of its first session. So unhappy was the Attorney General and Labour Minister that the federal seat of Toronto Trinity was being held open for him should he decide to resign and run for the House of Commons. Some of this tension between certain members of the Government and Roebuck rose because of the repudiation of the Quebec hydro power contracts which Roebuck strongly pressed. Some of it, however, was caused by the Attorney General's advocating legislation that provided for more government control over industry.

Before the Industrial Standards Act passed, Premier Hepburn publicly stated that the best way to help labour was not to regiment industry but to cut governmental expenses. After the Act had been in operation for about a year, one of Hepburn's small "c" conservative advisers, the federal member for Northumberland, William Fraser, wrote from Trenton to protest against the deleterious effects the Act was having on the clothing industry.[1] "Knowing you as I do," Fraser wrote the Premier, "I do not believe that the Act is consistent with your own ideas." Hepburn replied: "I am frank to confess that I never was enamoured with the Industrial Standards Act and have tried to keep the brakes on as much as possible."

From the time he had come to power, Premier Hepburn's attitude toward labour unrest and disturbances reflected the conservative-humanitarian sides of his make-up. In April, 1935, when hunger marchers complained to Queen's Park that their families

[1] Many of Mitch Hepburn's friends, the men who encouraged his leadership and supported his campaign for Queen's Park – men like Arthur Slaght, Percy Parker, Bethune Smith and Senators A. C. Hardy and Frank O'Connor – were, in many respects, small "c" conservatives. So, for that matter, was Hepburn's chief lieutenant in the government, Harry C. Nixon.

were starving, the Premier gave up part of his Easter holiday, toured their homes in Toronto's suburbs, spoke to their wives ("Good morning, Madam, my name is Hepburn. I just came to see how you and your family are getting along. Are you getting enough food?"), and returned to Queen's Park where he ordered that two thousand mattresses be distributed to the poor and that the government's relief allowance be increased.

That same month a disturbance at Crowland, near Welland, where relief recipients refused to continue public works until their allowance was further increased, revealed Hepburn's stern rural conservatism. He ordered extra provincial police into the area, visited the strikers himself to warn them against "outside agitators", and threatened their leaders with jail if there were any further disturbance. If they did not accept the Government's terms, "then it's war to the finish." When the strikers capitulated, the Toronto *Globe* congratulated the Premier for breaking the back of the Crowland strike. This rigid attitude toward labour unrest during his government's first session fitted neatly into Mitch Hepburn's aim to balance the budget. Labour agitation for higher wages and relief allowances must be put down because the first would threaten the primary industries like the mines on which the province's economy depended and the second would be an unwarranted drain on the treasury.

Furthermore, Mitch Hepburn never evinced much concern with, or understanding of, the aspirations of organized labour. These aspirations, such as a contract between employer and employees and the process of collective bargaining itself, were not recognized by the general citizen in the thirties to the extent that they later became acceptable. In those years, the word "union" was often a dirty epithet. Mitch Hepburn was much less concerned with the aims of labour than with its apparent threat to law and order and the province's economic well-being. Consequently, it was not surprising that when the United Auto Workers of America tried to organize the workers at General Motors' Oshawa plant in the spring of 1937, Mitch Hepburn, aware of the violence attributed to this C.I.O. affiliate in neighbouring Michigan, aware, too, of the threat higher wages posed to other industries especially the mines, came out flatly against the union.

Premier Hepburn's open support of management in the Oshawa strike was not a sudden "shift to the right." On the contrary, whatever else may be said of it in retrospect, Hepburn's anti-CIO policy was quite consistent with his rural conservative background and his previous statements on labour-management relations. That policy was merely the most dramatic demonstration that Mitch Hepburn's social and economic views, from the very beginning of his political career, had been basically conservative.

BIBLIOGRAPHICAL NOTE

The main sources of information on Mitchell Hepburn are the Hepburn Papers in the Department of Public Records and Archives of Ontario, the Diary of Senator Norman Lambert at Queen's University, Kingston, and contemporary newspapers. Periodicals like *Saturday Night* and *Canadian Forum* are also useful. The only book on Hepburn is Neil McKenty, *Mitch Hepburn* (Toronto, McClelland & Stewart, 1967).

PART III

Aspects of Ontario's economy

An Introduction to the Economic History of Ontario from Outpost to Empire[1]

H. A. Innis

This article followed closely upon Professor Innis's intensive study of the fur trade and the publication of his two volumes of documents on Canadian economic history. There is a sense in which these books with his history of the Canadian Pacific Railway launched Canadian economic studies. Work on Canadian staple production has since proliferated into histories, both scholarly and popular, of industry, transportation and immigration and into penetration of early records of fur trade and settlement.

Though it appeared more than thirty years ago, the article is as valid and fresh as when it was written. Subsequent studies have elaborated but not disturbed its conclusions. Its last two paragraphs forecast much of the recent history of Ontario in relation to other provinces and to the federal government.

M. Q. I.

In view of the important work on various phases of the subject considered in this paper it may seem presumptuous that one should use the title selected. On the other hand it is the plan of the paper to emphasize the essential unity of the subject and the underlying factors responsible for peculiar types of development, and it is perhaps not too much to say that from this standpoint the title might more accurately be made An introduction to an introduction to the economic history of Ontario. It is scarcely necessary to emphasize the enormous gaps in our knowledge of the economic history of Ontario. We have almost no thorough survey of any of our industries and we have no adequate history of agriculture. Extension of the subject is possible with increasing stress on the part of the archives, museums, and libraries, on economic material. The most serious weakness, however, is the lack of appreciation of the relative value of economic material or the lack of attention on the part of economists to the evolutionary character of economic institutions. Economics and history have suffered immeasurably from this neglect. These considerations are the justification and the danger of this paper.

An understanding of the main features of the geographic background of the province is essential to an appreciation of the main trends of economic development.

[1] **First printed in Ontario Historical Society, *Papers and Records*, XXX (1934), pp. 111-23. Footnotes have been deleted.**

Geological history is a prerequisite to the study of later history. The ice age left its stamp on the history of Ontario and of Canada. Retreating ice sheets contributed to the formation of large bodies of water. Lake Agassiz, (now dwindled to Lake Manitoba), Lake Algonquin (now the upper Lakes), and Lake Iroquois (now Lake Ontario), all with the northern outlets by Hudson Bay and the St. Lawrence river dammed by the ice, poured through southern outlets following respectively the Red River, the Mississippi, and the Hudson. Lake Algonquin flowed into the Mississippi, and then into Lake Iroquois, alternately by Niagara Falls and the Trent valley. The final retreat of the ice sheet opened the outlet of the St. Lawrence following Logan's fault line along the southeastern edge of the Precambrian formation. These shifting outlets have had a profound influence on economic development since trade like water has tended to flow at different periods through the same outlets but finally has tended to settle down to the St. Lawrence. Soil was again largely the result of the ice age. Earth was scraped from the Precambrian area, carried down and deposited in what is now southern Ontario, or it was held in Lake Ojibway by the retreating ice sheet, further north, to be deposited as the clay belt. The geologically recent emergence of the topography has been responsible for the broken character of the waterways especially in the Precambrian area, and in the serious obstructions evident in the rapids of the main outlet, the upper St. Lawrence. The existence of large bodies of water in the Great Lakes tempered the climate and occasioned long autumns and late springs.

Flora reflected the influence of soil and climate. Migration of species following the retreating ice sheet and the geographic background have been responsible for distinct zones, first the Carolinian zone in territory south of a line from Toronto to Windsor, and including such species as the hickories, oaks, chestnut, and walnut; second, the hardwood forest zone extending north to a line roughly from Anticosti to the head of Lake Winnipeg, or the northern limits of white and red pine, and including these conifers in addition to basswood, maple, ash, elm, birch, and beech; and third, the sub-arctic forest extending north of the second zone to the boundaries of the province, which includes the black and white spruce, Banksian pine, poplar, larch, and balsam. Fauna was determined in part by thermal lines and by flora. Fur bearing anmials flourished in the hardwood forest and sub-arctic forest zones.

The culture of the Indians indicated more broadly the effects of the geographic background. The agricultural tribes of the eastern woodlands, the Hurons, north of Lake Ontario, the Tobaccos in western Ontario, and the Neutrals north of Lake Erie, occupied the agricultural regions of southern Ontario; and the migratory tribes of the eastern woodlands, the Algonquins on the Ottawa, the Ojibway north of Lake Superior, and the Crees south of Hudson and James Bays occupied the Precambrian forested areas and depended primarily on hunting.

Recorded history begins with the appearance of Europeans in this setting. The importance of cheap water transportation to Quebec and Montreal accentuated dependence on staple products and led to the development of trade in furs with the hunting Indians. Exploration and trade led to penetration of the northerly forested Precambrian regions by the numerous tributaries of the St. Lawrence by the use of facilities such as canoes provided by these Indians. The territory which has become the province of Ontario begins roughly at the point on the St. Lawrence above which the river was practically inaccessible. It is significant that this area was approached by a tributary which later became its eastern boundary. Champlain went up the Ottawa, crossed the portage to French river and came down to Georgian Bay. The discovery of Lake Ontario was made from the north by Brulé on the Humber and by Champlain on the Trent system. Champlain might have descended the upper St. Lawrence before he ascended it.

Trade expanded to the north and was extended in the first half of the seventeenth century chiefly by the agricultural Indians marginal to the hunting regions, especially the Hurons in the vicinity of Lake Simcoe (Huronia). An alternative approach to southern Ontario was available by the old outlet of Lake Iroquois to the Hudson river. In competition, the Dutch, and later the English (1664), obtained furs from this region through the Iroquois. The struggle waged between the Iroquois and the Hurons was a prelude to the struggle between New York and Montreal, which dominated the economic history of Ontario. The Iroquois, with a strong agricultural economy as a base, trapped and traded along the north shore of Lake Ontario and carried war to the point of destruction among the Hurons, the Neutrals, and the Tobaccos.

To oppose this development, the French were obliged to take a more direct interest in trade to the interior. Radisson and Groseilliers were among the forerunners of traders who endeavoured to re-establish the trade broken by Iroquois incursions, and who built up first the trade carried on by Ottawa middlemen and later by coureurs des bois. Finally a direct attempt to check the Iroquois and the New York route was made by a journey up the difficult St. Lawrence rapids by La Salle and by the establishment of Fort Frontenac in 1673. Boats were built on Lake Ontario in 1677, and in 1679 the *Griffon* was launched on the Niagara River above the Falls and navigated the upper lakes and a post was established at Niagara. A line of defense was slowly built up by the St. Lawrence particularly with the energetic measures of Frontenac.

The Iroquois wars which were revived after 1684 and the massacre of Lachine (1689) and constant smuggling to the English were indications of the difficulties involved. Lahontan, an expert in military affairs, however disputed may be the merits of his work as an explorer, wrote on November 2, 1684, "In time of war I take it (Fort Frontenac) to be indefensible; for the cataracts and currents of the river are such, that fifty Iroquois may there stop five hundred French, without any other arms but stones. Do but consider, Sir, that for twenty leagues together the river is so rapid, that we dare not set the canoe four paces off the shoar; besides Canada, being nothing but a forrest, as I intimated above, tis impossible to travel there without falling every foot into ambuscades, especially upon the banks of this river, which are lined with thick woods, that render 'em inaccessible. None but the savage can skip from rock to rock, and scour thro' the thickets, as if 'twere an open field. If we were capable of such adventures, we might march five or six hundred men by land to guard the canows that carry the provisions; but at the same time 'tis to be considered, that before they arriv'd at the fort, they would consume more provisions than the canows can carry; not to mention that the Iroquois would still out-number em."

Development of forts along the lakes as a means of checking New York trade was accompanied by measures to check encroachment of trade from the north. In revolt at the restraint imposed on traders penetrating to the interior Radisson and Groseilliers deserted to the English and the Hudson's Bay Company, under their direction, established posts at the mouths of rivers flowing into James Bay. Competition from this direction was followed by the establishment of posts north of Lake Superior, designed to prevent Indians going to the Bay and by the capture of English posts. To the north and to the south, Ontario was being hammered by French policy into a fortified unit, guaranteeing control for the lower St. Lawrence.

In the half century following the Treaty of Utrecht (1713) the struggle became more intense and led to the fall of New France. The establishment of a post on Lake Ontario at Oswego by the English and the growth of the rum trade following increased trade on the part of the English colonies to the West Indies created serious problems. A strong post was built at Niagara in 1726 and this post as well as Fort Frontenac were subsidized as King's posts. In 1750 Fort Rouillé was rebuilt to prevent trade by the Toronto portage. The difficulties of transportation on the upper St. Lawrence continued and as late as 1736 the late arrival of the King's vessels made it impossible to forward from Kingston to Niagara goods from France. On the north, return of posts on Hudson Bay to the English under the terms of the Treaty of Utrecht necessitated renewed activity in the construction of posts in the interior. To check English trade at Port Nelson, La Vérendrye and his successors pushed exploration and the fur trade to Lake Winnipeg and the Saskatchewan. In spite of these aggressive advances, or possibly because of them, France proved unequal to the task. The English in the final campaign broke the southern line of fortifications by the capture of Fort Frontenac. Temporarily the New York route prevailed.

After the downfall of New France, English traders from Albany and New York pushed into the newly opened territory. Boats were used to transport goods along the south shore of Lake Ontario to Niagara and in turn to Michilimackinac and the interior. The New York-Great Lakes route became an effective competitor. On the other hand the advantages of the Ottawa route and of Montreal as a depot of skilled labour and technique continued to be of first importance.

With the beginning of hostilities in the American Revolution, traders were forced to abandon the New York route and to move to Montreal. Nevertheless the expansion of boat navigation on the Great Lakes in relation to the Albany route made possible a combination of the advantages of the St. Lawrence and the Ottawa routes. The canoe on the Ottawa and the boats and vessels in the Great Lakes combined to support a marked expansion of trade to the interior. At the close of the American Revolution the upper St. Lawrence had become for the first time a vital link in the development of the interior in relation to the lower St. Lawrence. The system of lake navigation built up from Albany and the development of boats on the upper St. Lawrence under the French were combined and improved in relation to Montreal. The agricultural beginnings at posts developed under the French régime on the Great Lakes, for example at Detroit, served as a base for the expansion of navigation and settlement under the English and especially after 1783.

With the improvement of navigation on the upper St. Lawrence fertile land along the north shore of Lake Ontario and in the Niagara district was opened to settlement. Moreover population in the form of disbanded regiments, the United Empire Loyalists, and settlers moving westward from the English colonies was available to settle new territory. That a large proportion of this population was in opposition to the colonies which had broken from British control was a favourable consideration from the standpoint of military consolidation of the outlying territory. In this sense Haldimand deserved the title of his biographer "the founder of Ontario." The new settlements, especially at Niagara, provided a stronger agricultural base for the Northwest Company. With the decline of the fur trade in the United States after Jay's Treaty (1794), traders moved to the Northwest and larger supplies of provisions and more adequate transport facilities were necessary to support the extended trade. By the end of the century goods were taken up the St. Lawrence, across the Niagara portage, and even by Yonge Street.

The emergence of a new community and the necessity for its protection were evident in the Constitutional Act in 1791 and in the energetic activities of Simcoe in the planning of roads and in reinforcing the new province against possible aggression from the United States. The capital was moved, roads were planned, and the general military strength of the colony placed in a position which successfully withstood the aggressions of the United States in the war of 1812.

As a result of increasing population, larger quantities of goods were taken up the St. Lawrence and the continued incentive to land speculators hastened immigration. Population advanced beyond the importing stage and in 1790 Patrick Campbell noted that 6000 bushels of wheat were bought at Kingston. In 1800 Elias Smith, the founder of Port Hope was engaged in selling flour in Toronto and in Montreal. By the turn of the century the problem of transportation on the St. Lawrence became serious and larger boats were introduced.[2]

The beginnings of settlement and of exports of wheat and flour coincided with the development of the timber trade. Square timber was floated first down the St. Lawrence, and about 1806 Philemon Wright succeeded in taking rafts down the Ottawa to Quebec. The American Revolution, the French Revolution, and the Napoleonic wars provided a powerful stimulus to the energetic development of settlement and of the timber trade. The importance of naval supplies and the decline of European and United States sources of supply led to emphasis on the British North

[2] A boat, probably a Durham boat (invented about 1750) was introduced between Chippawa and Fort Erie in 1799, which with six men carried 100 barrels and displaced the batteaux which with five Canadians carried only twenty to twenty-four. *Select documents in Canadian economic history 1783-1885* (Toronto, 1933) pp. 138-9. Writing at Queenstown on June 15th, 1801 to John Askin, Robert Nichol stated "Mr. Clark . . . . is building a Kentucky boat at the former place (Kingston) in which he intends going to Quebec with 350 barrels of our flour. It will (I imagine) be the first boat of the kind that ever descended the Saint Lawrence, and interests all the mercantile people of this part of the country very much . . . . The quantity of flour going down this year from the district of Niagara is immense, say upon a moderate calculation five thousand barrels, which for the first year is really very great." Mr. Clarke made the trip from Kingston to Montreal in this boat in ten days with 340 barrels of flour. *The John Askin Papers* II. 343, 353, also *Life and Letters of the late Hon. Richard Cartwright* (Toronto, 1876).

American colonies. Following the substantial preference of 1808, the timber trade increased with marked rapidity and with the more aggressive attitude toward settlement after the war of 1812 immigration provided a source of labour for the industry. Settlement of Upper Canada, preference on colonial timber, and the interrelations, by which emigration was supported by the timber ships and in turn agriculture and new supplies of labour supported the timber trade, were closely linked to imperial policy. Decline of the fur trade to Montreal after the amalgamation of the Northwest Company and the Hudson's Bay Company in 1821 and concentration on the York boat and the Hudson Bay route to the northwest necessitated increased emphasis on other commodities. New settlements such as the Talbot settlement, the Selkirk settlement, and the settlement which followed migration of Selkirk settlers from the Northwest as a result of the aggressiveness of the Northwest Company, and larger numbers of immigrants after the war of 1812 gave Upper Canada an additional labour supply for the expansion of trade in timber, wheat, and flour.

Imperial policy and its influence reached its peak and started on its decline in the period 1820 to 1850. The Rideau Canal, with its supporting canals on the Ottawa, was built by the imperial government and completed for navigation in 1832-3. After a slight reduction in 1821 the preference on colonial timber continued at a high level to 1843. The corn laws followed a similar trend. The decline was a result of far reaching changes which were traceable ultimately to the sweep of the later stages of the industrial revolution. Labour displaced by machinery was available for emigration and weavers moved to the district of Bathurst. Emigrants, assisted and unassisted, moved in ever increasing numbers to the new world. Under the auspices of the Canada Company, and of the British North American Land Company, capital was mobilized respectively for settlement on land in the Huron tract in western Ontario and in the Eastern townships.

The Welland Canal (1829) gave access to the upper lakes and provided for movement of population to western Ontario and for the growth of the Talbot settlement and of Goderich on Lake Huron. Roads were extended from Hamilton, Dundas, and Ancaster westward and from Toronto northward to meet the demands of new areas. In 1815 the first steamship the *Frontenac* was launched on Lake Ontario and in 1818 the *Walk-in-the-Water* was launched on Lake Erie. Access to the seaboard was provided on the upper lakes by the Erie canal, completed in 1826. On the Ottawa the first steamboat, the *Union* was built in 1822.

The timber trade emphasized the basic importance of large rivers and strengthened the position of the St. Lawrence and the Ottawa. Timber could not be handled by New York and as a consequence the St. Lawrence became essentially a monopoly route. Laurentia or the St. Lawrence drainage basin, which coincided roughly with the white and red pine areas, was the basis of the timber trade and in turn was linked to settlement and to trade by the lower St. Lawrence to Great Britain. Decline in importance of the timber trade followed exhaustion of the larger trees in the more accessible areas, the diminishing demand which accompanied increased competition in Great Britain from European sources, and the relatively minor importance of timber with the achievement of industrial maturity. Settlers had increased beyond the point necessary to meet the demands of the timber trade and of the westward movement for provisions and supplies, if not for labour, and the population of Great Britain demanded flour and wheat rather than timber.

Increase in population, the introduction of steam navigation on the upper lakes, increase in the production and export of wheat, the powerful influence of the commercial interests of Montreal, and the serious effects of the depression of 1835, which contributed to the distress culminating in the Rebellion of 1837, created problems which were solved by the recommendations of Durham's report, the consummation of Union of the two Canadas in 1840, and the building of the St. Lawrence canals.

By the end of the first decade after Union, a nine foot channel had been completed and steamships were able to go down to Montreal and return. These steamships were linked with the newly opened route for steamships below Montreal.

The rapid increase in the importance of agricultural produce and especially wheat precipitated the problem of the upper St. Lawrence. Steamships, canals, and wheat involved financial support of the state. Wheat, unlike lumber, was faced with competition from New York and in turn involved railways as supplemental to water transportation. Portage railways across the Niagara peninsula, from Toronto to Collingwood, and even the Grand Trunk, were developed in co-ordination with water transportation. Steam navigation and railways hastened immigration with the result that, by the end of the decade 1850 to 1860, the available, more desirable land was exhausted. Population began to pour through to the western states.

The decline of wooden sailing vessels and of the market for timber from Great Britain, the rise of Montreal as a rival to Quebec, and the coming of the iron steamship and the railway coincided with the depletion of forests in the eastern states, the growth of cities, and the migration of sawmills to the Ottawa and the district north of Lake Ontario. Water power and steam power made their impact on the lumbering industry. The Reciprocity Treaty, the Civil War in the United States, and the shift from square timber to deals for the British market hastened the growth of lumber mills. The trend was accentuated in turn by the decline in the number of small trees.

The rise in importance of wheat and agricultural products, and the emergence of steamships, canals, and railways coincided with and implied responsible government and the establishment of new devices for finance. The upper St. Lawrence waterways, which had needed government support by means of subsidized posts in the fur trade of the French régime and by an aggressive imperial policy in the timber trade in the English régime, continued to demand with wheat continued support. Capital investment on a large scale necessitated more direct responsibility and supervision and more adequate methods of finance. The Act of Union and Responsible Government provided the solution; and these in turn were involved in the problem of government guarantees and the tariff as means of acquiring revenue. The problems of the clergy reserves, of seigniorial tenure, of immigration and colonization roads, of railways and canals, and of money, credit, finance, and trade, were attacked directly and vigorously. The imperial nursery continued and became more efficient with the decline of commercialism and the rise of capitalism. Eventually the difficulties of finance which followed dependence on raw materials, particularly on wheat, and the accumulation and rigidity of fixed charges which accompanied government support to railways and canals; provided a powerful driving force toward Confederation and the creation of a new institution to carry the burden of debt of the United Province.

Exhaustion of the more fertile land areas, problems of continued cropping of wheat, improved transportation and navigation, and abrogation of the Reciprocity Treaty led to the development of the dairy industry in the sixties, and of the livestock trade in the late seventies. Specialized agriculture was facilitated and the varied geographic background supported the production and export of barley, fruit, dairy products, and live stock. Minerals were discovered and exploited in the agricultural area, for example petroleum and its successor, salt. The railways hastened urbanization and in turn directly and indirectly the growth of industries and the demands for iron and raw materials. Trade and finance flourished in the new metropolitan areas of Hamilton and Toronto. Ontario began to develop its own nucleus of metropolitan growth independent of that of the province of Quebec. The success of the struggle of Senator McMaster and The Canadian Bank of Commerce with E. H. King and the Bank of Montreal in the first banking legislation of the new Dominion was an indication of maturity. The aggressiveness of the new area was in direct descent from the aggressiveness with which imperial policy had supported the development of Upper Canada.

The problem of Confederation was that of linking together relatively isolated areas and of providing a new base for the support of debt lifted from the shoulders of the provinces. The Intercolonial to the Maritimes (1876) and the railway from St. Paul to Winnipeg (1878) corresponded roughly with the depression and the National Policy. The tariff was extended to provide revenue to support new capital investment and to guarantee control over new areas. Increase of population, the disappearance of free land, decline in wheat production, and fluctuations in the lumber industry released settlers for migration to new lands made available in the West. The economy of agricultural Ontario based largely on wheat was available to support expansion to the prairie provinces of western Canada. (Completion of the Canadian Pacific Railway in 1885 repaired the breach in control over the Northwest which followed the amalgamation in 1821 and enabled an area which had become diversified from a wheat base in relation to the effects of improved transportation to Great Britain to become in turn a support for the expansion of wheat production in the West). In some sense the prairie provinces paralleled in their development that of Ontario; and the difficult stretch of the railroad from Fort William to Winnipeg had its counterpart in the rapids of the upper St. Lawrence. Continued competition from the New York route and the difficulties of Montreal and the St. Lawrence necessitated further efforts in the improvement of navigation below Montreal and in the deepening of the upper St. Lawrence canals to fourteen feet.

The improvement of the Montreal route by the end of the century provided the base for rapid expansion in the production and export of wheat in eastern Canada. The turn of the century brought a violent development with the exploitation of placer gold in the Yukon (1896) and the opening of the Kootenay region following construction of the Crowsnest Pass railway. As a result of these developments and of free land, population poured into western Canada from the United States, Great Britain, Europe, and the older provinces. Immigrants from the old settlements of Ontario were replaced by immigrants from Great Britain. The demands of western

Canada had immediate effects on the industries of eastern Canada. The agricultural implement industry and the iron and steel industry illustrated the effects of western demands. The financial nucleus of Toronto, supported, through The Canadian Bank of Commerce and other institutions, and such men as Mackenzie and Mann, the construction of a rival road to that of Montreal, in the Canadian Pacific Railway. The ambitions of the Dominion and of the Grand Trunk were realized in the National Transcontinental. Increased urbanization was the result and in turn eastern agriculture shifted from an export to a domestic industry. Exports of dairy products and of livestock declined steadily in the first decade of the century. Production of butter and cheese for export was displaced by the production of milk for domestic consumption. Winter dairying expanded rapidly. The apple industry declined from the standpoint of exports but increased from the standpoint of consumption in Ontario and western Canada. Lumbering was stimulated by the demands of the construction industries. The embargo on exports of logs in 1898 hastened the growth of mills along the north shore of Georgian Bay. The effects of the increase in wheat production were accentuated by other developments. The railroad to western Canada necessitated penetration of the vast Precambrian area and led to the discovery and development of the copper nickel mines at Sudbury. It provided a base at North Bay for the construction of a railway supported by Toronto and government auspices to open the clay belt to settlement. The Temiskaming and Northern Ontario Railway (now the Ontario Northland Railway) led to the discovery of silver at Cobalt, and in turn of gold at Porcupine and Kirkland Lake, and of copper at Noranda (Quebec). Settlement in the clay belt and the spruce forests of the area north of the hardwood zone supported pulp and paper mills at Iroquois Falls, Kapuskasing, and Smooth Rock Falls. The decline in importance of pine in the region north of Georgian Bay and the embargo on the export of pulpwood from Crown lands hastened the growth of mills at Sturgeon Falls, Espanola, Sault Ste. Marie and in the vicinity of Fort William. With the mining industry and the pulp and paper industry, towns came into existence, agriculture was encouraged and the hydro-electric power development advanced with amazing rapidity. Extension of the Temiskaming and Northern Ontario Railway to Moosonee was followed by the development at Abitibi Canyon and the opening of the new north of northern Ontario facing on Hudson Bay.

The advance of industrialism which followed the opening of the West and of New Ontario was accomplished by the activity of the state and of private enterprise. The rapidity of development, the long tradition of state support dating to the French régime and linked to the problem of the upper St. Lawrence waterways, and the relatively late development of metropolitan areas as contrasted with Montreal were factors responsible for the part of the government in the formation of the Ontario Hydro Electric Power Commission and of the Temiskaming and Northern Ontario Railway. The peculiarities of the economy of Ontario are deep rooted and vitally related to her position as an outpost of the lower St. Lawrence.

The war period stimulated industrial growth and the post war period was dominated by the enormous speculative boom of the United States and by the later stages of the industrial revolution based on gasoline. Road construction, automobile factories, the tourist trade, with hotel construction and the decline of prohibition, were a phase of this revolution. Again the state assumed a role of direct importance in financing roads.

From this tentative outline we may venture to suggest the general underlying factors of the economic history of Ontario. The difficulties of the upper St. Lawrence and the importance of fur as a staple of trade with the hunting Indians of the northern forested Precambrian area were responsible for the development of the Ottawa river as an eastern boundary, and as a canoe route to the interior. Competition from New York compelled the state to support ventures to the interior by the upper Great Lakes in the form of subsidized forts. The effectiveness of this competition was evident in its contribution to the breakdown of French control and in the consolidation against New York in the combined effects of the activities of the British government, the importance of British manufactures to the fur trade, and the combination of canoe and lake navigation by the Ottawa and the St. Lawrence. Moreover it eventually forced the fur trade to the Northwest and contributed to the final adjustment of the boundary from Grand Portage along the main route of the trade. Competition from the Hudson's Bay Company through Hudson Bay and its tributary rivers finally broke the control of the St. Lawrence drainage basin to the interior. By 1821 the supremacy of Hudson Bay had indicated roughly the northwestern boundary of Ontario.

The determined efforts of the British government to maintain control over the upper lakes was followed by the development of lumbering and agriculture. The St. Lawrence and the Ottawa became ideal routes for the export of square timber. The problem of control was temporarily solved. Timber and an effective imperial policy involved settlement and in turn the shift to wheat. The difficulties of the upper St. Lawrence and of the Niagara River again became acute since wheat and an agricultural population demanded cheap transportation for imports. Competition from New York by Lake Ontario and by the Erie Canal again accentuated the demands for state support which implied the Act of Union, the building of canals, and the addition of railways. From this background emerged the problem of fixed charges for transportation improvements, the tariff for revenue and for protection, the demand for larger capital imports, Confederation, the Intercolonial and the Canadian Pacific Railways. The problems of the state in overcoming the difficulties of the St. Lawrence were met by the activities of the state in building and supporting a railway to western Canada.

Confederation provided for release and continued expansion in the upper St. Lawrence area. The Toronto-Hamilton metropolitan area assumed greater control with release from the out-grown clothes of Union. Ontario was determined to secure a substantial share of the trade from newly opened areas, and railways tapped the new transcontinental. She gained appreciably from the similarity of her economy to that of the newly opened West. Improved navigation in the form of deepened canals on the St. Lawrence system and shorter railway lines to seaboard hastened the expansion of the West and in turn of Ontario. Deepening of the St. Lawrence ship channel to 30 feet by 1906 brought to successful completion the long and determined struggle with New York. These improvements, the rise in prices which began with the turn of the century, the migration of mature technique from depleted resources in the

United States to virgin resources in terms of wheat, minerals, pulp and paper, and the growing interdependence of these industries were factors supporting the phenomenal boom from 1900 to 1914. Railways brought to the expanding metropolitan area of Toronto and Hamilton the results of expansion in minerals, pulp and paper, and hydro-electric power in Northern Ontario.

As a province, Ontario has gained enormously by the expansion of the Dominion and has been quick to press for advantage, and to undertake as government enterprises hydro-electric power and railways. The Temiskaming and Northern Ontario Railway, the Algoma Central and other lines tapped directly the lines to Montreal and the East. The disadvantages which arose with the dominance of water transportation have been converted into advantages. Rapids and falls have become sources of hydro-electric power. Competition of the New York route has been converted to an advantage by the lower rates for Ontario compelled by competition and water routes. The new staples pulp, paper, and minerals have been linked to railways and the continental development of the United States. The tapping of fresh resources has brought problems of exhaustion and of conservation. Integration has already brought its problems as shown in the establishment of the Ontario Research Foundation. We can already see the effects of competition in the pulp and paper industry. The uneven growth based on sudden improvements in transportation and in exploitation of natural resources will tend to be displaced by stability and increasing reliance on diversification. Ontario combined the development of furs, minerals, pulp and paper and lumbering, hydro-electric power and agriculture in northern Ontario with the development of wheat in the West. In turn industrialism and agriculture in the south gained from the expansion and from the possibilities of integration. The diversity of her geographic background has provided for specialized production, cheap power and low costs of transportation and the results have been evident in an efficient balanced and relatively elastic economy.

The emergence of Ontario to maturity has brought problems for the province as well as for the Dominion. The elasticity of the economy of Ontario has been based on a wealth of developed natural resources and has been obtained in part through inelastic developments which bear with undue weight on less favoured areas of the Dominion. The strength of Ontario may emphasize the weakness of the federation. An empire has its obligations as well as its opportunities.

BIBLIOGRAPHICAL NOTE

Innis, H. A., "Transportation as a Factor in Canadian Economic History," *Essays in Canadian Economic History* (Toronto, 1956), pp. 62-77.

———, *The Fur Trade in Canada* (rev. ed., Toronto, 1956).

———, ed., *Select Documents in Canadian Economic History, 1497-1783* (Toronto, 1929).

———, *Settlement and the Mining Frontier* (Toronto, 1936).

———, and Lower, A. R. M., eds., *Select Documents in Canadian Economic History, 1783-1885* (Toronto, 1933).

Jenness, D., *The Indians of Canada* (6th ed., Ottawa, 1963).

Foundations of the Canadian Oil Industry, 1850-1866

Edward Phelps

The oil industry of Canada had its humble origins in the heart of southwestern Ontario over a century ago. Research into the history of this industry has hitherto been left largely in the hands of local historians and company publicists, with plenty of factual material and but few scholarly studies being published as a result. In the nineteenth century, oil ceased to be a natural curiosity and became the basis of a well-organized and technically sophisticated industry. The extraction, processing, and marketing of oil therefore offers a rich and hitherto untilled field for the study of technological and business history.

The first two decades of the oil industry were marked by those vicissitudes which seem to be endemic to the early stages of the industrial development of any natural resource. Prior to 1850 petroleum was a scarce commodity for which there was little practical use save for medicinal potions. Between 1851 and 1858 its value as a lubricant and illuminant was definitely established. After 1858 the success of the oil pioneers led to the rapid exploitation of the oil-fields, in an orgy of speculation and waste. This turbulent period of adolescence was over by 1866, when the industry began to acquire a measure of stability under the leadership of a few far-sighted operators who elected to stay with the business and make it their life work.

Petroleum springs had been known to the Indians and the early settlers in various parts of North America. These springs generally took the form of seepages where the crude oil worked its way to the surface for centuries and impregnated the earth to form a sort of gumbo, which could be boiled down to extract asphalt and a very impure form of lighting oil. Thus David Zeisberger, the Moravian missionary at Fairfield, noted a spring of oil near the mission in April 1792, possibly the same location reported in the journal of Governor Simcoe's overland trip from Niagara to Detroit in 1793. Here the Indians collected oil from the surface of a small creek by soaking a blanket and then wringing out the oil. They recommended the bad-smelling, evil-tasting compound for various ailments of man and beast alike.

The earliest commercial uses for petroleum were for lighting and lubrication, in that order of importance. The discovery of oil, and, much more important, the ever-widening knowledge of its uses, accompanied and assisted the rapid industrialization of Ontario during the railway era of the nineteenth century. The principal modern uses of crude oil, as a basis for the manufacture of synthetic organic compounds, and a source of power (gasoline) and heat (fuel oil), were not discovered for some three decades, and, indeed, were only made possible by later technological developments. Until the introduction of hydro-electric power and light, kerosene distilled from crude oil provided the best universally available source of artificial lighting, although gas light, where available, was brighter. The major technical problems, however, were to produce a kerosene which would give an adequate, smokeless odourless flame without the danger of explosion, and then to develop safe lamps in which to burn it.

Before 1850, illuminating oil was rapidly becoming a necessity of life, with the increasing need to stretch out the normal hours of daylight to accommodate the multifarious activities of man. During the 1850's kerosene was distilled from coal and it appeared that coal would continue to be the main source of illumination unless petroleum, still relatively scarce despite many natural occurrences, could be found in sufficient quantity to replace it as a much less expensive, more appropriate, source of supply.

The search for a commercial supply of petroleum proceeded simultaneously in the United States and Canada after 1850, plagued by all manner of technical and financial difficulties. Both Canadians and Americans claim the credit for having drilled North America's first producing oil well but evidence unearthed by Canadian researchers, led by Col. Robert B. Harkness, indicates the existence of such a well at Oil Springs by 1858, and probably in 1857.[1] The first American well was brought into production on 28 August 1859 at Titusville, Pennsylvania, by Edwin L. Drake. The American claim therefore achieves priority only by ignoring the work of historians of the Canadian oil industry.

The south part of Enniskillen township, in the heart of Lambton county, provided the scene for Canada's, and Ontario's, first oil developments. Here the tell-tale gum beds covered half an acre, in the midst of a heavily-wooded swamp. The township surveyors missed finding the gumbeds in 1832 because of heavy rainfall in the area at the time. A few years later the first settlers came upon them, though to what extent they utilized the gumbo is not known. It is safe to say that their technology had probably not advanced beyond that of the Indians.

Canada's pioneering Geological Survey, ever on the watch for minerals of economic value to the country, gave the first impetus to the development of Enniskillen township oil. From the report for 1849-50 it appears that Earl Cathcart, Governor General during the years 1845-47, had sent the Survey its first sample of Enniskillen gumbo. Later, Hon. J. Woods, the M.L.A. for Kent (then including Lambton county) sent in a sample of over a hundred pounds. The gum beds at that time were two feet thick, the accumulation of centuries. The Provincial Geologist, William E. Logan (later Sir William) in his *Report of Progress for the Year 1849-50* noted that the gumbo was useful "for the construction of pavements, for

[1] R. B. Harkness, "Ontario's Part in the Petroleum Industry," *Canadian Oil and Gas Industries* (February and March, 1951). A contemporary American writer, John F. Tyrell, in his book *The Oil Districts of Canada* (New York, 1865) stated that in 1857 Williams found the first oil well in Canada when digging for water.

paving the bottom of ships, and for the manufacture of illuminating gases." Alexander Murray, the Assistant Provincial Geologist, directed detailed exploration of the gum beds in the seasons of 1850 and 1851. Murray owned a farm near Woodstock which he worked when not employed by the government. It is probable that he introduced his neighbour Henry Tripp, and the latter's brother Charles Nelson Tripp, of Bath, to the unusual phenomenon in Enniskillen.

The Tripp brothers were the first to grasp the economic possibilities of petroleum and to take steps to exploit it. In 1852 Charles Nelson Tripp organized the International Mining and Manufacturing Company (chartered in 1854). He purchased several hundred acres of land, including what proved to be the best oil-bearing territory at Oil Springs, and some property at the site of what later became Petrolia. In 1853 Tripp obtained a favourable report on samples of his bitumen from a New York chemist, Thomas Antisell, which he advertised widely.

Tripp's company set up primitive equipment for distilling the gumbo which they dug from the ground like peat. They may have dug wells to get to a source of freely flowing petroleum. From the gumbo they produced asphalt, which was sold to the shipping trade along the St. Clair River for water-proofing ship bottoms, and as some kind of lighting fluid. The high point of their enterprise was reached in 1855 when they were awarded an honourable mention for the sample of asphalt which they sent to the Universal Exhibition in Paris.

The Tripp enterprise, despite its auspicious beginning, was destined to failure, for the country was too little developed to make possible such a relatively sophisticated form of business enterprise. There was no railway within thirty or forty miles, and the only transportation was a shallow, meandering creek during temperate weather, and frozen trails in winter. It was therefore difficult, if not impossible, to import adequate equipment (which, in any case, had not really been developed) or to haul out the products, be they raw or finished. Speculators, sensing the significance of Tripp's explorations, forced up the price of oil-bearing lands during the early years, so that he was penalized by his own success when he came to buy more land! Refining techniques of the day could not turn out a safe enough lighting oil to make it universally attractive. These factors, as well as a falling-out among the partners, kept the company from showing the promise necessary to attract the volume of investment which could have overcome the difficulties.

By the summer of 1855 Tripp's creditors were pursuing their cause in the civil courts. They included Alexander Murray, who had first told the Tripps about the oil, and John B. Van Voorhies, one of the original partners, who presented the enormous claim of £1,500.[2] After 1856 Tripp had to part with his most promising asset, his real estate, to satisfy his creditors. Various individuals and groups took over parts of the oil territory. The Bank of Upper Canada forced the sale of 800 acres in 1857, and the last remnant went in 1858. For a time Charles N. Tripp worked for James Miller Williams, his successor, then moved to New Orleans where he died in 1866.

By 1857 James Miller Williams, of Hamilton, emerged as the leading figure in

[2] This information was provided by Mr. Leslie K. Smith of Sarnia, from his research among early land records of the oil field.

the Canadian oil industry. Williams had been a successful carriage and railway car builder, until in 1856 he sold this line of business in order to devote his energies to Enniskillen oil. He bought up most of the Tripp properties and brought to the enterprise a wealth of business experience and financial backing which it had previously lacked. His task was, however, much easier than Tripp's in one important respect: by this time the Great Western Railway had extended its Sarnia branch westward from London as far as Wyoming, only thirteen miles north of the oil field.

In 1857 Williams began to dig for oil, and in that year or the next brought in the first producing well in the country. Many more wells followed, numbering nearly 100 by the end of 1860. During 1859 (perhaps as early as 1857) a small distillate works had been built at the site to remove by heating the lightest and most dangerous fractions of crude oil, which were simply allowed to go to waste.[3] The treated oil was shipped to Hamilton by rail, where Williams had built a refinery at the foot of Wentworth Street. Oil from the Kelly wells, at the present site of Petrolia, was at first shipped to Boston, but a refinery was built at this site in 1861. By 1859 Williams was ready to offer his product to the public. A tempting advertisement in the *London Free Press* for September 15, 1859, described it in glowing terms:

CANADA EARTH OIL. SOMETHING NEW.
SUPPORT HOME MANUFACTURE.

A great deal has been said about the recently-discovered Earth Oils of Lambton, otherwise known as the Enniskillen Oil. In its pure state it is unfit for use. But, by the action of Chemistry, is rendered beautifully pure, transparent, and free from offensive odour.

Professor Crofts, of Toronto, after much labour, has succeeded in deodorizing the Oil, and rendering it useful as an article of commerce.

L. C. Leonard, Richmond Street, opposite the Post Office, Has been appointed by Messrs. Williams and Hawks the Sole Agent for London & the West, for the sale of this new Oil. He is prepared to treat with parties for a supply either wholesale or retail.

This Oil is superior to the Coal Oil in quality and durability; is free from unpleasant smell; and burns with a pure, bright flame. It burns longer, and is at least 40 per cent more economical than any Coal Oil now in use. Price One Dollar per gallon. Samples for trial can be obtained gratis of the Subscriber. Lamps for Burning the Enniskillen and Coal Oil always on hand, at wholesale and retail.

Although Williams was the most successful of the early Canadian refiners, neither he nor any of his contemporaries were able to cope with the basic problem affecting Canadian illuminating oil – the removal of the sulphur content, which gave off an unpleasant smell and left a crust on the lamp. For this reason Canadian refined oil was for a long time considered inferior to its American counterpart. The final solution was not achieved until 1887 when Herman Frasch, a noted chemist, patented a process for removing the sulphur completely. In the early days, refining consisted of rectifying (separating the illuminating oil from its lighter and heavier fractions)

[3] T. Sterry Hunt in his "Notes on the History of Petroleum," *The Canadian Naturalist*, VI (1861), pp. 241-55, states that Williams and his associates began to refine tarry bitumens from the gum beds in 1857 and implies that processing was done at the site. The *London Free Press*, Jan. 27, 1859, reports that distillate works were then in course of erection.

by repeated distillations, followed by deodorizing by an acid treatment, then washing in alkali compounds to remove the acid.

Williams was recognized by his contemporaries as the pioneer oil refiner and largest enterpriser. By 1864 he and his American partners had invested $50,000 in the business. As his product gained commercial acceptance, Williams offered oil for sale in ever increasing quantities, and gradually lowered the price. Refined oil fell from $1.00 a gallon in 1859 to 70 cents in 1860, and for the next five years fluctuated between 28 and 60 cents. The low prices prevailed during summer and fall, when the producing season was at its best, and the high prices through winter and spring.

As news of Williams' success with crude oil spread, the inevitable rush to the oil field took place, until a settlement developed, first named Victoria, soon called Oil Springs. It was Ontario's best example of a boom town, disorganized, fiercely competitive, unhealthy, and noisy. Hundreds of adventurous young men invaded the district, until by 1862 a community of 2,000 persons had sprung from the bush. These newcomers, of course, found the Williams group in possession of most of the known oil-bearing territory, which they were prepared to lease, but not sell, in half-acre plots, enough for two or three wells.[4] These early operators were mainly shoestring speculators, typical denizens of any boom town. Most of them had nothing to lose, lived on luck, and swiftly departed in search of greener fields when the boom slackened off. A few of the Oil Springs pioneers, however, stayed and rose to prominence through their natural ability and determination. One of these was John Henry Fairbank, who came to Oil Springs in 1861 with enough borrowed capital to dig only one well, and enough credit to pay for tools and living expenses. Successful in his first great gamble, Fairbank stayed with the oil field, pursuing a business career which lasted for half a century. He died in 1914, the wealthiest man in the Canadian oil industry. As one of its natural leaders, he participated in every public aspect of the business from 1862 onward.

Throughout the period from 1860 to 1866 many operators like Fairbank drilled successful wells not only at Oil Springs but all over western Ontario. A few spectacular but short-lived finds were made outside the Enniskillen field, and drilling still continues in 1966 in hopes of finding untapped sources. In the course of the drilling for oil, however, another important industry was launched when salt was discovered at Goderich, Sarnia, and Warwick. Several hundred surface wells were dug at Oil Springs into the so-called "upper horizon" or soil overlying the bedrock, by 1862. Many of the larger operations were carried out by wealthy American speculators from New York, Hartford, Boston, and other eastern cities. Their interest may be ascribed to the fact that the newly-opened Pennsylvania fields were not nearly productive enough to satisfy American demand and leave a surplus for foreign markets, while the Canadian field offered just such an advantage as well as the chance of new and greater discoveries.

[4] The *Sarnia Observer*, Feb. 21, 1862, describes the standard terms of these leases, whereby the lessee was bound to pay a yearly rent, work the well to its utmost capacity, and deliver to the lessor one-third of the oil pumped, in barrels.

While most of the wells at Oil Springs had been dug in the "upper horizon," some of the well-financed American operators, following Williams' lead, began to penetrate the limestone, or "middle horizon" with drills. This type of exploration led to the discovery of the flowing wells, which produced veritable rivers of oil and changed the whole picture of the industry. Ironically, the first such well was brought in by an obscure, near-penniless prospector named Hugh Nixon Shaw, who went hopelessly into debt and earned the derision of some of his contemporaries who thought he was foolish to gamble so much on an empty hole. When, on January 16, 1862, he struck an oil gusher at a depth of 208 feet, of which 158 feet was drilled in rock, the scorn of the community turned into emulation. Shaw's famous well spewed oil twenty feet into the air until it was finally capped and the flow brought under control. For over a year it flowed oil, as did many other deep wells immediately drilled in imitation. Throughout the year 1862 Oil Springs went mad with a frenzy of speculation, wasteful, heedless, and ruinous, for the price of oil tumbled to ten cents a barrel at the well-head. The purchaser, however, had to supply his own barrels, which were worth $1 each. Countless thousands of barrels of oil were lost through lack of control of the flowing wells, and the utter inability of the operators to store it properly.

The waste of oil was graphically illustrated by the recollections of one of the pioneer oilmen, who as a result was actually induced to come and make his fortune. In his evidence before the Royal Commission on the Mineral Resources of Ontario, John D. Noble explained:

> The way my attention was first called to the business was this: I was a vessel owner residing at Kingston. A schooner came back covered with oil and I asked the captain what was the cause of it. He said they had struck oil at Sydenham and could not stop the wells flowing, and that it was coming down the river a foot thick on top of the water. I considered there might be something in it, so I came immediately to look into the matter. What the captain referred to was caused by the flowing wells of Oil Springs. When I got here they had just struck oil at Petrolia; I fancied the place and bought some land . . .

Thus began one of the more successful careers in the oil business. Noble, like Fairbank before him, was attracted by the prospects of oil and stayed for the rest of his life.

Throughout this period of dynamic though irregular growth, Williams refined oil in Hamilton, far removed from the scene of the frenzy. With his own wells already established, there was no need for him to drill more, since the country could not possibly absorb the vast surplus of oil that built up in 1862. In any event, he was assured of a portion of the new supply through leasing his property in Oil Springs in return for one-third of the oil, barrelled and delivered for shipment. With the benefit of his adequate finances and the help of Dr. Abraham Gesner, a noted authority on oil refining, he improved his output and won two gold medals at the International Exhibition in London, England, in 1862, one for being the first to produce crude oil, the other for his samples of refined oil.

In the meantime, a business structure grew up on the wealth produced by the exploitation of this natural resource. Refineries sprang into being along the important transportation routes, farther and farther away from the source of supply, so they could in turn exploit their own commercial hinterland. The ease of converting crude to refined oil, and its attractive selling qualities, made men almost as eager to build refineries as they were to drill wells. By 1863 there were 10 refineries in the field at Oil Springs, and others nearby at Petrolia, Bothwell, and Wyoming. They had spread eastward from Sarnia along the railways to important distribution and junction centres – London, Ingersoll, Woodstock, Brantford, Hamilton, Port Credit, and Toronto. Indeed, the cut-throat competition among refiners had its inevitable results, just as among producers; by the end of 1863, twenty-five percent of the available refining capacity could have supplied the entire Canadian demand for oil. Despite the warning of a financial critic that "a very considerable sum of money has, therefore, been unprofitably invested," the situation did not dissuade more producers from erecting refineries.[5] Among them was J. H. Fairbank, who, having secured a steady flow of crude oil, was anxious to try his hand at refining in order to take the maximum advantage of the oil market. Three years' experience with a primitive and unsafe little plant convinced him, however, that his forte lay in the production of crude oil.

The growing surplus of oil, accumulated throughout the year 1862, led the producers to co-operate in two important, and perhaps obvious respects. They tried, not too successfully, to limit output and raise prices, and to export crude oil to Great Britain for manufacture there. On 12 May, 1862, the Enniskillen producers banded themselves together as the Canada Oil Association, the first price-fixing ring in the industry of which record has survived. It followed only five months after a similar organization had been tried in the American oil field and had immediately failed. The Association was formed as a one-year partnership among the subscribing producers, who agreed to market their oil exclusively through their management, who in turn negotiated prices and filled orders through a levy on the members according to the rated capacity of their wells. From the paucity of recorded evidence it is difficult to say what effect the Association had on the price of oil. Certainly not all the producers joined the Association; among the notable stand-outs was James Miller Williams, the pioneer.

The Association did not live out its allocated span of one year. A later observer quoted in the *Sarnia Observer* of June 1, 1865, bemoaned its fate:

> The combination . . . fixed the price at 50¢ per barrel. [It] failed from lack of means and from the pressing necessities of its members; but considering its very moderate demands, it surely deserved a better fate. What other monopoly . . . was so liberal in its terms as this one? It failed, not having the power of cohesion among its members sufficient to withstand the offers of buyers provided with ready money, who came determined to buy cheap for cash, and who in most cases overcame the scruples of even conscientious members of the Association with their tempting offers of "cash down."

The producers addressed themselves with vigour to the second of their objectives, eliminating as much as they could of the glut on the home market by export-

[5] William J. Patterson, *Report on the Trade and Commerce of the City of Montreal for 1863* (Montreal, 1864), p. 62.

ing the surplus. In March, 1862, the first known trade convention in the industry convened at Oil Springs. Toronto's enterprising mayor, John G. Bowes, headed a delegation of businessmen, accompanied by a well-known scientific expert, Dr. Henry Y. Hind, to Oil Springs where they met with a party from Sarnia, and the local oilmen. Mayor Bowes suggested that a company be formed to promote the export of oil to Europe.

The oilmen were not slow to test the project so thoroughly aired at the conference, for various well-financed local merchants and producers began to send cargoes of oil to England almost at once. Barrels of oil were floated down the Sydenham River and loaded onto schooners such as the three-master *Prince of Wales*, which carried 3,000 barrels. In all, seventeen ships laden with oil left Montreal during the shipping season of 1862, fourteen bound for Great Britain and one each to Germany, British Guiana, and Australia. Unfortunately, not all the oil sent abroad was properly deodorized so that the quality of the product was not uniformly attractive to the customers. By 1864, bad quality had effectively ruined the Canadian export market for oil.

The winter of 1862-63 saw the decline of the great flowing wells, and the dissolution of the Canada Oil Association. The Shaw well stopped flowing in January, 1863, almost a year to the day of its dramatic beginning. Shaw himself was drowned in his well on 11 February, 1863, while trying to retrieve a lost tool. At the same time, the Bothwell field, located about fifteen miles southeast of Oil Springs, came into production. It had a brief, hectic boom lasting three years and paralleling that of Oil Springs, until in 1866 it too sank into oblivion which lasted thirty years. The cessation of production had left a vast surplus which sustained the market throughout 1863. Late in 1863, however, the accumulated oil was finally used up and the price of oil rose dramatically, briefly touching \$7.50 a barrel before it settled at around \$3.50 to \$4.00. Refined oil then fetched 50 cents per gallon. The high prices encouraged further drilling, and many old wells which had been neglected because of their low production, were re-opened. Many local refiners who could not pay the high prices for crude oil, or who could not get any, faced ruin.

With the price of oil again rising to \$6 a barrel in 1865, several large and wealthy companies with capital, skill, and good business management moved into the field. They drilled deeper wells throughout the townships of Enniskillen and Dawn. While the Oil Springs field was not revived, since the drills did not penetrate to the "lower horizon" which remained undiscovered until 1881, the Petrolia field showed great promise. During the early years drilling there had been confined to the banks of Bear Creek, a tributary of the Sydenham River, since the American prospectors thought they could find oil only near a water-course.

The Petrolia story illustrated an important cyclical trend in the early development of the oil industry. A high price for crude oil invariably brought more operators into the picture, who extended the known limits of the field by their endless search for oil. As soon as the inevitable discoveries were made, a great rush of drilling activity took place, with the result that the price tumbled again, and a surplus developed. In the course of a year's drilling at Petrolia, during which time the settlement sprang into being and assumed the aspects of a boom town by the fall of 1866, the price of crude had fallen from $8 to $3 a barrel. In the meantime, many of the American operators, fearing that the Fenian Raids could develop into another war, had taken their capital and gone home.

Even at three dollars a barrel, however, crude oil held enough profit for drillers, producers, speculators, and refiners alike. During this time, a Canadian operator, Captain King, was busy drilling wells for the Northeastern Oil Company of St. Catharines, deep in the bush two miles west of Petrolia and Bear Creek. On November 24, 1866, he was rewarded with overwhelming success, when he struck a well which flowed 800 barrels per day at the outset. His work convinced his fellow oilmen that they could safely leave the banks of Bear Creek, and soon they joined him to prospect the north and west regions of Petrolia. A host of new wells resulted from their work, some even more prolific than Shaw's almost legendary gusher at Oil Springs. The price of crude oil fell below one dollar per barrel for a year, then gradually recovered as exports began anew, especially to the United States where the Pennsylvania field was in a period of low production, between the peaks of great discoveries, just as the Canadian field had been.

The five years that followed were among the most productive and prosperous in the history of the Canadian oil industry. Fortunately, the oil rush at Petrolia was more carefully controlled than it had been at Oil Springs a few years earlier. Means were found to store the surpluses and prevent the tremendous waste which had marred the record at Oil Springs. Under the leadership of men such as J. H. Fairbank, E. D. Kerby, H. W. Lancey, John D. Noble, and W. H. McGarvey, the producers acted together from time to time to secure an adequate return on their investment, and to ensure that the quality of the oil remained high. The new field proved to be much more permanent than the first, for it yielded oil steadily for over forty years under the influence of deeper and more widespread drilling. Through the later years of the nineteenth century combinations similar to the Canada Oil Association rose and fell. Export markets were gained and lost more than once; technological improvements gradually lowered the cost of production and refining so that the industry became far more efficient than in its early days, and yielding a steady, and sometimes substantial profit for the entrepreneurs. Late in 1866 Petrolia and the oilfield were finally linked to the outside world by a railway line, a blessing that oilmen had coveted for fifteen years. Petrolia drillers were soon in demand all over the world as new oilfields were discovered, many of them far richer than those in Canada.

In the years after 1866, the petroleum industry of Enniskillen developed along with the country to become one of Canada's important home-owned industries, for the wealth which it generated locally made an important contribution to the national economy. The lessons taught the oilmen by the experiences of their first hectic years at Oil Springs, and later Petrolia, remained with them as they went on to greater successes, and as they achieved fame and fortune, they were wont to remember their humble origins with nostalgia.

BIBLIOGRAPHICAL NOTE

Fairbank, C. O., "The Petrolia Story," *Northwest Oil Journal*, vol. 2, no. 1 (1953), pp. 5-13.

Harkness, R. B., "Ontario's Part in the Petroleum Industry," *Canadian Oil and Gas Industries* (February and March, 1951).

Hunt, T. S., "Notes on the History of Petroleum or Rock Oil," *The Canadian Naturalist and Geologist*, VI (1861), pp. 241-55.

Kerr, James, "The Oil Belt," Toronto *Mail*, Dec. 1, 1888; republished as "An Early View of Petrolia, Ontario," *Western Ontario Historical Notes*, XVIII, no. 2 (Sept., 1962), pp. 57-91. (Authorship subsequently attributed to a Mr. Beach, a reporter for the *Mail.*)

Lauriston, Victor, *Lambton's Hundred Years, 1849-1949* (Sarnia, 1950).

"One Hundred Years of Oil, 1858-1958," *Oil/Gas World* (June, 1958), pp. 39-66.

Ontario. Royal Commission on the Mineral Resources of Ontario, *Report* (Toronto, 1890), "Petroleum," pp. 153-67.

Purdy, G. A., *Petroleum: Prehistoric to Petrochemicals* (Toronto, 1957).

Ross, Victor, *Petroleum in Canada* (Toronto, 1917).

Saywell, John T., "The Early History of Canadian Oil Companies; A Chapter in Canadian Business History," *Ontario History*, LIII (1961), pp. 67-72.

Whipp, C. B., and Phelps, Edward, *Petrolia 1866-1966* (Petrolia, 1966).

Williamson, H. F., and Daum, A. R., *The American Petroleum Industry: The Age of Illumination, 1859-1899* (Evanston, 1959).

Of the surviving newspapers, the files of the Sarnia *Observer*, the Petrolia *Advertiser* and *Topic*, the London *Free Press*, and the Toronto *Globe* are probably the most useful.

Serial publications, such as *Annual Reports* of the Geological Survey of Canada and the Ontario Department of Mines, often contain items of historical restrospect.

Of the trade publications, the *Imperial Oil Review* has carried the largest number of historical articles over a period of many years.

The Impact of Hydro on Ontario

R. N. Beattie

In a chapter about Ottawa in *Picturesque Canada* (2 vols., Toronto, 1882), there is a vivid picture of the lumber mills driven by the waterpower of the Chaudière Falls:

> The scene at night – for work continues both by night and day – is extremely novel and picturesque. Some of the lumbering firms now use the electric light, and the effect in that pure, clear glare, is of the most Rembrandt-like character.

That was probably written in 1882 and relates to the earliest industrial use of electricity in Ontario. The electrical revolution had begun, and within a few years it would spread to almost every populated locality in Ontario. Within a quarter-century it would bring The Hydro-Electric Power Commission of Ontario into being. This province-wide electrical utility, long familiarly known as Hydro, is a unique example of co-operative municipal enterprise and one of the most significant economic achievements of Ontario's first century.

Street lighting by means of arc lights was in the van of electricity's conquering advance against darkness and manual drudgery. The arc lights were suitable for lighting large public buildings and commercial or industrial premises as well as streets. In some municipalities, venturesome businessmen or investor-owned companies installed arc lighting equipment in mills or factories, and obtained contracts from the municipalities to supply street lighting as well.

The claim to have been the first municipality to light its streets electrically has been advanced on behalf of a number of Ontario towns and cities, including Pembroke, Hamilton, and Ottawa. It seems most likely that the honour properly belongs to Toronto where, early in 1884, the City Council arranged for a three-month trial for two competing companies, each of which was to erect 25 lights in a specified area. This interesting competition produced its blaze of light on May 15, 1884. Peterborough's electric street lights were turned on only eight nights later. The new lights were soon welcomed enthusiastically into town after town across the province.

Light bulbs for incandescent lighting, elements for electric heating, and electric motors to drive machines, all appeared on the market even while arc lights were still a novelty. The electrical industry grew and spread very rapidly during the years between 1883 and 1900. Almost every city and town saw the introduction of electricity to replace gas for street lighting. Electric lighting became fairly common in factories, hotels, stores, theatres, and new homes. Electric street railways appeared in most cities. Many electric inter-urban railways were built, and many more were planned. Especially where waterpower was available as the motive power for the electric generators, the use of electric power for turning the wheels of industry was growing steadily.

The possibility of using hydro-electric power extensively for Ontario's industry appealed strongly to manufacturers. Coal for factory steam engines as well as for railways and heating fuel had to be imported, often at very high prices. The young and growing electric power industry mostly used coal-fired steam engines to drive its generators. As soon as the transmission of electric power for more than a few miles became technically feasible, businessmen, working through their local boards of trade and municipal councils, sought to encourage investment in electrical generating and transmission plants, just as their predecessors in pre-Confederation days had pressed for roads, canals, and railways.

In some localities, however, investors were unwilling to risk their capital, even in small, coal-fired systems. Occasionally a company, having made a brave start, failed. In some cases, contracts for street lights were not renewed because of disputes over rates and the quality of service. Faced with the need to establish or maintain lighting service, the city or town government took over the task of supplying electricity, sometimes just for street lighting, but in other cases for lighting commercial and residential buildings, and even, to some extent, for electric motors.

When a municipal government undertook to own and operate an electrical utility, it had to assign the management of it either to a committee of council or to a separate commission. Legislation empowering a municipality to establish a commission to operate a public utility had existed since before Confederation. The Municipal Institutions Act of 1858 was a thorough revision of previous legislation and was intended to be "a complete code for all municipal purposes". Among its new provisions was one enabling cities and towns to pass by-laws,

> for providing for the appointment of three commissioners for entering into contracts for the construction of gas and water works, – for superintending the construction of the same, – for managing the works when completed, – and for providing for the election of the said commissioners by the electors from time to time and at such periods, and for such terms as the council may appoint by the by-law authorizing the election.

This power to establish commissions was included in an 1883 act to authorize cities, towns, and villages to provide gas and other means of lighting and heating "and to manufacture and supply electric, galvanic, or any other artificial light or heat, either in connection with gas or otherwise."

The provisions of the Act of 1883 remained in force until 1913 when the Public Utilities Act succeeded it and other related legislation. Sections 34-43 of the Public Utilities Act relate to the election of public utilities commissions, the power of commissioners, etc.

Many Ontario municipalities became the owners of their public utilities during the first generation after Confederation. This is clearly shown in a legislative committee report published in 1903. The municipalities had been asked to list the "reproductive undertakings" in which they had invested, the date of commencement, the amount of investment, and the average annual income. Of the 94 municipalities that responded, 39 reported that they owned and operated electrical utilities, mostly for street lighting. Municipally-owned waterworks were more numerous, at 79. The two oldest electrical utilities, in Orillia and Goderich, had both commenced operation in 1887. Twenty towns and cities reported commencement dates between 1899 and 1902.

The report does not tell us how many of these utilities were under commissions and how many under committees of municipal councils. It appears that in some municipalities, commissions were formed for the purpose of planning and constructing facilities which were later handed over to the municipality for operation and administration. This was what occurred, for example, in Hamilton where the Board of Water Commissioners was appointed at the beginning of 1857 and where the waterworks were transferred to the city in 1861. In Toronto, the waterworks were operated by a commission from 1871 to 1877 but were then taken over by a municipal department.

The development of municipal electrical utilities did not follow a standard path. In Orillia, the Fire and Water Committee of Council assumed the management of the town's arc light plant in 1887. By 1899, when Orillia became the first Ontario municipality to build its own hydro-electric generating station with long-distance transmission, the committee had been renamed the Fire, Water, and Light Committee. It was not replaced by the Orillia Water, Light, and Power Commission until 1913.

In Barrie, electrical service was supplied by a succession of four organizations – first, the Barrie Electric Light Company from 1888 to 1898; second, the Electric Light Department of the Town of Barrie, 1899 to 1901; third, the Barrie Water and Electric Light Commission (independently) 1902 to 1913; and finally, the Barrie Public Utilities Commission (as a cost contract municipal electric utility associated with Ontario Hydro, 1913 to the present). Gravenhurst was supplied with arc and incandescent lights by a private company from 1892. In 1903 the town bought the plants, and in the following year provided for the election of waterworks and electric light commissioners. Peterborough, after a long history of water, gas, and electrical companies, set up a waterworks commission in 1902 but established neither an electric department nor a commission until 1913.

When the twentieth century began, Ontario had 29 cities and towns with populations exceeding 5,000. Of these 12 owned and operated their own electrical utilities before 1906, the date of the founding of Ontario Hydro. The group of 17 cities and towns which were served by investor-owned electric companies included Toronto, Hamilton, Ottawa, and London. (Ottawa had recently bought an investor-owned competitor of its main supplier, Ottawa Electric.) These were by far the largest municipalities in the province. Nevertheless, there was a great deal of support for the idea of municipal ownership of utilities even in Toronto and in other cities where it had not yet been established.

Another factor of great importance in the background of Ontario Hydro was a widespread feeling, particularly strong in southwestern Ontario, that the Canadian share of the waterpower of Niagara Falls was a great natural resource and potential source of power that should be available to all of the people of the province who were within reach of it, rather than to private business or the inhabitants of any particular locality. This opinion seems to have been based on fear and envy of business interests in the United States and in the cities of Toronto and Hamilton.

The provincial Liberal government, successively under Mowat, Hardy, and Ross, had defended the province's right to water and waterpower within the province, including the Canadian share of boundary waters. However, under George W. Ross, the government was opposed to undertaking the development of Niagara power as a provincial project. At the same time, it was willing to authorize municipalities interested in Niagara power to form some kind of co-operative union for the purpose of obtaining it.

As a result, the Ontario Power Commission was appointed in 1903 by the municipal corporations of Toronto, London, Brantford, Stratford, Woodstock, Ingersoll, and Guelph. The Commissioners were "to enquire into the question of the municipal development of power at Niagara Falls and to report thereon in accordance with the requirements of the Municipal Power Works Act." The report of this Commission was presented in March 1906. It enthusiastically recommended a co-operative municipal enterprise.

A second advisory commission, called the Hydro-Electric Power Commission of the Province of Ontario, was appointed in 1905 by the Conservative government, under James P. Whitney, which had recently defeated the Liberals under Ross. This second Commission's function was to investigate the hydro-electric resources and the probable demands for electric power throughout the province, not merely in the vicinity of Niagara Falls.

Adam Beck, the mayor of London, was a member of the first advisory commission and the chairman of the second. He was subsequently appointed first chairman of a third commission created in 1906 to give effect to the recommendations of the advisory commissions. The Hydro-Electric Power Commission of Ontario was to be a corporate entity, a self-sustaining public enterprise endowed with broad powers with respect to electricity supply throughout the province of Ontario.

The Power Commission Act invited action: "Any municipal corporation may apply to the Commission for . . . electrical power or energy . . . for lighting, heating, and power purposes."

The first applicant to enter into an agreement with the new Commission was the city of Ottawa. On July 31, 1907, arrangements were completed whereby the Ottawa and Hull Power and Manufacturing Company agreed with Ontario Hydro to supply Ottawa with 1,500 horsepower from its plant on the Gatineau, a Quebec tributary of the Ottawa River. Ottawa had established a municipal distribution utility to compete with the Ottawa Electric Company two years earlier.

Ontario Hydro's main objective from the beginning was, of course, to obtain power at Niagara Falls and transmit it to the municipalities in southwestern Ontario which had worked together during the previous half-dozen years for the establishment of a co-operative system. But first, contracts had to be signed with fourteen municipalities, a system of transmission lines and transformer stations had to be designed and built, and 100,000 horsepower from the Ontario Power Company at Niagara Falls had to be bargained for. Operations began officially on October 11, 1910 when Hydro power was switched on in Berlin (now called Kitchener). A series of official ceremonies brought 19 more municipalities into the Niagara system by the end of October 1911.

Elsewhere in the province, while the Niagara system was being organized and built, the bases were being established for other systems too remote from Niagara Falls to be served by Niagara power. For example, two pioneer systems were originated to serve Port Arthur at the western end of Lake Superior, and Midland and Penetanguishene on Georgian Bay. These systems ultimately grew into the Thunder Bay and Georgian Bay Systems. Other new systems were formed here and there. Later on, many of the small systems were amalgamated into larger systems.

The initial wholesale purchase of 100,000 horsepower from the Ontario Power Company had seemed overly optimistic to some of Adam Beck's critics. Soaring demands during the 1914-18 war, however, required the securing of additional sources at Niagara and elsewhere. Then came the building of the Queenston plant (now the Sir Adam Beck Niagara No. 1) which was for several years the world's largest hydro-electric generating station.

Demand continued to grow. Ontario turned between 1926 and 1930 to hydro-electric resources in neighbouring Quebec, and still purchases from suppliers there a sizeable proportion of the energy it distributes in Ontario (about 15 per cent in 1965).

After the second world war, most of the province's remaining hydro-electric resources were developed. On the Ottawa, Niagara, and St. Lawrence Rivers in particular, huge generating stations were built to raise total dependable capacity from less than two million kilowatts in 1945 to more than four million in 1954.

Part of the increased capacity was in Hydro's first large thermal-electric generating stations, one in Toronto and one in Windsor. It became clear that Hydro's future growth would call for more and more thermal-electric capacity and therefore increased imports of fuel. It was decided to explore two other sources of power for the southern Ontario economy: first, long distance transmisson at 500,000 volts to draw on the potential power of rivers flowing into James Bay, far to the north; and secondly, nuclear energy derived from uranium, of which Ontario has extensive resources. Ontario Hydro, in collaboration with Atomic Energy of Canada and Canadian General Electric, built a small (20,000 kilowatts) Nuclear Power Demonstration station at Rolphton which started operation in 1962. The second nuclear station at Douglas Point was placed in service early in 1967. Its 200,000 kilowatts of installed capacity will be dwarfed by the third nuclear station now under construction at Pickering near Toronto, where the installed capacity will be 1,080,000 kilowatts.

The process of growth, change, and consolidation that began in 1910 has been continuous. Now there are only two systems, East and West. One of the Commission's most recent policy announcements concerns a transmission link between the East System, serving southern and northeastern Ontario, and the West System, serving the northwestern and western parts of the province. This link, which will strengthen both systems, is also a phase of Ontario Hydro's co-operation with other North American utilities in the establishment of a continent-wide grid through which each utility is able, in emergencies, to depend upon the reserve capacity of the others.

But, to return to the situation in 1910, the co-operative municipal enterprise headed by the Commission naturally entered into competition with established investor-owned companies, of which there were a great many, large and small, scattered throughout the province. Where a company operated entirely within the bounds of one municipality, the municipal government usually bought the company's lines and stations and handed them over to a municipal commission established to distribute Hydro power from Niagara or elsewhere.

In other cases, however, the privately-owned utilities were serving districts containing several municipalities. In such cases, the purchaser was usually the provincial Commission – or the provincial Commission in co-operation with one or more municipalities. The first such purchase occurred in July 1914 when the Commission bought out the Simcoe Railway and Power Company which had a small hydro-electric generating station at Big Chute on the Severn River and a few miles of transmission line to serve neighbouring municipalities.

A much larger purchase was made in March 1916 when the provincial government bought out the Electric Power Company, a holding company controlling 23 subsidiary utilities in the central Ontario district stretching from Oshawa to Kingston and north to the fringe of the Haliburton Highlands. The company had begun in 1910 to supply power from hydro-electric plants located at some of the locks of the Trent Canal. The long-range plan was to build more plants along the Trent to replace the small steam-powered stations which provided electric lighting in most of the communities served by the 23 subsidiary utilities. The government assigned the operation and management of the utilities to Ontario Hydro. Later, the Commission purchased from the province the generating and transmission plant, and one by one the municipalities purchased their distribution systems and joined the Hydro league by entering into contracts to be supplied at cost. Eventually the Central Ontario System was merged with neighbouring systems.

In April 1917 the Commission bought the generating station and transmission lines of the Ontario Power Company at Niagara Falls. This had been the original source of supply for the Niagara System. Although supplementary sources had been secured, the system's load had outgrown the supply so the Commission soon proceeded to enlarge this property.

In December 1920 the Commission also acquired the generating station belonging to the Toronto Power Company, which was a close neighbour of the Ontario Power Company plant. This latter purchase was just one part of a comprehensive arrangement whereby a syndicate of Toronto financiers also disposed of the Toronto Electric Light Company, the Toronto Street Railway Company, several suburban and interurban railways, and a transmission line from Niagara Falls to Toronto.

The Toronto Electric Light Company had been incorporated on September 25, 1883, with a paid up capital of $175,000. In 1884 it had won the first contract to light Toronto streets with electric arc lights. In succeeding years it had absorbed competitors, moved into incandescent lighting and power supply, and in November 1906 first received power for its customers all the way from the Toronto Power Company's plant at Niagara Falls. By 1920 it had become a major part of the power and transit organization which cost Toronto Hydro, the Toronto Transportation Commission, and Ontario Hydro nearly $33 million.

Ten years later, in 1930, a similar complex of electric power and electric railway companies ceased to operate in Hamilton and its neighbouring municipalities when Ontario Hydro and the municipalities concerned divided between them the property of the Dominion Power and Transmission Company. The group of companies in this case owned a pioneer hydro-electric generating station at DeCew Falls near St. Catharines which was linked in 1898 by a 35-mile 22,000 volt transmission line to Hamilton. This was nearly twice as far (at twice the voltage) as the Niagara-Buffalo line which had aroused continent-wide interest less than two years earlier. The Cataract, as the enterprise was popularly known, also included distribution utilities in Hamilton, Burlington, Oakville, and Brantford, and electric street and interurban railways.

The electrical history of Ottawa after 1910 was somewhat unusual. The Ottawa Electric Company, which had been founded in 1895, not only withstood the competition of older and younger companies, but also of the municipal utility which was founded in 1905. Although the municipality, as already noted, entered into the very first power-at-cost contract with the provincial Commission in 1907, the investor-owned company and the municipal electrical utility competed side by side until 1951 when the municipal system finally took over to serve the whole city.

There are still several investor-owned electric utilities operating in Ontario. Some of them serve customers in remote pulp and paper or mining communities. Cornwall and Sault Ste. Marie are the only large urban centres not included in the Hydro family of municipalities. Ontario Hydro provides about 90 per cent of all the electrical energy distributed in the province.

How can one explain the success of the power-at-cost, co-operative league of municipalities in meeting and supplanting its investor-owned rivals in a business community which is otherwise characterized by free enterprise? In most respects, Ontario is far from being either radical or socialistic. During most of the sixty years of its existence, Ontario Hydro has operated within a political environment in which the provincial government has usually been Conservative. Perhaps the investor-owned companies in Toronto and Hamilton lacked vision and confidence and therefore lost firm public support. Assuredly, the leadership given to Ontario Hydro by its first chairman, Sir Adam Beck, and a tradition that Hydro engineering and administration should be of a high order were very significant factors. One cannot overlook the fact that rates to customers have been well below North American averages and that Hydro's resources have usually been adequate and secure. Up to now, Hydro has undoubtedly fulfilled the principal aim of its founders – abundant power for an industrial economy throughout a province with virtually no fossil fuel of its own, but with magnificent waterpower resources. It faces its future, in which fossil fuels and nuclear energy will grow in importance, with confident optimism.

The Changing Patterns of Tourism in Ontario

R. I. Wolfe

I

There is very little to be said about tourism in Upper Canada, and little more about tourism in Canada West; but almost immediately after Canada West became Ontario tourism as a well-defined activity began. That is, in Ontario the history of tourism is almost exactly coextensive with that of Confederation.

The resorts of Canada as a whole developed within a fundamentally unchanged pattern during the two middle quarters of the nineteenth century. The chief resorts of the period are well summarized, for the benefit of tourists from the United States, in a travel book published by Henry Beaumont Small in the year of Confederation. With few exceptions, these resorts were in Lower Canada, on the banks of the St. Lawrence. But things were changing:

> In the days of yore the Summer Tourist through the country had no easy means of access to the quiet nooks in the "back country," or the many pleasant resorts our railways have opened out. The old hackneyed journey was as follows: A few days at Niagara Falls, a hurried trip through the "ambitious little city of the West," Hamilton, a cursory glance at Toronto, a night on Ontario in the close stateroom of a steamer, a hurried run through the Lake of the Thousand Islands, a day or two in Montreal and Quebec. . . . and the Canadian Tour was complete. But now, thanks to the iron horse and its accessories, wild forest-lands, smiling villages beside rivers teeming with the finny tribe, the scenery of Superior and Huron, the Saguenay, the St. Francis, the St. Maurice, all are easy of access – all worthy of a visit, and only awaiting some painter's hand to bring them prominently forward in their beauty.

It took time for this new pattern to establish itself. As long as thirty years after Confederation Charles G. D. Roberts was still describing Cacouna, on the St. Lawrence below Rivière du Loup, as probably the most famous resort in Canada. (Who knows of it today? Yet in its time it was visited each season by many thousands of vacationists from the United States and Canada.) During these thirty years, however, the people of Ontario, instead of seeking their recreation elsewhere, turned more and more to the resources within their own province.

The development of Ontario's summer resorts in the nineteenth century, which I have described in *Ontario History*, LIV (1962), pp. 149-60, may be summarized as follows: The resorts of Ontario were of little consequence until the 1870's, and indeed everything that came before 1890 was little more than a prelude. But by the 1890's the people of Ontario first joined vacationing visitors from the United States in making intensive use of their own wilderness for recreation. The first boom in Ontario tourism came with the economic boom that started in 1896, but in a sense it was a restricted boom, because only the well-to-do participated. This was the era of the society resort, and newspapers carried pages of the names of socially prominent people to be found summering in the hotels of Muskoka and the private cottages on Lake Simcoe, or taking part in regattas on Stony Lake.

Depending as it did on the prosperity of the moneyed class, the well-being of Ontario's fashionable resorts was closely tied to the economic state of the country. When, in 1912, the crops failed in the Canadian West, and the resulting depression was felt in Ontario the following year, the society resorts suddenly collapsed. Whereas the newspapers had formerly abounded in chatty news from the resorts, they were now completely silent. The reader going through the files of the newspapers of more than half a century ago is stunned by the suddenness of the transition.

With the coming of war a year later, the quiet of the resorts continued undisturbed.

II

During the war years a new element entered the recreational pattern. This was the automobile. By 1917 there were enough auto-borne tourists on Ontario's gravel county roads to make them both a nuisance and a boon to farmers. (A nuisance and a boon is what resorters have been to the surrounding rural population at all times; occasionally they have even had catastrophic, demoralizing effects, as many writers have pointed out.)

"MOTORISTS BRING PROFIT TO FARMERS; Wayside Signs Almost Always Bring Trade from the Tourists," were the headings over one article published in a Toronto newspaper in 1917. "CITY MOTORISTS BECOME BURDEN TO THE FARMERS. Their Week-End Visits to Country Relatives Not Appreciated. Spoiling Rest Day. Women Work in Fields all Week and Then Feed Visitors on Sunday," read those over another: "Why, country roads are black with them on Saturday afternoons and Sundays. There is scarcely a farm in the neighbourhood that doesn't have at least one load over Sunday since the auto came in style." Good or bad, the effect of the automobile and the road was to bring city and country together.

The farmer brought his burdens (and his opportunities) on himself, for he was largely responsible for starting the network of rural roads that was later to serve the tourist. At the beginning of the century there were only two hundred cars in all of Ontario, and good roads were the concern, not of the city-dweller, but of the farmer. He agitated for them, and he provided much of the money for building them. Twenty years later over one third of the passenger vehicles in Ontario, 64,000 out of 182,000, belonged to farmers. In all the cities of Ontario there were fewer than 69,000 passenger cars. But among the cottage-owning class of that day – professionals, merchants, businessmen – there were precisely as many cars as among farmers: 64,000. The network of provincial highways did not as yet do justice to their numerical importance. It served agricultural and urban Ontario, but on the road map recreational Ontario remained a blank. Of all the lakes in the interior, only Lake Simcoe and Lake Couchiching were served by roads of provincial standard. Still, the recreational lands were served by roads of a sort, which could now be easily reached via the better provincial roads. The rising crowd of car owners took advantage of them with a rush, and the resort boom of the 1920's was under way.

III

The character of recreational land use in the Ontario of the 1920's, during the second tourist boom, was radically different from that at the beginning of the century. In this decade of the Coolidge prosperity the workers were at last coming into their recreational own. Great numbers of them owned cars – registration in Ontario reached the quarter-million mark in 1925 – and if the number of cottage owners among them was much smaller, still they could afford to buy tents, and go camping on lakeside resorts. Here was foreshadowed the most striking change that recent years have brought to the pattern of outdoor recreation in Ontario, the vast increase in the number of campers and of the provincial parks needed to accommodate them. Today over one million people camp in provincial parks each year, and the number of parks has increased within twenty years from perhaps half a dozen to nearly a hundred.

The 1920's saw a reversal in the relative positions of railway and highway, a return to conditions that had prevailed nearly a century before. In England, as we know from the delectable descriptions of stage-coach travel that permeate the works of Charles Dickens, the highway was of great importance at the end of the pre-railway era. So it was in Ontario. The railway gained the ascendancy in the 1850's, and, as Small perceptively noted, was chiefly responsible for the opening up of most of Ontario's resort lands. Railway and steamer were still the chief means of travelling to and about these lands during the first boom. In the twenties the automobile reasserted the dominance of the road. It would take another two or three decades before it all but wiped the railroad and the steamer off the recreational scene.

The egalitarian society was much closer in the twenties than it had been during the first recreational boom. Though news of the resorts again began to appear in the newspapers, it had lost its society tone, and lists of distinguished guests at the fashionable resorts, if they were presented at all, were relegated to the society page. This was the decade in which the workingclass resorts, particularly those on Lake Simcoe, Georgian Bay, and Lake Erie, began to develop. It was also the decade in which once-fashionable resorts on Lake Ontario and the St. Lawrence, such as Niagara-on-the-Lake and the outgrowths of the Methodist camp meeting, Grimsby Beach and Thousand Island Park, followed Cacouna into near-oblivion.

Travel into and out of Canada rose steeply in the latter part of the decade, and Ontario assumed the dominant position in Canadian tourism – as the destination of two out of every three vacationists from the United States visiting Canada – that has remained virtually constant ever since. There is conflicting evidence as to the economic proportions that tourism into Canada attained. One authoritative source maintains that expenditures in Canada reached a peak of over $300 million in 1929, a figure that according to other sources was not reached until 1953. An even more authoritative source placed this 1929 peak at the more believable figure of just under $200 million, or about a quarter of what the figure is expected to be in this Centennial year. In either case, the tourism of the pre-war, pre-car days had been left far behind. But the simile of the rocket and the stick is nowhere more apt than here; for rapid as was the rise until 1929, the fall after that date was even more rapid.

The coming of depression ended the second recreational boom, as it had ended the first. In the United States, where the boom psychology was far more greatly developed than in Canada, resort lots were vastly oversold. The accomplished confidence man "Yellow Kid" Weil was able to "give away" Michigan bogs, some of them under two feet of water, as Elysian fields, to gullible Chicagoans. In Wisconsin the market was so drastically oversaturated that responsible scholars, examining the undeveloped riparian lands there, were led to the conclusion, which time was to prove unwarranted, that the day of the cottage was over; that people would henceforth refuse to let themselves be tied down to a plot of ground on a lake, for the pattern of American life was changing, and Americans would from now on want to see their country from their cars.

In Ontario during the depression there was little inclination to think of buying summer property, but the cheapest lands, those inhering in the Crown, did receive even more interest than during the boom of the twenties.

IV

The thirties saw the beginning of a very important change in the pattern of commercial resorts. In spite of severe economic strains, the number of automobiles in Ontario decreased very little – much less than during the war that followed. After faltering slightly in the early thirties, the curve of car ownership once more began to climb, with the same speed as during the early twenties. Travel across the border in both directions fell much more drastically, but it too began its recovery after the depth of the depression had been passed.

Yet money was still in short supply, and the resort hotels were too costly for most travellers. To meet the demand for cheap food and accommodations, and to take advantage of the increasing use of the automobile for touring, the snack stand and the roadside commercial cabin began to appear. In the United States the cabin rapidly developed into the motel, though it would be a long time before it became the huge, elaborate, luxurious, and ubiquitous establishment that we know today.

One further characteristic marked the resorts of this period. This was an intangible, and a most disquieting one. At no previous time had racial discrimination been given overt expression at the resorts. It was there, but it expressed itself in action rather than verbally. In the 1930's discriminatory announcements became a prominent part of the summer-resort scene, and were numerous in the resort advertisements carried by the daily newspapers. Part of the cause, no doubt, was the strain put on society by the depression. Much more directly responsible was the example of Nazi Germany, allied to the growing size of the Jewish community in Toronto.

Whatever the reason, in 1934 the open expression of discrimination appeared in newspaper advertising for the first time, and persisted for more than a decade thereafter. In deference to anti-discriminatory legislation, it has almost disappeared in recent years. Discriminatory *practices* have, we can be sure, diminished much less.

The second world war, with its unsettled populations and its restrictions on gasoline and building materials, further inhibited the growth of Ontario's resorts. But with the end of the war there immediately began not only the greatest economic boom in the country's history, but with it, inevitably, the greatest boom in recreational land use, a boom that with minor fluctuations persists to this day.

This boom has brought fewer radical changes to the pattern of tourism in Ontario than did either of the others. Instead, it has brought an intensification of trends that were already in existence. In large part this can be attributed to the continuing, but again intensified, dominance of the automobile in American life. Resort lands on the Precambrian Shield are beginning to fill up, and a movement has begun into areas that were once inaccessible by car, but that have now been opened up by virtue of the extensive program of highway construction that has been underway during the past two decades. The airplane has become increasingly used for vacation travel, but, except for the small privately-owned plane that flies to isolated lakes in the north, it is of much greater significance for travel out of Ontario – to Europe in the summer and the American South in the winter – than it is for travel into or within Ontario. As elsewhere in North America, there has been an astonishing increase in the number of power boats cluttering recreational waters. The beautiful Canadian winter is coming into its own, as more and more people turn to skiing. As has already been mentioned, there has been a vast increase in the number of campers and of provincial parks. But the summer cottage remains, as it has been almost since the time of Confederation, the single most characteristic and desired place of recreation for the people of Ontario and for the vacationing visitors from beyond its borders.

Agricultural Settlement on the Canadian Shield: Ottawa River to Georgian Bay

Florence B. Murray

The Canadian or Laurentian Shield circles the Arctic in the north and three thousand miles to the south drives a wedge of rock between the Ottawa River and Georgian Bay. From the days of the voyageurs to the present time, in one way or another it has been a determining factor in the industrial and social development of Canada: until the building of the railways the rough terrain that separates the Ottawa and Georgian Bay formed a barrier to trade between the St. Lawrence and the Canadian and American West; in the latter half of the nineteenth century its pine trees afforded one of the most profitable of Canadian industries; and for a few years the promise of free grants on the Shield lured the land-hungry native Canadian and immigrant alike.

The wedge between the Ottawa River and Georgian Bay includes the administrative areas now known as Muskoka, Parry Sound, Haliburton, Nipissing, and Renfrew, and the northern townships of certain counties to the south. The altitude varies from roughly six hundred to seventeen hundred feet, and, although the local relief is seldom more than two or three hundred feet, here and there a hill rises so abruptly, dramatically, that custom attributes to it the title of mountain. It is a land of lakes and ponds, creeks, and swift rivers obstructed by rapids and falls. From the height of land in the central area, rivers such as the Muskoka and Magnetawan fall west to Georgian Bay; the Gull and Burnt rivers find their way south through the Trent system to Lake Ontario; and on the east the Madawaska, Bonnechere, and Petawawa flow to the Ottawa.

The land, typical of the Canadian Shield, is rough and broken, granite rock alternating with swamps and with fertile patches that often occur on the beds of former lakes. The soil is generally a thin cover of vegetable mould which was quickly eroded when the protecting timber was removed by the lumberman or settler, or by the bush fires that only too often raced through the country. The climate is more extreme than in the lands bordering on Lake Ontario. In winter the snowfall is high and the temperature drops occasionally to forty or more degrees below zero. The original forest included red, white, and jack pine, spruce, balsam, hemlock, tamarack, cedar, birch, poplar, and some sugar maple. After an area had been stripped of its pine and burned in one of the innumerable forest fires, or cleared and abandoned by the settlers, the new growth was mainly poplar and birch.

The first exploratory surveys across the heavily wooded land between the Ottawa and Georgian Bay, south of Lake Nipissing, arose from military rather than economic motives. The war of 1812 pointed up the necessity of a water connection, shorter and more navigable than the fur traders' old route, and as a result a series of explorations were carried out by officers of the Royal Engineers. In 1819 Lieutenant Catty crossed from Lake Simcoe to the Ottawa by way of the Madawaska, and in 1826 and 1827 a number of officers searched without success for a navigable waterway through the Muskoka-Haliburton area.

By the 1820's the development of a water route had an economic as well as a military importance. Settlement on the American side of the border had reached the upper Lakes and an extensive commerce was developing between that area and the Atlantic seaboard. Unfortunately for the Upper Canadians, the 1820's were a time of canal building in the United States. The Erie Canal opened in 1825 with the Oswego feeder in 1828, and these, by carrying the commerce of the rapidly expanding West directly to the American ports threatened the commercial dominion of the St. Lawrence. A new water route from the upper Lakes to the St. Lawrence was essential if Upper and Lower Canada were to share in the rising prosperity of the period.

Charles Shirreff and his sons, Alexander and Robert, of Fitzroy Harbour on the Ottawa were strong advocates of the development of a waterway somewhere south of the old Lake Nipissing route, and so were among the first proponents of settlement on the Canadian Shield. Charles Shirreff believed that a canal could be built from the Ottawa to a river which he called the Moose (probably the Moon) which falls into Georgian Bay. The Shirreffs were not idle dreamers. In 1829 Alexander Shirreff made an exploratory trip across the Shield from the Ottawa to Penetanguishene and back to the Ottawa, and unlike his predecessors the Royal Engineers he studied the quality of the land for settlement. His report[1] was enthusiastic, though one suspects that it may have been affected by preconceived conclusions.

Alexander's brother, Robert Shirreff, was even more interested in the possibility of land settlement and formed a connection with an English company that was attempting to obtain a large grant of wild land in Canada. A group of English and Irish gentlemen in London, operating under several corporate names, such as the Ottawa Land Company, and the North American Colonial Association, tried desperately to obtain from the British government a tract of land somewhere south of Lake Nipissing and in the rear of the then-existing Newcastle and Midland Districts. With such a grant, they argued, they could afford homes for the destitute of the British Isles and at the same time open communications between the Ottawa and Lake Huron. Negotiations, however, came to an abrupt halt in 1835 when the British

[1] Alexander Shirreff, "Topographical Notices of the Country Lying between the Mouth of the Rideau and Penetanguishine on Lake Huron," Literary and Historical Society of Quebec, *Transactions*, 1st Series, II (1831), pp. 243-309, and map at end of vol.

government announced that it was not expedient to establish any new land company in Canada.

Meanwhile the government of Upper Canada had not been entirely inactive. On January 4, 1834, the House of Assembly requested that the Lieutenant Governor, Sir John Colborne, send out an exploring expedition to survey the land from Lake Huron, fifty or sixty miles into the heart of the country, and that it examine the soil, timber, and water, as well as geology and mineralogy. In 1835 a party under Lieutenants John Carthew and F. H. Baddeley carried out extensive survey work north from Lake Simcoe into the Parry Sound district. Following this, in a further search for a water route, David Thompson, of western Canadian fame, explored the Muskoka and Madawaska in 1837. Thompson, who continually observed the quality of the soil, had high praise for some regions, but discouraging comments on others. His conclusion, however, was optimistic: that there were 1,024,000 acres of land along the Muskoka fit for settlement, which would provide 200 acres to each of 5120 families.

Less dramatic than the explorers were the land surveyors who as early as the 1820's were gradually working north from the comparatively level lands of the south, and west from the Ottawa onto the edge of the Shield. As adventurous settlers spread up the Ottawa River, townships were surveyed and organized, McNab, Horton, Ross, and Westmeath being among the first. Surveyors in the southern part of Muskoka and Haliburton in the 1820's were critical of what they saw, and their unfavourable reports, combined with the Rebellion of 1837 and the Union of the Canadas in 1841, seem to have turned the attention of the government from the unsettled lands for a considerable number of years.

One problem that brought anxiety to governments and settlers alike when other areas were opened for settlement, especially in the American and Canadian West, was absent in the Ottawa-Georgian Bay tract. Although certain Indian bands laid claim to the land, they lived mainly south of the Shield, and were accustomed to go north only at certain seasons of the year to hunt, trap, or make maple sugar. In 1850 the Robinson Treaty with the Ojibways cleared the government's title from Penetanguishene to Lake Superior and included hitherto unceded lands in Muskoka and Haliburton. Two years later the Legislative Assembly requested of the Governor General that a survey be made of the newly-ceded territory, and that certain sections be set aside as free grants.

Any verdict on the wisdom of opening these lands on the Shield must be made in the light of political and economic conditions prevailing in the 1850's, not in that of the agricultural economy of the twentieth century. By the middle of the nineteenth century the best lands in the southern part of Upper Canada were settled, and the diminishing waste lands at the disposal of the government had become of immediate concern. The unemployed in the older parts of the province, the farm labourers, the benevolent societies disturbed by poverty in their own cities and in the British Isles, all looked speculatively to the north. Even if the government had opposed the opening of the land it is doubtful how long it could have withstood the importunities of the citizens. But members of the government and the business community had little desire to oppose it. Across the border they saw the growing population and rising prosperity of the United States, while they watched with dismay British immigrants going directly to the United States or lingering in Canada for only a brief interval before moving on to promises of higher wages or cheap farms.

When the government decided to open the northern lands for settlement it realized that it must provide some reasonable means of access to the grants. Accordingly, in 1854 a plan of road building was announced that would open the whole tract from the Ottawa River to Georgian Bay. The Ottawa-Opeongo Road was to run from the Ottawa to the mouth of the Magnetawan on Georgian Bay, and Bell's Line was to parallel this road part of the way, some distance to the south. However nothing but the eastern section of the Ottawa-Opeongo was completed; Bell's Line was replaced by the Peterson Road still further south, which in turn never reached the goal of its planners. More successful were roads that led directly to the desirable areas for settlement, such as the Hastings, Bobcaygeon, Muskoka, and Parry Sound Roads.

The roads were a constant source of trouble between settlers and government authorities. Naturally the settlers, busy clearing their farms, did as little free labour as possible, while the government grudged the mounting expenses for roads that brought little political acclaim. Road-building techniques which had been developed in the more level lands to the south were not suitable among the rocks and hills of the Shield, and almost as soon as a road was completed it was cut to pieces again by the heavy loads of provisions for the lumber camps or by the settlers' possessions. Bridges were carried away by spring floods or burned in the frequent forest fires. Swamps posed a special problem, and the solution – the corduroy road – received the same abuse in these regions as it had received in an earlier day in the south. Many roads, indeed, were so bad that they were known as "winter roads", passable only when ice and snow had congealed the swamp, and carpeted the corduroy, stumps, and rocks. If the road were not in constant use, undergrowth rapidly reclaimed the land.

For good or ill, in 1859 a number of townships in Muskoka and Haliburton were opened for sale. The terms of settlement at that time were determined by the "Act to Amend the Law for the Sale and the Settlement of the Public Lands" (1853), under which the price of land was fixed from time to time and certain free grants were permitted to settlers in the vicinity of a public road. As soon as the townships were opened would-be home owners selected their lots and proceeded to take possession. They were not, however, the first inhabitants in the area. Fur traders had long been accustomed to hunt and trap there and a few had built cabins that served more or less as permanent homes. Certain adventurous settlers had even entered the still restricted lands and cleared small farms at strategic spots on the major waterways, or at mill sites, or on some of the pockets of rich soil; a few had located on the roads leading to the timber limits where they grew provisions for the camps. Surveyors and road builders found many squatters who had been in possession of their land for a number of years.

In spite of the publicity in Canada and abroad the number of settlers increased slowly and many of those who did purchase land had no way to earn the few dollars required for payments. Influenced by these circumstances, in 1868 the province of Ontario passed the "Free Grants and Homestead Act" which opened certain areas in Algoma and Nipissing, and between the Ottawa River and Georgian Bay, to all settlers who "shall have cleared and have under cultivation at least fifteen acres of the said land, whereof at least two acres shall be cleared and cultivated annually during the five years next after the date of the location, to be computed from such date, and have built a house thereon fit for habitation at least sixteen feet by twenty feet, and shall have actually and continuously resided upon and cultivated the said land for the term of five years." The government advertised its free lands widely in the British Isles and in Europe and even assisted the immigrants with passage money.

Meanwhile another plan had been developed to hasten the settlement of the country. On January 13, 1859, "Regulations for the Sale and Management of the Public Lands" announced that land would be sold "en bloc" at one half dollar per acre. The lumber manufacturers of the Ottawa viewed the scheme with "anxiety and alarm", but in spite of their protests the government went ahead. After lengthy negotiations the Canadian Land and Emigration Company of London, England, obtained ten townships, of which one, Longford, was in Victoria county, and nine were in Haliburton: Dysart, Dudley, Harcourt, Guilford, Harburn, Bruton, Havelock, Eyre, and Clyde. Although the Company offered settlers some advantages not available to those who obtained their lands direct from the government, purchasers were few. The area was remote from transportation, the soil was typical of the Shield, and after 1868 the lure of free grants in other parts was almost irresistible. The Canadian Land and Emigration Company was never financially successful and finally after the second world war it surrendered its charter.

The government's action in opening for settlement lands not suitable for farming, was more than matched by its inept handling of the forests. The timber on the Ottawa-Huron tract was almost priceless in value and should have provided an enduring asset for future generations, but almost nothing was done to preserve it. Forests were ruthlessly destroyed by lumberman and settler alike. The cutting of the pine and the clearing of farms that went on side by side during the latter half of the nineteenth century gave rise to a tangle of relationships between lumberman and settler that were both good and ill. The lumberman needed shantymen for the camps, as well as a supply of hay and oats. If no settlers were in the neighbourhood, men and supplies had to be brought long distances over the "tote" roads such as the one leading from the Ottawa River to the upper reaches of the Petawawa. The settler, in turn, often found that he could not live on the produce of his farm and that he was dependent on work in the camps for his livelihood. When the timber had been cleared the settler lost his market and his winter job at the same time, and often had to abandon his clearing and follow the lumberman.

There were less desirable aspects to the relationship. Each blamed the other for the forest fires that destroyed the timber and the settler's home, and for the heavy loads that cut the roads into deep ruts. The ownership of the pine on the settler's land was a constant source of friction. The law in force in 1853 gave the ownership of the timber on the grant to the settler even though the land might be within the boundaries of a timber limit already under license for cutting. Bogus settlers made one payment on the land, cut the pine, and moved on to another lot. Progressively such abuses and the lumbermen's protests led to the curtailment of the settlers' rights. By the "Free Grants and Homestead Act" of 1868 the settler's right to cut pine on his land before issuance of the final patent, was limited to those trees necessary for building fences or for clearing the land. The emotions of the settler who saw lumbermen strip his land of pine, without any compensation, need not be described.

When the settler took up his newly-acquired grant he met problems not very different from those of earlier settlers to the south, but aggravated by the rough terrain and the extremes of climate. With his belongings, perhaps accompanied by wife and children, he rode to the end of the railway, then proceeded by water or road. Even if wagons were available, lack of money sometimes forced him to walk and carry his provisions on his back. When he reached the grant, the first task was to make a small clearing and put up a log shanty. Gradually a few acres were chopped, logging bees were held to burn the fallen timber, and crops were planted between the charred stumps.

Every season of the year brought its own problems. The bitter cold of winter was a new experience for many of the settlers, who soon learned that even a one-room cabin required incredible quantities of fuel, and that sheep and cattle had to be provided with shelter and food if they were to survive the cold and snow. The frosts that lingered late in May and returned in September restricted the variety of crops. Spring brought the inevitable hordes of insects, especially black flies and mosquitoes, and the violent storms in summer struck terror into the heart of the settler's wife who feared not only the lightning but the likelihood of falling trees. Town people and tourists could talk of the health-giving properties of the climate, but the newcomer on the free grant, often inadequately supplied with shelter, clothing, and food, must often have longed for a more temperate land.

The settler, when he began to clear the land for his first crop, came face to face with the actuality of the Canadian Shield: rock, stones, and thin soil. One of the bitterest critics, Joseph Dale, wrote in his *Canadian Land Grants in 1874* (London, 1875): "Those spots, which by desperate labour have been cleared by hand, reveal to the emigrant nothing but rock, rock, rock, covered here and there with a thin stratum of vegetable mould, without any secondary strata whatever". At the other extreme were claims such as "a squash that would fill the bottom of a small Donkey cart . . . cucumbers a yard in length", and three hundred bushels of turnips grown from two ounces of seed.

Although promoters of the district and sportsmen constantly talked of the fish and game, few of the settlers found it of much help. Here and there a man made a little money by trapping or hunting, but the majority had neither the time nor equipment necessary. Mrs. H. B. King, author of *Letters from Muskoka, by an Emigrant Lady* (London, 1878), said: "the truth must be told that when settlers, gentle or simple, are engaged in the daily toil of grubbing, and as it were scratching the earth for bread, it is difficult to find a day's leisure for the gentlemanly recreation of shooting."

One of the settlers' greatest enemies was loneliness, the loneliness of a small clearing hemmed in by dark, towering forests. Women left on the farms with small children, when the men went to camp in the winter, were much affected by it, as were the well-to-do families who had known a very different social life in England. As Mrs. King wrote,

> None but those who have experienced it can ever realise the utter weariness and isolation of Bush-life. The daily recurrence of the same laborious tasks, the want of time for mental culture, the absence of congenial intercourse with one's fellow-creatures, the many hours of unavoidable solitude, the dreary unbroken silence of the immense forest which closes round the small clearings like a belt of iron; all these things ere long press down the most buoyant spirit, and superinduce a kind of dull despair.

Like all people in a new land the settlers tended to re-establish the life they had known before. Some, who had come from city slums or poverty-line farms, were satisfied with nothing more than food and shelter, supplemented only too often with whiskey, the bane of pioneer settlements. Many others, however, were well-educated, from middle class families, and even though the new home was only a two-room cabin, and the furniture home-made, it was as clean and comfortable as the women could achieve. Scarcely were the walls raised when there was talk of a school and a church. Often a group of families at first could do no more than gather the children together for lessons from some educated member of the community, and on Sundays meet for Christian worship in one of the homes. As time passed, Protestant and Roman Catholic churches were built, and clergymen ranged over the wilderness visiting remote settlers and the men in the lumber camps.

Social life developed rapidly, differing in form from one neighbourhood to the other according to the ethnic origin and cultural background of the leading families of the community. Raising bees, logging bees, wool-picking bees, socials, dances, amateur dramatics, cricket matches, and regattas were common. Newspapers were established in the larger villages, and libraries were set up at several centres, sometimes under the auspices of the Mechanics Institutes. Fortunately, too, not everyone who settled on the Shield tried to make his living on a farm. Villages grew up at strategic points, especially at the junction of a road and a waterway, and attracted labourers, tradesmen, and professional men. Few of these endured the hardships of the settlers on the land grants.

In the early days the settlers were mainly from Ontario and the British Isles, with lesser numbers from countries such as Germany, Iceland, Norway, Sweden, Denmark, Switzerland, and surprisingly, the United States. French Canadians were found in many sections, but especially in Renfrew county. Groups of families, non-British in origin, often settled together, such as the Germans in Ryde and Morrison townships, Icelandic settlers in Watt and Cardwell, Scandinavians in Watt and Monteith.

Considerable variety developed in patterns of settlement. In Ryerson township the government offered farms for sale on which a few acres had been cleared and a house built ready for the settler and his family. In Parry Sound village "Governor" Beatty who had acquired most of the land, sold it only to those who would agree to a regulation prohibiting the sale of alcohol. Here and there an enterprising Englishman offered to teach newcomers the art of scientific farming for two hundred pounds a year, and incredible as it may seem, found pupils.

Business men and farmers alike realized from the beginning that nothing more than a hand-to-mouth existence was possible without railway connections with the markets to the south. Lumbermen and settlers forgot their differences and worked together for the establishment of railways – railways to run east and west to connect the Ottawa River and Georgian Bay, railways to run north into Muskoka, Parry Sound, and Haliburton. Unfortunately, though it was an age of railway building, the Shield had many years to wait. The Northern Railway reached Gravenhurst only in 1875, Bracebridge in 1885, and Huntsville in 1886; the Victoria Railway Company did not reach Haliburton until 1878, and it was not until 1896 that the Canada Atlantic finally connected the Ottawa River with Parry Sound on Georgian Bay.

The development of railway transportation in Canada contributed to the small, temporary success of agriculture on the Canadian Shield, but eventually also contributed to its decline. Railways opened rival lands – the prairies, level, treeless, fertile, and free of stones. The West beckoned, and many a family in Muskoka, Haliburton, and Renfrew lost its young people, even the more adventurous of its older people, to Manitoba, Saskatchewan, or the Red River valley of Dakota. Farms that had taken years to clear often found no purchaser and were abandoned. In time, the soil, no longer protected by the forest, was washed away, leaving bare rock and stones, and on the more fertile land, the trees grew again, obliterating both farm and road.

Not only did the railway open the rival lands of the West, but with its twentieth century allies – the motor car, paved road, and airplane – was a major factor in revolutionizing the agricultural economy. With the development of specialized farming and mechanization of equipment, little place was left for the self-sufficient, marginal-subsistence farm found only too often on the Canadian Shield. For some of the rural townships such as Cardwell, Stisted, Christie, and Ryerson, census returns show an almost continuous drop since the beginning of the century.

A decline in the lumber trade coincided with the loss of rural population. For the first half century the lumber trade had given a false impression of the success of settlement, not only by providing the farmers with winter jobs and markets for their produce, but by building sawmills which encouraged the growth of villages. When in the early 1900's the best of the forests had been cut, and less and less timber came down the streams in the spring drives, the mills closed one by one. While the population of Ontario increased over seventy-two per cent between 1901 and 1941, Haliburton, Muskoka, Parry Sound, and Renfrew recorded only a negligible gain.

Business men realized that if the area was to prosper new sources of revenue had to be found. From the earliest days promoters had been pointing to the water power resources and to cheap land as inducements for industry, and the more optimistic had never abandoned hope of discovering mineral wealth in the Precambrian rock. Of more immediate monetary importance, however, were the beauty of lakes and rivers in summer and autumn, the deep snow of winter, the fish and game, combined with the proximity of a thickly-populated district to the south from which to draw visitors. The tourist trade developed from an occasional vacationer in the 1860's to a major industry at the present time. The wisdom of the government of Ontario in setting aside Algonquin Park in 1893 to some extent atoned for the inept handling of the area a half century before.

Lumbering and farming, though less evident than in the early days, are adjusting to the changed economic conditions. Markets have developed for woods that were despised in the heyday of the red and white pine, and reforestation is reclaiming once-cleared land. Farms on the fertile soil found in wide areas of Renfrew county and in more scattered sections of other districts continue successfully with stock raising, dairying, and field crops, but many of the farms on barren soil have long been unoccupied. Since the second world war the population that had remained almost stationary for decades, is once more rising as it did a hundred years ago, but this time it is no longer dependent on an indiscriminate agricultural settlement that wasted the resources of the Canadian Shield.

BIBLIOGRAPHICAL NOTE

Cummings, H. R., *Early Days in Haliburton* (Toronto, 1962).
De la Fosse, F. M., *English Bloods, by Roger Vardon* (Ottawa, 1930).
Greening, W. E., *The Ottawa* (Toronto, 1961).
Lower, A. R. M., *The North American Assault on the Canadian Forest* (Toronto, 1938).
Murray, F. B., ed., *Muskoka and Haliburton, 1615-1875; A Collection of Documents* (Toronto, 1963).
Price, Mrs. Carl and Kennedy, C. C., *Notes on the History of Renfrew County* (Pembroke, 1961).
Saunders, Audrey, *Algonquin Story* (Toronto, 1947).

Original sources for exploration and settlement are found mainly at the Public Archives of Canada in series such as C and C.O.42; at the Ontario Department of Lands and Forests in surveyors' papers; and at the Ontario Department of Public Records and Archives in Crown Lands Papers, Colonization Road Papers, and other series. Many of the documents relating to Muskoka and Haliburton are printed in F. B. Murray, *Muskoka and Haliburton*, listed above.

PART IV

The Ontario outlook

The Upper Canadian Religious Tradition

John S. Moir

In the course of Ontario's history the period from 1825 to 1850 has an essential unity in both secular and religious spheres. It has its own characteristics that mark it clearly as being different from what went before and what came after. In general terms, the period of the frontier, of scattered and lonely settlement, of early struggle with the Canadian environment, was over by 1825. In the next quarter century Upper Canadian life was dominated by a settled agricultural pattern. It was a period of relatively sophisticated, if rural, living. After 1850 the face of Canada changed rapidly under the impact of a series of interrelated revolutions – revolutions in communication, transportation, politics, economics and every-day living. The age of the railway, the telegraph, daily newspapers, free trade, the political party system, urbanization and industrialization reached Canada at the middle of the nineteenth century. But the years between 1825 and 1850 were still the era of rough roads, horse and saddle, weekly papers, factional politics and, above all, of the farm as the backbone of the Upper Canadian way of life.

The religious scene in the period from 1825 to 1850 displays several distinct features, most of which have become part of a living Canadian tradition. In the first place, Upper Canada was almost exclusively a Christian community. The pagan Indians were the only notable exception to this characteristic. The Christian churches, of course, were and still are transplants from Europe, although significant adaptations had been made to meet the challenges or demands of the North American environment. The next characteristic is that Upper Canada was predominantly Protestant, with a strong strain of puritanism. Further, from the earliest days of settlement, Canadian religious life was also pluralistic – there was no single national church, but instead many denominations were represented. This fact in turn gave strength to one of the most powerful of Upper Canadian religious beliefs – the belief in voluntarism, or the separation of church and state. Canadians have never pushed this belief to its logical conclusions with the thoroughness of the Americans, but during these twenty-five years, voluntarism did displace any conviction carried from Europe that a church establishment should, or could, be created in Canada. Voluntarism was only one aspect of the drive for religious equality that periodically convulsed the province, embittered religious and political life, and had a direct bearing on the Rebellion of 1837. Equal treatment for all denominations, privileges for none – this was the battle cry that carried religion into the politics of Upper Canada. The right of all clergy to perform marriages and burials, equality of opportunity in education, and a total end to the clergy reserves and rectories, those fruitful sources of dissension – these were the main specific issues that arose in the period and gave it a flavour of denominational bitterness that is still too lively a tradition.

This close interconnection of religion and politics, from the appearance of John Strachan's Ecclesiastical Chart in 1827 to the secularization of the clergy reserves in 1854, has created another tradition that needs qualification. That popular tradition equates religious reformism with political reformism in Upper Canada, a generalization based on historical part-truths. True, Upper Canadian Methodists and William Lyon Mackenzie were the most vocal exponents of reform until the Rebellion of 1837, but their objectives were parallel rather than identical. They agreed on the need for religious freedom and equality, but beyond that the basically conservative Methodists had little interest, and indeed, much objection to Mackenzie's radicalism. Two years after the Rebellion a prominent Upper Canadian Reformer stated that the supporters of his party were voluntarists almost without exception, that they included Baptists, Methodists, secession Presbyterians, Congregationalists and Quakers, while Anglicans, most Roman Catholics, and members of the Church of Scotland were usually Tories. There is no reason to reject this political categorization by denominations, but it must be kept in mind that it is a generalization. Robert Baldwin, leader of the post-Rebellion Reform Party, was a staunch Anglican, as were many other Reformers. The one ideal that united men of all churches, but particularly the so-called dissenters, was voluntarism.

The most marked characteristic of Upper Canadian life was, however, piety. To a greater or lesser degree – usually greater – all Christians in Upper Canada were devout, God-fearing and church-going. More than this, they made their religious beliefs and their religious practices a part of every-day life, as opposed to a Sunday-only religion. Every event, every custom was put into a religious framework and this "religiosity" is still very much in evidence. A related aspect of the Upper Canadian religious outlook that was basic to all these specific attitudes was the generally accepted belief in the operation of Providence. Many events which a scientific mind would credit to mere chance were in that day assumed to be the workings of divine Providence.

Religious attitudes have an important bearing on people's tastes. If luxury is sinful, rough furniture should be godly furniture; plain and modest clothing will be preferred to fopperies; the human voice raised in praise will be more acceptable than any swelling anthem from a great organ; and a log chapel will seem more becoming than an ornamented stone church. Examples of such interrelation of faith and physical surroundings were conspicuous on every hand in Upper Canada. No doubt the more simple life of a rural society, and a pioneering society, reinforces such appearances, and Upper Canada was just such a rural and pioneer colony in that period. This, when joined to the predominance of Protestantism in Upper Canada, meant that the religious climate was generally uncongenial to the development of the decorative arts. Only in the Roman Catholic Church, and to a minor extent in the Church of England, are religious sculpture, art and church ornaments and ornamentation to be found. Compared to Quebec, the Ontario heritage of religious art is very poor indeed.

It may seem contradictory to speak of rugged individualism in an age of collective social enterprises such as barn-raising bees. Nevertheless, the Upper Canadian who enjoyed the fellowship of a camp meeting was also a rugged individualist in religion. He believed that his relationship to God was peculiarly his own, however strong the pressure might be to belong to one denomination. This is commonly reflected in the writings of pioneer clergymen. Each writes as though he alone was engaged in the salvation of souls. One gets the false impression that there are no other clergymen and no other denominations to be found in the vineyard where he is labouring so mightily. One also gets the misleading idea that society in that age was unspeakably depraved, that Upper Canada was New World Sodom and Gomorrah. Such fulminations against sin have, of course, been heard from pulpits in all ages and the people of Upper Canada were probably no better or worse than most generations are. Perhaps it is only that the clergy were more outspoken then. But certainly there seemed to be more attention to sins of the flesh than to sins of the spirit.

There is one more tradition that stems from the individualism of that age. In a day when educational opportunities were severely restricted, when pioneer life put a premium on individual initiative, and the practice of do-it-yourself was a necessity rather than a hobby, clergymen were commonly the equals, not the superiors of their congregations. There were very practical advantages in having ministers who preached in every-day language, who understood the problems of sinners. All these factors created a North American tradition, albeit a minor tradition, of religious anti-intellectualism, of reliance on God-ordained rather than man-made and highly educated ministeries.

Two religious objects found in most Upper Canadian homes were a Bible and a portrait of Queen Victoria. I include the Queen's picture because from Victoria's accession a cult of loyalty and devotion to the young monarch existed that had all the fervour of a faith. Disrespect to the royal ikon was considered almost as sinful as mutilating a Holy Bible. A third religious object less frequently seen before 1850 was a picture of King Billy crossing the Boyne. Within the Protestant household the Bible served as a centre of family devotions. Roman Catholic homes would have a cross or crucifix on the wall, but there is no evidence that religious pictures were common. Since card playing, dancing, the reading of novels and even ice skating were widely denounced as dangerous if not sinful pastimes, the Bible was popular reading material in Upper Canada. Biblical allusions sprinkled personal conversation and parliamentary debates in the same way that Victorian England cited the classics.

Personal relations and even household routine in the Upper Canadian family were governed by the religiosity found in Victorian novels. They remembered the Sabbath and kept it holy. On Sunday the whole family, ignoring the extremes of Canada's weather, might walk many miles to church service. But by the 1830's the romantic log chapel was rapidly being replaced by brick structures. The thirties and forties saw tremendous church building activity, probably unequalled in Ontario's history until the period after the second world war. Log churches, built of green timber without any foundations, deteriorated rapidly and were becoming the exception by 1850. The new imposing and permanent churches that reflected the stability and growing affluence of Upper Canada after 1825, still were simple and unadorned inside, Roman Catholic churches being an obvious exception. Outside, the style of architecture showed elements of romanticism – a trend towards such Gothic revival elements as pointed arches and slim buttresses. The short-lived classic revival as it influenced church architecture through collonaded fronts appeared in few Upper Canadian churches and apparently never in rural churches.

The typical "Dissenter" service laid great emphasis on congregational singing, usually unaccompanied, on inspiring and long sermons and on spontaneous prayer. The formalized liturgy of the Anglican and Roman Catholic churches were, of course, exceptions to such spontaneity in church services. The decorum in church we now take for granted was frequently lacking in earlier days. Enthusiastic listeners who punctuated a sermon with loud Amens and Hallelujahs were not the only interruptions. Dogs – valuable assistants and guardians to the pioneers – were often brought into the church where they snarled, snapped and fought for preferred positions around the box stoves that roasted the nearest worshippers but left much of the church miserably cold. When the collection was taken, the average Canadian displayed another characteristic, namely miserliness. All the denominations complained about the small givings of the congregations. One Methodist preacher got the magnificent sum of twenty-five cents for travelling expenses to cover several months. After 1825 poverty could not be used as an excuse for such stinginess, but clergy salaries were unbelievably low – one hundred dollars a year for married Methodist clergy.

The Methodists were mainly responsible for introducing and perpetuating revivalism in Upper Canada. That North American phenomenon, the protracted camp meeting with its fervent praying, dynamic preaching and violently emotional reactions had been known to a generation of Canadians before 1825. In Canada the camp meeting was more conservative than in the United States, but still an unruly affair in the opinion of some contemporaries. The same streak of religious conservatism was even more marked among Canadian Presbyterians, who rejected entirely the American practice of camp meetings. If the original camp meeting promoters had acquired a somewhat more sober gentility by 1850, new evangelical groups had appeared to continue the tradition. Yet after 1850 growing urbanization would transmute the rural camp meeting into the city revival meeting, and, further indication of changing times, the camp meeting would soon take on an interdenominational appearance. So both the memory and the spirit of the camp meetings endured beyond 1850. The Presbyterian long communions that inspired the camp meetings, were common in all parts of North America. They too lasted for several days. Metal communion tokens are one physical relic of the Presbyterian closed communion. The Methodists in turn, as they became more highly organized, practised closed communion – that is, for full members only – and admission was obtained with pasteboard tickets.

Other religious aspects of that second quarter of the nineteenth century were the temperance movement, the founding of the public school system and the growth of denominational colleges. Grain was the main agricultural product of the age, a goodly portion of which was converted into hard liquor. Breweries and distilleries were almost as common as churches, and excessive drinking was undeniably a social problem of great magnitude. By 1851 one hundred distilleries in Upper Canada were producing 1.17 million gallons annually, most of which was consumed by a population of only 952,000, including children! (In the same year Upper Canada had forty-nine breweries.) And that hard liquor was fifty per cent higher in alcohol content than the modern product. Liquor was cheap and readily available. Whiskey for fifty cents a gallon was available at the ubiquitous local taverns or directly from the local distiller if he were closer to hand. From the demon drink stemmed most of the too-prevalent violence and poverty. The interdenominational temperance movements that began in the late 1820's were the popular reaction to this very real, very serious social problem.

In the 1840's the modern relationship of religion to primary education became firmly established in Ontario. The European tradition of denominational schools that had been brought to Upper Canada by the early settlers was replaced by Egerton Ryerson's system of nondenominational public elementary schools. This did not mean that religious influences were excluded, that education became secular. Religion was very much a part of Ryerson's educational plans, but it was Christian in the ecumenical sense rather than sectarian. Bible readings and prayers formed a daily exercise for the pupils; denominational classes in religion were provided for in the weekly school timetable; all clergymen were *ex officio* school visitors, and half of the members of the provincial Board of Education were prominent churchmen.

Part of the pattern of higher education in this province was also established in these years. That colleges should have some religious affiliation was taken for granted by most Canadians, and by 1850 the Churches of England and Scotland and the Wesleyan Methodists had each established one college while the Roman Catholic Church had established two. Admittedly, the Reform Party favoured entirely secular higher education and in 1850 actually nationalized Anglican King's College. But the connection between religion and higher education was already so firmly grounded that the years after 1850 saw the pendulum swing strongly in that direction as other denominations created their own denominational colleges. A minority of Upper Canadians believed that the denominational principle should be extended to elementary education too, but the controversy over separate schools really belongs to a much later period.

If any doubt still remains that the second quarter of the nineteenth century was an age of belief in Upper Canada, there is one final article of proof, drawn this time from the field of geography. One need only look at a map of southern Ontario to discover a rich religious heritage of place-names that reflects the Christianity of those years. How many hamlets in the Ontario countryside bear Biblical names? Salem, Beulah, Hope, Kedron, Zion, Shiloh, Bethel, Bethany, Bethesda, Ebenezer, Korah, Hebron – these are a dozen examples to begin with. Underlying all these factors was the close relation between geography and religious expression in Upper Canada before 1850. Specific areas were settled at different times by settlers who usually had much in common. It is no accident that low church Anglicanism and Free Church Presbyterianism were strongest west of the Niagara Escarpment, that some eighty per cent of one smaller Methodist body were concentrated in Darlington and Clarke townships, that Gaelic sermons were commonly heard only in the regions of Glengarry and the Grand River basin, or that wakes persisted in regions with heavy Irish or Scottish settlement.

It was, then, a period in colonial life when religion was a serious, all pervading – but not necessarily always effective – influence. Religious experience in that period was deeply emotional, expressed in spiritual, mystical terms rather than practical. This fact, when linked to the puritanism of the settlers, explains the scarcity in quantity and quality of religious objects which have survived – all so plain when contrasted to the flamboyant expression of religion in Lower Canada. The quarter century marks the move from sect to church in terms of attitudes, organization and church buildings. As the community consolidated, religion became more genteel – the church one attended, the clothes one wore there, and the propriety and good taste of the worship service acquired social and religious significance.

But even before gentility and decorum appeared, religious expression had always been more conservative than in the United States. The churches were in North America – they reflected North American experience to some extent – but they were, above all, British North American. The twenty-five years from 1825 to 1850 are not birth pangs but growing pains of the churches of Ontario. By 1850 the clergy were becoming professionalized, church buildings were more substantial although not much more ornate, services were becoming more formal and 'decent', but laity remained as miserly as ever. The churches and religious expression of present day Ontario belong far more to the mid and late Victorian age than to the period 1825-1850. Nevertheless, one cannot understand either modern or mid-Victorian Ontario without examining religious attitudes of the early 1800's, for religion is intimately connected to the art, architecture, artifacts and general way of life of every age.

BIBLIOGRAPHICAL NOTE

There is a large body of historical literature regarding religion in Upper Canada before Confederation, but most of it was published many years ago and is therefore out-of-print and rare. Also, most of the writing was specifically denominational, and probably at least half of the volumes concern the Methodists. Several denominations have no printed histories and others are very inadequately served. The study of intellectual history is only in its infancy in Canada, and the number of problems begging for investigation seems endless.

Of modern books, two in particular, are of value for the general reader. They are *The Churches and the Canadian Experience*, edited by John W. Grant (Toronto, 1963), a small paperback volume of essays dealing with various religious traditions, and *The Social Teachings of the Canadian Churches, Protestant . . . before 1850* by William H. Elgee (Toronto, 1964), a well documented examination of religious attitudes on various problems. John S. Moir, *Church and State in Canada – Basic Documents, 1627-1867* (Toronto, 1967) contains three chapters dealing with this aspect of Upper Canada's religious history. Allan Gowan's *Building Canada, an Architectural History of Canadian Life* (Toronto, 1966) contains general material on church architecture, but, in contrast to the Quebec scene, there is a dearth of writing on Ontario church buildings or Ontario religious art or music.

Of the many histories of Canadian Methodism, the best is John Carroll's *Case and his Cotemporaries* (5 vols., 1867-77) which contains much descriptive and anecdotal material. A recent scholarly book, *Parsons and Politics* (Toronto, 1962) by Goldwin French compares Methodist development in Canada and the Maritimes to 1855.

William Gregg's *History of the Presbyterian Church in the Dominion of Canada* (Toronto, 1885) and his *Short History of the Presbyterian Church* (Toronto, 1892) are formal accounts with few references to religious opinions or practices. Better descriptive material on Presbyterian life can be found in W. D. McIntosh, *One Hundred Years in the Zorra Church*, (Toronto, 1930). Roman Catholic religious life is described in detail in W. P. Bull's *From Macdonell to McGuigan* (Toronto, 1939) and in W. R. Harris' *The Catholic Church in the Niagara Peninsula* (Toronto, 1895). The only comprehensive account of the Baptists is E. R. Fitch's *The Baptists of Canada* (Toronto, 1911) but it is too brief to be able to deal with problems in depth. There is no history of the Congregationalists in Canada. A good introduction to the various "Plain Folk" groups is G. E. Reaman, *Trail of the Black Walnut* (Toronto, 1957; Toronto, 1966). A recent useful book by A. G. Dorland, *Former Days and Quaker Ways* (Picton, 1965) is an interesting account of this group. *The Cross in Canada* (Toronto, 1966) edited by John S. Moir, is an anthology of short readings on various aspects of the life of the Christian Church throughout Canada's history.

The largest source of religious history in Ontario is still the numerous biographies of church figures – too numerous to list here. With the exception of C. B. Sissons' *Life and Letters of Egerton Ryerson* (2 vols., Toronto, 1937-47), these are invariably old and generally of limited historical value, but extensive reading of these books will reveal much detail about religious attitudes and practices that has never been extracted and organized. For specific subjects in the religious field consult the *Encylopedia Canadiana.*

Educational Leadership in Ontario, 1867-1967

Robert M. Stamp

The formative years in the history of public education in Ontario are the years before Confederation. Under the guidance of Superintendent of Education Egerton Ryerson, acts of the Legislature in 1846 and 1850 had begun the establishment of the Ontario elementary school system as we know it today. Similar steps had been taken to organize the provincial secondary school system through legislation in 1853 and 1865. Ryerson's legislative triumphs in 1871 merely added the finishing touches. In that year the "common" schools were officially designated as "public" schools, the financing of elementary education at the municipal level was made entirely dependent on a compulsory property tax, and minimum attendance laws were introduced. At the secondary level, the old "grammar" schools became "high" schools or collegiate institutes, and a broader curriculum was introduced.

The division of authority between the provincial department of education and the local school boards was also clearly delineated by the time of Confederation. Ryerson had set up a strong central authority to prepare regulations and curricula and to control the quality of teaching through certification and inspection. But he also believed that no system could be successful without involving the citizens of the local community; he had left to municipal boards such responsibilities as the engagement of teachers and the maintenance of schools.

Many of the emotional battles over education had been settled by 1867. In the struggle between church and state for control of schools, the state had emerged with a clear victory. Under Ryerson's system of government-controlled education henceforth there would be no special privileges for the Church of England, and the Roman Catholic separate schools were an integral part of the provincial system. Likewise, the struggle between American and British influences was largely a thing of the past. Ryerson had shown that it was possible to incorporate into the Ontario school system the best ideas from the United States, from Britain, and from other countries of the world. If it was too early to call the Ontario system a "Canadian" system of education, nevertheless the province was well on its way to developing such a system.

There is virtually no question of Ryerson's leadership in educational matters in pre-Confederation Ontario. When he visited district or county conventions he came as a lawgiver, either to explain existing regulations, promulgate new ones, or obtain assent for those for which he wished to secure legislation. Only after the grammar schools became efficient did Ryerson meet at teachers' conventions men who were intellectually his equals and who were ready to criticize his policy and, when necessary, to give him wholesome advice. Robin Harris' recent essay "Egerton Ryerson" in *Our Living Tradition*, Third Series, proves quite convincingly that Ryerson deserves the title of "father of the Ontario system of education" in every sense of the term – that he was responsible for conceiving the system as well as establishing and administering it.

. . . . .

It is true that the pre-Confederation years in Ontario educational history have considerable appeal to the historian and to the general reader. Ryerson's accomplishments and his dominant personality have continued to attract the attention of later generations. Not content to confine himself merely to school matters, as so many later educators did, Ryerson moved as a giant back and forth among the fields of education, politics, and religion. The political and religious problems with which he concerned himself seem infinitely more appealing to the student of history than the practical pedagogical issues with which later educational administrators had to deal. So much attention has been paid to these earlier years at the expense of the later ones, that the important developments in Ontario education during the past ninety years since Ryerson's retirement have tended to be overlooked. The only post-Confederation educational issues that have been adequately treated are those dealing with such sensitive cultural and religious issues as Roman Catholic separate schools and French-language schools.

And yet a brief examination of the period reveals some equally interesting themes in Ontario educational history that could profitably be explored. With the political, technological, economic, and social changes of the past century have come profound changes in educational thought and practice. In the late nineteenth century the impact of Canadian nationalism, of science, of industrialization, of urbanization, of the temperance movement, of the movement for women's rights, all had their effects on Ontario education. So did the pedagogy of educational reformers such as Pestalozzi, Herbart, Froebel, and Dewey. Moving later into the twentieth century, the expansion of democracy, the impact of two world wars, the most serious economic depression of modern times, and a complete revolution in the world-wide balance of political power, have all affected the philosophy and practice of education in this province. The pre-Confederation years in Ontario educational history have been well examined; the time has come to look in more detail at the past hundred years.

One aspect of Ontario educational history, and its relation to general historical development, that has not been explored is the question of educational leadership in a widening democracy. Over the past century political democracy has expanded to such an extent that today there are few barriers in the way of universal participation in the democratic process. At the same time the system of public education has been democratized. This is especially true at the secondary level. One hundred years ago the secondary schools of this province were catering almost exclusively to the needs of the few who were bound for university; today they seek to provide equal educational opportunities for all the children of all the people. What is the connection between a broadening political democracy and a broadening democratic spirit in education?

Who are the individuals in Ontario educational history who have kept the schools moving along a democratic path in tune with the widening political democracy of society as a whole? The system has not stood still since Ryerson's retirement, ninety years ago. New men have appeared with each succeeding generation and have fashioned education in accordance with their own views in the light of new developments. This paper will examine the leadership of five Ontario educators – George Paxton Young, George Ross, James Hughes, John Seath, and John Althouse – in an attempt to show how each has brought to the educational system the educational principles that society as a whole has increasingly embraced over the past century.

. . . . .

George Paxton Young (1819-1889), Presbyterian clergyman and later University of Toronto philosophy professor, was a contemporary of Ryerson's who exerted a decided influence over the democratic evolution of the Ontario high school in the years immediately following Confederation. Ryerson had concentrated more on the elementary or common schools than on the secondary schools, but Young attacked the problem of the aristocratic high schools following his appointment as grammar school inspector in 1864. Young's reports for the years 1865, 1866, and 1867 are landmarks in Ontario educational history; they exposed the defects of the existing system and suggested the necessary changes. Generally his reports were merciful to the teachers and put the blame on the laws and regulations which permitted the schools so often to be filled with pupils who could not profit by the instruction given. The most potent cause of trouble was the Act of 1865 which apportioned the government grant to grammar schools on the basis of the number of pupils in each school who were taking Latin. Throughout the province the curriculum remained predominantly classical, English was neglected, and pupils were being admitted prematurely in order to swell the enrolment.

The solution Young advocated was to revolutionize the aim and purpose of the grammar school. "The time has come," he reported in 1867, "for the organization of a different sort of school, from either the existing Grammar School or the existing Common School." The idea of a classical high school for the elite must give place to a high school for the people, laying stress on the more practical subjects such as English and science. Most of his suggestions were incorporated into the Acts of 1871, 1874, and 1876. The name "grammar" school, with its aristocratic and elitist connotations, was changed to the more democratic-sounding "high" school. Largely under his guidance, the secondary schools of Ontario were given a degree of uniformity and centralized control, and a more modern purpose and curriculum, that enabled them to fill the educational needs of a greater proportion of the population.

But men of Young's type were not to be satisfied with the erection of a system. His criticism of secondary education went far deeper. Young was acquainted with the Herbartian thesis that history and literature are subjects of pre-eminent importance in developing good human relationships and good citizenship. Thus in the teaching of classics, English literature, and history, Young championed teaching for the sake of understanding and appreciation, rather than for the sake of learning by rote abstract grammatical laws and historical facts. Similarly, what he prized in science was the method of scientific study; he believed that a single scientific subject adequately taught could give an insight into the principles of logical reasoning which were of great general value. Thus, in his attempts to modernize the curriculum, his object was not necessarily to ensure a larger range of subjects, but a more thorough and mature training in what was taught.

George W. Ross (1841-1914) is best remembered in Canadian history as Premier of Ontario from 1899 to 1905 and later as Liberal party leader in the Senate at Ottawa. But for sixteen years prior to his term as premier Ross served as Minister of Education in the provincial cabinet. Ross had more practical experience with the schools than any other education minister has had in Ontario history. For fifteen years before entering politics he had been a teacher and inspector in the western part of the province; he had worked under Ryerson and was familiar with his policies. As minister he became such an indefatigable promoter of the Ontario education system as the world's best that many people came to take his boastful claim for granted without question.

Ross' regime is usually remembered because of the controversies over French-language schools, Catholic separate schools, and religion in the public schools that arose at the time. Ross came under heavy criticism from the increasingly militant Protestant extremists in the legislature and in the press. They deplored his failure to stamp out French-language schools in the Ottawa valley, his extension of privileges to Catholic separate schools, and his willingness to accept suggestions from the Catholic bishop of Toronto regarding Bible readings in the public elementary schools. But Ross should also be remembered as the person who did more than anyone else in the years following Ryerson to ensure that the products of the Ontario schools could play a useful and vital role in the new Canadian democratic nation that was being created.

Ross had been a member of the Dominion Parliament for eleven years prior to his assumption of the provincial education portfolio in 1883. During these years the movement for a wider franchise was under way; before his death he was to see the attainment of virtually complete manhood suffrage and the movement for women's votes become a live issue. Was the Canadian public prepared for the responsibilities that universal suffrage would bring? Were the schools doing as much as they might to prepare young people for participation in the democratic political process? Ross emphasized the fact that "it must not be forgotten that public and high schools are public institutions, maintained for the purpose of developing the highest type of citizenship." The school system must prepare young people "to be better citizens than their fathers and to prepare them for the duties of national life which are pressing upon us." People should be educated "in order that they might rightly discharge their political obligations."[1]

Ross was also aware of the lack of patriotism and national feeling that existed in the new country. His years at Ottawa had given him more of a national vision than most Ontario educators possessed. He witnessed with dismay the decline of the young nationalist group known as Canada First; he deplored the willingness of so many Canadians to embrace the idea of commercial union with the United States; and though intensely proud of his Scottish ancestry he could not support the idea that patriotism to Ottawa would somehow weaken the imperial bond. Again he turned to the schools: were they doing all that they might to foster a sense of pride in the new Canadian nation? In his presidential address to the Ontario Teachers' Association in 1884 he deplored the fact that Canadian history was almost entirely ignored in Canadian schools, and he believed that in ignoring it we were depreciating our country and its heritage. During his administration the teaching of Canadian history was made compulsory in Ontario elementary schools and a long step forward was taken to stress Canadian achievements in the schools in addition to British achievements.

James L. Hughes (1846-1935), inspector of public schools for the city of Toronto from 1874 to 1914, was responsible for introducing the kindergarten into Canadian education. The kindergarten concept was based on the pedagogy of Friedrich Froebel, and Hughes became one of the leading disciples of Froebel in North America. Froebelianism stood for the "child-centred" school, for growth through creative and expressive activity. On this continent, especially, it led to a new concept of education concerned with every aspect of the pupil's growth and maturity, or, as it came to be phrased, with the development of the whole child. Hughes believed that Froebel's method of introducing the young child to schooling through play and self-inspired activity was a necessary beginning step in helping the individual develop his full potential in a democratic society. Canadian educators before Hughes had been at least aware of the child as the forgotten factor in education, but more sympathy for the children in school had been shown by the medical profession than by teachers or educational administrators.

Hughes faced a formidable task in selling the kindergarten concept to the Toronto public. The idea of education "for" the child rather than "of" the child was unintelligible to most people at the time, and many who did comprehend felt that the "play" approach in the kindergartens was not serious enough to be called education and thus a waste of taxpayers' money. Yet as soon as he dared, Hughes included in his annual report the recommendation of kindergartens as the only solution to the unsatisfactory nature of primary education. Each year he ended his report with the identical wording: "It must ultimately become part of our system, and I trust it may soon."

[1] Ontario Educational Association, *Proceedings*, 1896 and 1897.

But since Hughes was the outstanding Canadian exponent of Froebel, it is not surprising that Toronto could claim to be the second city in the world (after St. Louis, Missouri) to make the kindergarten a part of its regular school system. As early as 1878, through Hughes' promptings, the two morning newspapers of the city carried arguments in favour of the adoption of Froebelian principles through the establishment of kindergartens. After an exchange of visits with kindergarten experts in St. Louis, a Toronto teacher who had been sent there for training took charge of the first public school kindergarten in Canada in 1883. The number of kindergartens multiplied year by year and spread to other cities. By 1900 there were 120 kindergartens in the province attended by over 11,000 pupils; within the next decade the number had risen to 194 classes with 20,667 pupils.

The establishment of kindergartens made Toronto, and Hughes, famous throughout the English-speaking educational world. In the course of years Hughes spoke at scores of American school conventions and was instrumental in the adoption of kindergartens by school boards throughout the United States. Hundreds of delegations of American educators visited Toronto schools during these years to see the kindergartens, and Hughes, in action. Perhaps the peak of his influence came in 1891 when he persuaded the National Education Association of the United States to hold its annual meeting in Toronto. His influence on American education dispels the notion that the interchange of educational ideas between Canada and the United States has always been a one-way street. At times, American educators have had much to learn from the Canadian experience.

"He pulled the Toronto public system from a backward and lagging pace in the educational march to the very forefront of the educational procession," relates the official history of the Toronto Board of Education. "Long before he resigned office, Toronto's leadership in education was felt far beyond the province."

John Seath (1844-1919), superintendent of education in the provincial ministry from 1906 until his death, continued the work begun by Young a generation before in broadening the course offerings of the secondary school to suit the needs of a changing society. By the late nineteenth century the effects of the Industrial Revolution were apparent throughout Ontario. The trends towards urbanization and large-scale factory enterprise were in full bloom. As work opportunities in industry increased, more people with practical training were needed. Keen competition in world trade was developing, yet the decline of the apprenticeship system in Ontario left a gap in the providing of skilled tradesmen for industry.

Seath's main idea regarding the Ontario educational system was that, as the schools had been providing a life training for the professional classes, it was their duty now to provide it for the industrial classes as well. The schools had been concerned about the intellect; now it was time to think also about the hand. The country had spent large sums of money on the education of doctors and lawyers; why should it not do the same for carpenters, mechanics, and farmers? Of course this was not a new idea; what was new to Ontario was that Seath did not allow the idea to remain as a mere notion but that he set out diligently to make it a reality.

Following his appointment as superintendent, Seath visited Britain, France, Germany, Switzerland, and the United States, as he had done before, to study vocational education in operation in those countries. Then Seath brought out his famous report, *Education for Industrial Purposes* (Toronto, 1911), a landmark in Canadian educational history. "In any system of primary and secondary education," argued Seath, "both the hand and the brain should be trained to act together and to help each other. Without this training the education would be incomplete." He recommended the immediate establishment of technical high schools, the appointment of a Director of Industrial and Technical Schools for the province, and joint financing of the programme by municipal, provincial, and federal governments. Upon Seath's report and the Seath-inspired Industrial Education Act of the Dominion Government in 1911, the technical education system of Ontario was founded.

Had Seath never joined the provincial department and championed vocational education, he would be remembered as one of the most outstanding high school headmasters in late nineteenth century Ontario. He had made his reputation as principal of St. Catharines Collegiate Institute between 1874 and 1884, when he had made the school one of the best secondary schools in the province. As it turned out he contributed even more to twentieth century than to nineteenth century education. His successful campaign for vocational education in the high schools destroyed the "ladder" concept in Ontario education – the belief that the sole function of each rung on the educational ladder was to prepare the climber for mounting the next rung. No longer were the secondary schools of the province able to concentrate solely on preparing their students for university entrance; now the needs of the technically oriented students who would "matriculate" into the labour force must be considered as well. "These new subjects have come to stay," Seath had prophesied at the turn of the century, "and it would be well for all of you – Classical, Mathematical, Science and Moderns men – to realize the fact, and use the movement, as it may be used, for the proper ends of education."[2]

John George Althouse (1889-1956), chief director in the provincial ministry from 1944 until his death, presided over the destiny of Ontario education in the years of post-war expansion and burgeoning school enrolments. Althouse faced the difficult task of maintaining quality education in the light of rising demands that the secondary schools provide wider educational opportunities for all. Though a classicist by training and a teacher of the university-bound students in his earlier days, he realized that the school "has the additional duty of outlining for others, less able or less willing to devote themselves to professional service, appropriate courses to prepare them to live usefully and with satisfaction." He repeatedly spoke of the need to provide appropriate training for "*all* those who wish to complete four or five years of secondary schooling."[3] "We know enough about individual differences," he wrote, "to realize that equality in development is attained through variety,

[2] *Ibid.*, 1902.

[3] J. G. Althouse, "Significant Trends in Education in Ontario," *University of Toronto Quarterly*, XXV (1955), pp. 232, 238.

not through uniformity."[4] It was in this post-war decade that the Ontario department of education first gave serious consideration to the idea that the high school should serve the educational needs of children of all aptitudes and talents for as long as they wished to remain in school.

Althouse gave leadership to the re-organization of rural secondary school districts as one answer to the problem. He successfully promoted the idea of the large district secondary school to replace the small and remote high and continuation schools that had dotted rural areas of the province in earlier days. To Althouse, the larger district schools with their greater resources and better facilities would bring a greater degree of equality of educational opportunity to the pupils of Ontario.

Althouse believed that the democratic spirit in education should also be extended to the teachers. For ten years prior to his appointment as chief director, he had been Dean of the Ontario College of Education, University of Toronto. At the time this was the only college for preparing teachers for the secondary schools of the province. Through his hands during that decade passed hundreds of student teachers who were later to hold important positions in education in the province. Coming from a family of teachers, having taught secondary school himself, and having done his doctoral dissertation on the teaching profession in Ontario during the nineteenth century, Althouse had always been interested in the teacher as a major figure in the educational process. He believed that the very foundation of a successful school system rested upon the sound preparation of teachers. Later, in 1949, in his position in the provincial department, he took the first major steps towards encouraging teachers to assume a greater degree of professional responsibility in curriculum planning than they had ever done since Ryerson's centralizing process began 100 years earlier.

Paul Nash in 1961 placed Althouse in the school of Canadian educators that leaned more towards an American than a British orientation, and cited three ideas of Althouse for this conclusion: the necessity for a system of education to reflect the democratic values of an egalitarian society; his questioning of the traditional hierarchy of subjects; and his belief that adaptability to meet unpredictable situations is more to be valued than factual information.[5] Nash is correct as far as he goes: certainly Althouse's advocacy of the regional high school proves his concern for equality of opportunity in a democratic society. But he was as much concerned with "quality" as with "equality" in education. He believed that only through the larger school units could "quality" in education be provided. Althouse responded to the challenges of education in a widening democracy by seeking to provide a quality education for all the children of all the people.

A brief examination of democratic leadership in Ontario education during the past century is but one pathway into the vast unexplored areas of Canadian educa-

[4] Althouse, "Organization of a School System," R. M. Saunders, ed., *Education for Tomorrow* (Toronto, 1946), p. 26.

[5] Paul Nash, "Quality and Equality in Canadian Education," *Comparative Education Review*, vol. 5, no. 2 (1961), pp. 113-29.

tional history. It is significant that of the five individuals selected for detailed study, only one, J. G. Althouse, made his contributions in the second half of the 100-year period under consideration. As the years have passed, as society has grown more complex, as the educational organization in Ontario has become larger, more centralized, and more bureaucratic in nature, it has become increasingly difficult for the individual to dominate the field and to flavour the entire system with his own personality and ideas.

Educational leadership in the pre-Confederation era was much more clear cut than it became later. From the turn of the century in 1800 down to the Rebellion of 1837 the name of John Strachan stands out; from the 1840's to the 1870's it is Egerton Ryerson. Yet the names of Young, Ross, Hughes, Seath, and Althouse also stand out in considering educational leadership in the widening democratic society of the past hundred years. In this sense they are as important to twentieth century Ontario education as Strachan and Ryerson were to the nineteenth century.

BIBLIOGRAPHICAL NOTE

Althouse, J. G., *Addresses* (Toronto, 1958).

———, *Structure and Aims of Canadian Education* (Toronto, 1949).

Bell, Walter N., *The Development of the Ontario High School* (Toronto, 1918).

Cochrane, Honora M., ed., *Centennial Story: The Board of Education for the City of Toronto, 1850-1950* (Toronto, 1950).

Guillet, Edwin C., *In the Cause of Education: Centennial History of the Ontario Educational Association, 1861-1960* (Toronto, 1960).

Harris, Robin, "Egerton Ryerson," McDougall, R. L., ed., *Our Living Tradition*, 3rd Series (Toronto, 1959), pp. 244-67.

———, *Quiet Evolution: A Study of the Educational System of Ontario* (Toronto, 1967).

MacPherson, W. E., "George Paxton Young, Inspector of Grammar Schools," Ontario Educational Association, *Proceedings*, 1916 (Toronto 1916), pp. 448-58.

McCutcheon, J. M., *Public Education in Ontario* (Toronto, 1941).

Moir, John, *Church and State in Canada West* (Toronto, 1959).

Ontario, Department of Education, *Education for Industrial Purposes*, ed. John Seath (Toronto, 1911).

Ontario, Royal Commission on Education, *Report* (Toronto, 1950).

Phillips, C. E., *The Development of Public Education in Canada* (Toronto, 1957).

Pierce, Lorne, *Fifty Years of Public Service: A Life of James L. Hughes* (Toronto, 1924).

Putman, George, *Fifty Years at School* (Toronto, 1938).

Ross, G. W., *The School System of Ontario* (New York, 1896).

Ross, Margaret, *Sir George W. Ross* (Toronto, 1923).

Semple, Stuart W., "John Seath's Conception of Vocational Education in the School System of Ontario, 1884-1911," unpublished M.Ed. thesis, University of Toronto, 1964.

Shortt, Adam, and Doughty, A. G., eds., *Canada and Its Provinces* (23 vols., Toronto, 1914-17), vol. 18.

Sissons, C. B., *Church and State in Canadian Education: An Historical Study* (Toronto, 1959).

———, *Egerton Ryerson: His Life and Letters* (2 vols., Toronto, 1937-47).

Squair, John, *John Seath and the School System of Ontario* (Toronto, 1920).

Walker, Franklin A., *Catholic Education and Politics in Ontario* (Toronto, 1964).

Captain Charles Stuart, Abolitionist[1]

Fred Landon

Few people in Canada or in the United States have ever heard the name of Captain Charles Stuart, though he spent years in each of those two countries. Nor is his name known in England where, as in the other two countries and in the West Indies as well, he was an active participant in the anti-slavery movements of the first half of the nineteenth century. His name is not to be found in any recent history of the United States nor in any account of the British emancipation movement and the *Dictionary of American Biography* gives only a few lines to his career.

Yet here is a man who after retirement from army service with the British East India Company was active as a lecturer and pamphleteer during the anti-slavery crusade in England, gave like service to the movement in the United States and in his later days was an officer in the Anti-slavery Society of Canada when it was organized in 1851.

Moreover, he is the man whose influence brought Theodore Dwight Weld into the American struggle. The name of Weld is no longer absent from American histories but today stands high in the roll of those who brought about the freedom of the slaves in the United States. In the revision of the American anti-slavery movement which has been going on during the last two decades the contribution of Weld as organizer and propagandist assumes steadily greater importance.

Those who knew Charles Stuart in his lifetime paid tribute to his deeply religious character. "One of the most devoted Christians I have ever known and an unwearied advocate of the oppressed African," was the judgment of James Cropper, the English philanthropist. "A true man of God, a perfect being" was Theodore Weld's judgment of his friend. There are other similar tributes.

For most of his life a bachelor, he ever went about doing good and despite the austerity of his life and his many eccentricities he was always beloved. "He was the children's friend," said a contemporary, "for with the tenderness of a woman he had the spirit of a child."

During two periods of his life he resided in Canada. Between 1817 and 1822 he lived at Amherstburg on the Detroit River. There he first became acquainted with American slavery through his contact with the numerous fugitives who came to that terminus of the underground railroad. From the early fifties until his death in 1865 he resided at Lora Bay, a little inlet on Georgian Bay, not far from the

[1] First published in *Western Ontario History Nuggets*, no. 24, 1956. Footnotes have been deleted.

village of Thornbury and in Thornbury Union Cemetery his grave may be seen today. He was in his eighty-fourth year when the end came.

Stuart's reasons for leaving the service of the East India Company are explained in a brief sketch of the man which is among the Weld papers in the William L. Clements Library at the University of Michigan. He was born in Jamaica in 1783, the son of a British army officer who had fought in the American Revolution. His parents were Scottish Presbyterians of an extreme Calvinistic type and the mother in particular deeply influenced the boy's character. He was educated in Ireland and at the age of eighteen received a commission in the service of the East India Company. At retirement in 1815 he was "a captain in the 1st Battalion, 27th Regiment, and native infantry." So he described himself when taking the oath of allegiance after coming to Canada.

During his service in India he was seriously wounded while assisting in the quelling of an insurrection and carried a bullet in his body to the end of his days. At a later date a new colonel came to the regiment and invited his officers to dine with him on a Sunday, announcing that all his official dinners would be held on Sunday. Stuart declined the invitation and told the colonel that he regarded his action as a profanation of the Sabbath. From this time Stuart was regarded with an evil eye by his superior officer and, though he was respected by his fellow officers and by his men, his influence was covertly destroyed. Feeling utterly baffled he eventually resigned his commission and returned to England where through the influence of friends he was granted a pension of $800.

This explanation of his retirement differs from that which was given by Dr. John J. Bigsby who met him at Amherstburg around 1821 and is entirely different from the story which was current following his death in 1865. According to these versions he was in disfavour because of some stand he had taken over the mutiny at Vellore in 1804. According to one story he had protested against the cruelty in connection with the suppression of the outbreak and had been sent home. But as the mutiny at Vellore was in 1804 and Stuart did not retire until more than ten years later there does not seem to be a connection between the two. Probably the version given in the Weld manuscript, and which appears to be in Weld's handwriting, is correct. No one knew Stuart better than Weld or was more in his confidence.

There is no record of Stuart's activities between the time of his return to England and his departure for Canada. There is some indication that it was a period of intense religious conflict which came to a crisis when he was at Montreal. "Many are the places," he wrote in his *Emigrant's Guide*, "which are endeared to me by melancholy or by pleasing recollections; but over Montreal, a memorial of struggle and of anxiety, of peace and hope, of truth and holiness, and love, of obedience and of conflict, of tears and joy, throws an influence more dear and sacred to my soul, than it ever before had experienced. In reviewing the days which I spent there in retirement . . . as an unknown stranger, and desiring not to be known, a peculiar emotion is on my heart."

Stuart already had a sister in Upper Canada and had been promised a land grant if he wished to settle in the province. He arrived early in 1817, bearing a letter from Henry Goulburn, under-secretary of state for war and the colonies, to Sir John Sherbrooke, Governor of Canada, and also authorization for a grant of land. Governor Sherbrooke sent a copy of the letter to Francis Gore, lieutenant governor of Upper Canada, recommending Stuart to his notice and protection.

"The object of this gentleman," he wrote, "is to become a settler in Upper Canada where he already has some friends. One of my correspondents acquaints me that Captain Stuart's precise reasons for quitting the Madras establishment are not known to him, but that he is assured they are such as reflect no discredit upon him, either professionally or individually; that he was very desirous to have procured orders in the Church of England previous to his quitting England; but neither his own efforts or his friends could effect this object, it having of late been considered objectionable to ordain a soldier or sailor."

Stuart's land grant was promptly approved but for the time being he settled at Amherstburg on the Detroit River. From that place he wrote to Gore's successor, Sir Peregrine Maitland, expressing his desire to enter the Church. Rev. John Strachan, the rector at York, had, he said, suggested that he seek official approval for a license to read prayers and preach, and he himself, so he informed Maitland, looked forward to eventual ordination.

There was one impediment, however, that this pious bachelor put before Maitland. "My sentiment," he wrote, "is that intermarriage of uncles and nieces is perfectly consistent with God's Holy word and will; and that restraints placed upon it in society, are the mere fabrications of that kind of reason which brings Divine wisdom to its own bar, and can believe a human inference more infallible than the Word of God."

Maitland, passing upon this theological question, saw no error in Stuart's views but soon another question arose. Stuart wrote to say that while he would gladly have received ordination from other hands he could not accept it from Bishop Jacob Mountain "because I believe him to be an exceedingly antichristian overseer; a secular, not a spiritual character. The feelings and principles I would try to establish would be at decided variance with his principles and his life."

Stuart went to England in the autumn of 1819 and was absent from Canada for almost exactly a year. While abroad he published his first work, *The Emigrant's Guide to Upper Canada; or Sketches of the present state of that province, collected from a residence there during the years 1817, 1818, 1819. Interspersed with reflections.* It was a curious production. Edward Allen Talbot in his *Five Years Residence in the Canadas* said that it might be much more appropriately entitled "The Pilgrim's Guide to the Celestial Regions." While crediting the book with presenting some honest and valuable information respecting the country, Talbot's comment was that it contained "such a confused medley of polemical theology, whining cant and complimentary bombast, that it would require as much patience to travel through this duodecimo volume, as to make a pedestrian tour through the whole of the Upper Province."

Returning to Upper Canada in the autumn of 1820 Stuart reopened correspondence with Maitland, offering copious advice on a variety of subjects until the lieutenant governor, wearied by the letters, said so in rather plain terms. But Stuart was not easily suppressed. Writing in January, 1821, he said that he was both pleased and distressed by Maitland's words; pleased by its candid and gentle style but regretful of the condemnation pointed at him.

"I have always been aware that you have no time for fruitless correspondence," he wrote, "and I distinctly perceive that my correspondence with you has been worse than useless." Then he added a few further suggestions for bettering the welfare of the province.

But Maitland was not the only one who was wearied by Stuart. At Amherstburg, where he had become a magistrate soon after his arrival in Upper Canada, he became involved in a heated dispute with one of the officers of the Fort Malden garrison over their respective jurisdictions in dealing with civil offences by members of the garrison. Colonel J. P. Hawkins wrote to the authorities at Toronto:

> Do pray endeavour to prevail on Sir Peregrine to cause instructions to be sent to this troublesome magistrate, not to interfere unnecessarily with matters that are purely military, as he really seems inclined to be troublesome.
>
> Believing him to be a good-hearted man, I have, hitherto kept on tolerable terms with him, tho' he has more than once before interfered improperly. In one instance he committed one of the men to gaol, and kept him there for many weeks before he could be tried, after all of which the man was acquitted on trial. You are doubtless aware of Captain Stuart's eccentricity of character, but perhaps not of his having a strong propensity to meddle with the affairs of other people; even, I believe, to the almost neglect of his own.

Stuart tendered his resignation as a local magistrate in October, 1821, and peace descended upon the Detroit River community.

There is no evidence that Stuart's desire to enter the Church advanced further. His wish was to serve as a missionary to the Indians in whose welfare he was deeply interested, as we see from his repeated communications to the lieutenant governor. He admitted that he had little talent for acquiring languages. This would have militated against him as a missionary. After he returned from England, however, he found a new outlet for his religious and humanitarian zeal in the fugitives from Southern slavery who were about him at Amherstburg. He has recorded that between 1817-22 about 150 Negro fugitives came to the village. "I became more or less acquainted with them all," he wrote in *The West India Question*, "and found them quite equal to any class of laborers in the country . . . one of them, a man named Adams, was one of the most interesting persons with whom I have ever met."

A more pleasing picture of Stuart than that by the officer of the Fort Malden garrison is given in *The Shoe and Canoe* by Dr. John J. Bigsby, who was attached to the British section of the commission occupied in the survey of the international boundary. Bigsby met Stuart at Amherstburg and has left this description of the man and his activities:

> Although Captain Stewart [sic] resided at Amherstburgh, and was still not thirty-five years of age, he had passed many years in India, and had had some concern with the mutiny at Vellore; but his part in the affair must have been small; for his jealous

masters dismissed him with full pay for life. He was handsome, frank and energetic. His iron frame was indifferent to luxuries or even comforts, any hut was a home, and any food was nourishment, provided he could be doing good to others; for he was, and is, a working Christian.

Bigsby found Stuart engaged in what he described as "waging successful war with the Negro slavery of the United States." He was providing homes for the fugitives from slavery by setting up a Negro colony on a small tract of land in the rear of the village. There the refugees became his tenants. "The negro village and the clearances were then but just begun," says Bigsby. "As it was a very rainy season, the land seemed to be a swamp, and the huts very indifferent affairs, but were thought to be palaces by the freemen who inhabited them. Subsequently heavy crops were obtained from their farms. Captain Stewart had the goodness to walk over some of them with me; and I am glad that I had the discernment to cheer him on in his difficult undertaking."

Bigsby met Stuart again later in the year near the mouth of the St. Clair River. While watching the flooded waters of Black River three men on horse-back, with large-caped greatcoats, came to the opposite bank and shouted for the ferryman. As none was there, Bigsby took a large "pirogue" (a hollowed tree trunk) and with a broad, heavy paddle drove it to the opposite shore. In three trips he took the party across. It was Stuart and two American clergymen on their way to establish a mission among the "Saguina" Indians on the fertile banks of a river of that name emptying into Lake Huron.

Stuart's first period of residence in Canada terminated in 1822 when he went to Utica, New York, as principal of the Utica Academy, an institution which received its charter in 1814 and was opened in 1818. It was an important move for Stuart. Henceforth his life was to turn in new directions and through his friendship with Theodore Dwight Weld he was to become one of the noteworthy figures in the anti-slavery cause. Stuart first met Weld at the home of Erastus Clark, a brother of Weld's mother. Clark, one of the founders and a trustee of Hamilton College, had undertaken to finance his nephew's education. When Clark died in 1825 Stuart at once offered to take on this financial obligation, making but one condition, namely, that young Theodore should report quarterly, in writing, on his spiritual progress, doubts and difficulties. It was the beginning of an almost life-long friendship.

During the later twenties, when Rev. Charles G. Finney, the great revivalist, was stirring all western New York by his preaching, Stuart and Weld came under his influence and were converted. Both joined Finney's "Holy Band" as assistant revivalists, touring the country, preaching and exhorting. It was a prelude to their later labours in the cause of emancipation.

The curious relations between Stuart and Weld, which began at almost their first meeting, were closer and more intimate than would have been the case had they been father and son. They demonstrated their piety and their friendship in these early years by a daily sunrise "heart meeting" praying each for the other. In the letters which the older man wrote there are expressions of fervent love. "Theodore," he wrote, "you are mine and I am yours. God made us one from the beginning . . .

I know that you love me in spite of my unmeetness and unworthiness, and I love you the more for your love." Young Weld, in his turn, with deepest reverence could say of Stuart: "While yet a boy I became acquainted with him, and from that time till now our intimacy has been almost that of an indivisible existence; and yet our creeds and speculative opinions, doctrinal views and philosophical belief are as far apart as the poles. We are always disagreeing in opinion."

This friendship, beginning in the twenties, continued unshaken until the early sixties. By that time Weld was going over to Unitarianism and Stuart, believing that this would prevent their meeting in the next world, ceased to correspond with him though in writing to others he still protested his deep love for the younger man. He had first probed Weld's views rather fully by putting to him a series of questions on doctrine. Finally, writing to Weld's brother and sister on Sept. 9, 1861, he declared: "Although Theodore has entirely separated himself from me except indeed I would prefer him to Christ and I have ceased in consequence to correspond with him; yet have I never forgotten our former love and I ever mourn over his presently culpable apathy." During the remaining years of Stuart's life there appears to have been no correspondence between the two men whose friendship had hitherto been closer than that of brothers.

Stuart had entered the United States in 1822 but took no part in any anti-slavery effort at this time. Indeed, the decade was one of the most barren in the history of the struggle. The conflict between 1818-20 over the entrance of Missouri as a slave state had weakened the movement and the anti-slavery societies which had flourished earlier, even in the South, tended to disappear at this time. Benjamin Lundy was almost the only man holding up the anti-slavery banner until the appearance of Garrison and *The Liberator* in 1831. Elsewhere, however, a great struggle was under way. In England the agitation for emancipation of the slaves in the British Colonies was making progress and in 1829 Stuart decided that he would offer his help. He returned to England and enlisted as an agent and pamphleteer.

Discussion of the slavery issue had been under way in England for some time before Stuart's arrival but there was widespread ignorance of the nature of the institution in the overseas island possessions. The Anti-slavery Society consequently took upon itself to educate public opinion and sent out lecturers to proclaim the simple principle that "the system of colonial slavery is a crime in the sight of God, and ought to be immediately and forever abolished." The report of the agency committee of the Society, presented in 1832, showed that six lecturers, of whom Stuart was one and George Thompson another, had been actively engaged, Stuart having spoken in twenty-six towns. Soon speakers were sent out in opposition by the Society of West India Planters and Merchants. In contrast to these defenders of slavery who were liberally paid, Stuart met all his expenses from his own pocket. He gave even wider service to the cause by writing several of the most effective pamphlets which appeared at the time. The best-known was *The West India Question: Immediate emancipation safe and practical* (London, 1832). This was reprinted again and again both in England and in the United States and in the republic became the approved statement of creed of the American Anti-slavery Society.

The Old Buildings of Ontario

W. S. Goulding

Much of the character of man-made Ontario is given by fine 19th century buildings.

St. George's Cathedral and Old Post Office, Kingston

The Rev. Daniel Wilson's Study, Sharon

In the 19th century romantics built in many styles. The new federal capital was high blown Gothic; but a small sect of singing Quakers built a tabernacle in their wilderness paradise.

West Block, Parliament Hill, Ottawa

Sometimes it is not a single building which delights us . . .

but a group of buildings or a street, for example the townscape of Perth.

Buildings of interest can be found all across the province.

Summer cottage designed by Frank Lloyd Wright, Desbarats, Algoma

Such buildings as this deserve respect and care and continued use.

Old house, Port Hope

We need to know more accurately what good buildings we have, so we need to make an inventory of them . . . and we need to encourage private and public support for preservation and restoration.

County Courthouse, Hamilton

Scott and Wellington Streets, Toronto (now parking lot)

The 20th century need not destroy the 19th. Both the present and the future qualities of our communities will be the richer if we can keep a sense of continuity.

Anon., *S.E. View of Port Talbot, 1803*. Water colour. Sigmund Samuel Canadiana Gallery, Royal Ontario Museum, University of Toronto

George Heriot, *Joseph Brandt's on the Ouse*. Water colour, *c*. 1810. McCord Museum, McGill University, Montreal

William von Moll Berczy, Jr., *Huron Indians leaving residence near Amherstburg, Upper Canada, on a hunting excursion.* Water colour, *c.* 1820-30. Private collection

R. G. A. Levinge, *The "43rd Light Infantry," as they "turn out" in their sleighs; at the "Falls of Niagara." — 1839*. Coloured lithograph.
John Ross Robertson Collection, Toronto Public Library

William Buck, *Penetanguishene*. Oil on canvas, *c*. 1840. The National Gallery of Canada, Ottawa

John George Howard, *Parliament Buildings, Toronto*. Water colour, *c*. 1835. John Ross Robertson Collection, Toronto Public Library

James Hamilton, *London, Ontario, 1844*. Water colour. John Ross Robertson Collection, Toronto Public Library

Robert Whale, *View of Hamilton*. Oil on canvas, 1853. The National Gallery of Canada, Ottawa

Anon., *Sunbeam, Grand Sweepstake Horse*. Oil on canvas. Sigmund Samuel Canadiana Gallery, Royal Ontario Museum, University of Toronto

F. A. Hopkins, *Parliament Buildings, Ottawa, 1866.* Water colour. Sigmund Samuel Canadiana Gallery, Royal Ontario Museum, University of Toronto

Stuart entered into yet another phase of the great conflict and aided the anti-slavery forces in the United States by completely discrediting the efforts of the American Colonization Society to secure approval and support in England for its work. This Society was organized in the winter of 1816-17 with the purpose of transporting emancipated slaves to Africa. The little republic of Liberia was the fruit of the Society's activities but it soon lost the confidence of both emancipationists and slaveholders. Elliot Cresson, its agent, wrote in 1831 in unhappy tone to Gerrit Smith complaining of the violent attacks made upon the Colonization Society's principles and practices by "Captain Stuart, a disciple of Lundy and Garrison, who not satisfied with trying to print us down, has now added public denunciation." By 1832 the Colonization Society was in general bad odour in England and all chance of support from that quarter was gone.

Official gratitude for Stuart's services was expressed in the 1832 report of the Anti-Slavery Society which described him as "a persevering, uncompromising friend of the cause." Uncompromising he had plainly shown himself to be, never hesitating to condemn those in high places who had any connection with slavery. In a long letter addressed to the Archbishop of Canterbury and published in *The Abolitionist* in 1833 he remonstrated over the fact that the great missionary organization of the Church of England, The Society for the Propagation of the Gospel, was itself a slave-holder and had been since 1710 through ownership of the Codrington College Estates in Barbados. Even the use of the driving whip had been admitted by the Society as late as 1829 – six years after its abolition had been recommended by the British Government. Stuart ridiculed the familiar excuse, repeated in the Society's annual report, that the slaves were not ready for freedom, though they were being gradually brought to that state. "I look in vain," Stuart wrote, "for a ground on which to support the untenable position that the right way in which to prepare a poor, ignorant man for liberty is to keep him a slave; especially when his preparation is conducted in a land of slavery and entrusted to distant stipendiaries."

In an appendix to *Remarks on the Colony of Liberia and the American Colonization Society*, one of the pamphlets which he published while in England, Stuart presented the Wilberforce Colony, near London in Upper Canada, as an alternative to Liberia. If the Negroes were to be encouraged to leave the United States it was preferable, he contended, that they go to Canada where the coloured man was encouraged to do all he could to help himself. Included in this appendix was a testimonial from Sir John Colborne, lieutenant governor of Upper Canada, to the character of Rev. Nathaniel Paul, agent of the Wilberforce Colony, who was then in England soliciting funds, particularly for the establishment of a college for young Negroes.

This idea of establishing a college in Upper Canada was a sequel to the refusal by the municipal council of New Haven, Conn., to permit the establishment of such an institution in that city. "When they persecute you in one city, flee to another," wrote Stuart. "The free colored people have done so; they have abandoned New Haven to her white man's christianity; and they have now fixed upon Wilberforce, in Upper Canada, as the place of their choice. There they are preparing to erect their college. There, amidst the Canadian forest wilds, they are preparing to place upon our brow a gem of the purest lustre, which the United States have proudly dashed away. They need and implore our help."

During the whole period of his mission in England Stuart corresponded with Weld, sending him copies of the pamphlets and other publications which were appearing and urging him to enter the struggle in the United States. John Quincy Adams once wrote to James Monroe saying that the influence of British Emancipation "may prove an earthquake on this continent," and among the strongest influences upon the Tappans and other philanthropists at this time were the contemporary British debates upon emancipation, material which was placed in their hands by Stuart and Weld.

Stuart returned to the United States in 1834 after five years of anti-slavery labour in England. For the next three years he gave his services to the crusade in the United States in close association and correspondence with Weld. He was one of the famous "Band of Seventy" sent out as lecturers in 1836 by the American Anti-slavery Society and had his share of the abuse and violence which these doughty warriors encountered. There are frequent references to his activities in the anti-slavery journals and newspapers of the time.

Prior to his departure for England in 1829 Stuart had met Cordelia Weld, a sister of Theodore, and had conceived a romantic affection which might have developed further had he remained in the country. But when he returned in 1834, while his admiration for Cordelia had not lessened, he realized that they were not destined for one another. In August, 1834, he wrote to Theodore: "She is not to be mine. There is altogether too great a discrepancy of temper and of mind between us. I see the fact now glaringly and wonder that I did not formerly perceive it." Cordelia's name does not appear further in the published correspondence.

When he left once again for England in August, 1837, Stuart endeavoured to persuade Weld to go with him but the latter was unwilling to leave the struggle in his own land. Stuart had intended to stay a year in England but his plans were changed soon after arrival in the homeland and instead he sailed for the West Indies to observe at first hand what was happening under the new conditions created by emancipation. He was in the Barbados in December, then went on to Jamaica and other islands and returned to England in 1839. While in the Barbados he learned of the insurrection in Upper Canada and wrote to Weld asking him to ascertain the situation of his relatives and provide them with aid if needed. He was back in England in time to attend the World Anti-slavery Convention called to consider the state of slavery in every land, especially in America, and to formulate a programme for universal emancipation. Stuart received special recognition at this time, his friends in Parliament securing his promotion from the rank of retired captain to retired major with an attendant increase in his pension. He was also made an honorary life member of the British and Foreign Anti-slavery Society. He was continuously active and his stay in England lengthened into years.

We get only fleeting glimpses of Stuart during this later period spent in England. He was active in British anti-slavery circles, concerned about the apprenticeship system in the West Indies, about conditions in the East Indies and always deeply interested in what was going on in the United States. During 1846-7 he engaged actively in relief work in famine-stricken Ireland and finally, in 1850, sailed directly to Canada.

"Duty seemed plainly to forbid my coming thro' the United States," he wrote on Nov. 5, 1850, from Toronto to Weld, "and I lost the privilege of seeing you all, on my passage." In the same letter he writes: "I myself am now residing with my eldest sister (Mary Rankin) in this place. I expect, the Lord pleasing, to remain here until February, when it is my purpose to remove to the North and pursue the improvement of my property there; as well as to seek to serve, in love, the settlers around me."

In a letter to Weld from Lora, St. Vincent P.O. Canada West, dated April 22, 1852, he writes: "I am settled here for the present – direction as above –; and have been lately married to a distant relation, whom I have known and loved as a pure and noble-minded woman, for upwards of thirty years . . . Her father and two sisters, all lately from Ireland, are living with us and we form a little society."

Before leaving Toronto for his northern property Stuart became the first corresponding secretary of the Anti-slavery Society of Canada when it was organized in Toronto in February, 1851. He was chosen for this office, we may surmise, because of his wide acquaintance with the leading anti-slavery figures in both England and the United States, but his name does not appear on the list of officers after the first year. He made occasional visits to the United States. Thus we find it recorded that both he and John Brown were at an abolitionist convention in Syracuse in 1855 and Frank B. Sanborn, another of the American abolitionists, has recorded that Stuart and Brown were at the home of Gerrit Smith on the night of February 22, 1858, when Brown unfolded his plan for a blow at slavery. In his *Recollections of Seventy Years* Sanborn tells of going out for a walk with Smith while "Brown was left at home by the fire discussing points of theology with Charles Stewart [sic]". This was less than three months before Brown held his convention at Chatham, Canada West. Sanborn says that Brown arrived at the home of Gerrit Smith on the evening of February 18th and in an upper room unfolded his plans for a campaign somewhere in slave territory east of the Alleghanies. He read to his friends the draft constitution drawn up by him in Frederick Douglass's home in Rochester for the government of the territory large or small which he might rescue by force from slavery.

Life at Lora Bay was peaceful. Writing to James G. Birney in March, 1855, Stuart could say: "My present situation is replete with mercies . . . The country where I am, is a fine and growing one – much I suppose like that near Saginaw Bay, tho' not so far advanced yet, in improvements. We at present feel confined here, by duty; but we do not expect to remain here many years, should my life be so prolonged."

The Lora Bay property had originally been opened up by Charles Rankin, a relative, who had surveyed for the government the wild lands west of Simcoe County. The location was lot 37, concession 11, Collingwood Township, and Rankin was the township's first settler. Charles Stuart apparently took over the property before his return to Canada in 1850 and on removing to the place after his marriage built a commodious one story log house with a veranda the full width of the home. There were several large rooms, each with a stone fireplace, and smaller rooms in attached wings. The grounds were neatly planted with shrubs and flowers. At the rear was an addition in which Major Stuart had his sitting room and study. The ruins of the house were still visible many years later.

Traditions have come down of the life at Lora Bay and of the relations of Major Stuart with his neighbours. His servant came regularly to the nearest post office to pick up his mail which continued to be extensive. Letters and papers were securely locked in a large leather military pouch. The story is still told that when the major himself came into the village his servant would open the doors of the shops and announce his arrival. Stuart loved children and animals and assisted in a local Sunday school. He found outlet for his reform instincts in the temperance cause and occasionally spoke with old-time fire at community gatherings. He was stoutly opposed to the use of any product of slave labour such as sugar or cotton and substitutes had to be found by his family for these articles.

Stuart died at Lora Bay on May 26, 1865, just a few weeks after the close of the Civil War and the assassination of Abraham Lincoln. The thirteenth amendment abolishing slavery had already been passed by Congress and at the time of Stuart's death was before the states for ratification. He had lived to see the cause to which he had given his best years victorious both in his own homeland and in his adopted country. He could say, as did one of old: "Now lettest thou thy servant depart in peace . . . for mine eyes have seen thy salvation." His confidential servant, Charles Grant, made the coffin out of pine boards hewn on the place and covered it with black cloth. He was buried on May 29 on a hill on his farm, the grave being surrounded by a fence. Later his body was removed to the Union Cemetery at Thornbury, Ontario, where the grave was marked by a plain stone bearing first the name of his sister-in-law, Isabella Watt, and, below, Stuart's name and the date of his death. At the base of the stone are the simple words "The sweet remembrance of the just will flourish when they sleep in death."

BIBLIOGRAPHICAL NOTE

For information on Stuart and Weld see: Gilbert H. Barnes, *The Antislavery Impulse 1830-1844* (New York, 1933); Benjamin P. Thomas, *Theodore Weld, Crusader for Freedom* (New Brunswick, N.J., 1950); Gilbert H. Barnes and Dwight L. Dumond, eds., *Letters of Theodore Dwight Weld, Angelina Grimké Weld and Sarah Grimké Weld 1822-1844* (2 vols., New York, 1934); Dwight L. Dumond, ed., *Letters of James Gillespie Birney 1831-1857* (2 vols., New York, 1938). The Weld-Grimké and Birney manuscripts are in the William L. Clements Library at the University of Michigan.

Landscape Painting in Upper Canada

J. Russell Harper

Niagara Falls has been the most popular Canadian landscape subject through the years. A Recollet friar, Louis Hennepin (*c* 1640-1701) stopped there while travelling up the Great Lakes with La Salle in 1678 and sketched "that vast and prodigious cadence of waters which falls down after a surprising and astonishing manner, insomuch that the universe does not afford its Parallel." The print from his sketch was published in 1697 and is the first known landscape showing an Ontario view. Various painters lured by the romantic charm of Niagara have worked there during succeeding generations. For a century following the Seven Years War, dozens of English officers on garrison duty in the New World were attracted by tales of its awesome fascination, and many stayed long enough to paint Niagara. Hundreds of sketches were made by travellers and tourists from near-by towns and foreign parts. To paint the Falls was the ultimate ambition of every Victorian lady amateur in that age when painting was an indispensable social grace. In those same years the brush of almost every professional artist in Upper Canada set down Niagara, that never ceasing source of wonder and amazement. These different painters who came to the Niagara are representative of the various artists who recorded the Upper Canadian landscape.

Paintings of Upper Canada during the early settlement period are all in the water colour medium. Most artists in the province were British by birth and brought to America that technique of the English amateurs. One artist painted Joseph Brant's portrait in oil in a landscape setting before 1800, but otherwise the first Upper Canadian oil landscape is evidently a Toronto harbour view of 1817. Water colours were much more practical for the traveller than oils, being cheaper and more easily carried through the Canadian woods. Only during the 1830's and 1840's when town living became a part of the pattern of life did oil landscapes become common.

All students of the local pioneer scene will know and love the landscapes of those regions fronting the American border by British officers. These men painted the majority of the Upper Canadian views dated before 1812, and indeed a goodly proportion until after the 1837 Rebellion. Their sketches are in the late English eighteenth-century water colour tradition of Crome, Varley and a host of others who painted the spring morning's freshness or atmospheric effects of a passing storm in a manner universally understood and admired. Many officers were amateur painters who set down new surroundings both to while away the hours of boring garrison duty and as mementoes for friends and relatives at home. Hobbies were good for the morale. Other officers (and gentlemen) wrote journals or composed poems as useful diversions. Some acted in the garrison theatres despite the unimaginative Governor John Graves Simcoe who only once went to see one of their plays and then left disgusted that Guards' officers should pass their time in such an unseemly manner. Army engineers and artillerymen were trained as topographical draughtsmen while studying at the Royal Military Academy in Greenwich, since map-making was one of their professional duties. The British government hired Paul Sandby and other celebrated English painters as teachers; some of these instructors extended the topographical training into a virtual art school course. Consequently amateur officers' works in Canada are of high quality, as are those from other regions where the British army was stationed.

The first officer-painters in Upper Canada served with troops sent to settle the displaced Loyalists in new townships following the disastrous American Revolution. James Peachey (active 1781-91) painted the heart-rending scenes as men, women and children arrived in the St. Lawrence wilderness. He was attached to the office of Samuel Holland, Surveyor General, and laid out their new subdivisions. Several of his superb paintings and coloured etchings have survived and are characterized by a light quality which is almost ethereal. In 1789 he drew both Niagara Falls and Mrs. Brant's portrait; Peachey was evidently a particular friend of Brant and illustrated his Mohawk Prayer Book which Brant published in 1787. Thomas Davies (*c* 1737-1812), a Greenwich-trained man, is best known for his superb Quebec views and Indian studies along the St. Lawrence. He first came to Canada during Wolfe's Louisbourg campaign of 1758, but years later travelled over the old French River waterway to Georgian Bay and painted it in a series of blue monochrome sketches. Henry Rudyerd (active 1788) of the Royal Engineers is virtually forgotten, but his series of upper St. Lawrence River views were marvels of unrivalled freshness, and have an exactitude of draughtsmanship which resulted from officers' training as accurate observers.

George Heriot (1766-1844) and Edward Walsh travelled about in Upper Canada during the first decade of the nineteenth century. Heriot is the better known, for while both published their paintings as prints, he wrote a popular book illustrated with superb aquatints engraved from his own sketches. But by then Heriot was no longer an army man, having resigned from the accounts department after his appointment as Postmaster General of British North America. This new duty necessitated inspection of all local post offices from Halifax on the Atlantic to Chippawa in the west. His leather-bound sketch books were with him on all his tours, and he painted at every opportunity. These water colours are freshly laid down in opaque colours with a very luminous quality and with that quiet gentleness and harmony which characterizes contemporary European neo-classic painting. One of Fort Chippawa above Niagara, where the commandant used Heriot's visit as an excuse for a party, is in full colour. Another in blue monochrome shows the Mohawk Village on the

Grand River below Brantford much as it was when Basil Hall visited there a very few years later and wrote:

> The Mohawk Village stands on a little plain looking down upon the Grand River, upon the alluvion of which the inhabitants raise their crops, chiefly of Indian corn. Their houses are built of logs, rudely put together, and exhibiting externally a great appearance of neglect, and want of comfort; some few are in better condition: the house belonging to Brandt's family resembles that of a petty English farmer; Dr. Aaron's was neat and clean.

Dr. Aaron, an Indian, had been ordained a Church of England minister; he applied bright vermilion spots to his face before preaching on Sunday, but his dissertations were long and monotonous.

Edward Walsh (1756-1832), an army surgeon with the Herefordshire Regiment, was on American frontier duty at Sault Ste. Marie, Detroit, Forts Erie and George and possibly Toronto between 1803 and 1805. At each place he painted local views and detailed buildings whose appearance is otherwise unknown. Black flocks of passenger pigeons fly overhead in his Fort Erie sketch. This is a unique record of those beautiful birds which provided food for so many pioneer settlers; early farmers described them as so numerous that the flocks darkened the sky for hours in passing overhead.

A third generation of army men left an equally varied record of Upper Canada during the '30s and '40s. James Cockburn (1778/9-1847) is best known for no other reason than the sheer number of sketches and coloured prints which he produced. There are distant views of Kingston with inns and inn signs on a quiet Sabbath, the corduroy road from Toronto to Hamilton, perhaps chosen as a subject because it was a nightmare for all stage coach travellers including the artist, and Niagara Falls sketched from every conceivable angle. At Quebec Cockburn sketched so much, whether on picnics at Montmorency or Ste. Anne's Falls or merely wandering about the city, that Lady Aylmer, wife of the governor, wrote to her English nieces that his indefatigable labours made him a model for industry. His sketches were quickly executed; his tree trunks are less correct anatomically than Heriot's, but they have a free swing of line attuned to the newly emerging romantic spirit in art gaining preponderance during that generation.

E. Y. W. Henderson (1821-1896) as a young subaltern drew with the topographer's hard calligraphic line a large drawing of himself and a penniless friend in their fashionable sleigh as it flew down a Kingston street. Light water colour tinting was added. Henderson lived to become a well-known painter. Sir James Alexander (1803-1885) and his wife both sketched while he was stationed in London, Ontario. The sketches illustrated Sir James's book on Canada. Lady Alexander published a coloured lithograph of a military steeplechase in London during 1843 which is one of the first Canadian sporting prints. J. E. Woolford (1778-1866), who retired from the army to spend his later days in Fredericton, travelled down the French River and left a series of sketches of the same shorelines as had Davies. Philip Bainbrigge (active 1832-80) after serving during the Rebellion in Lower Canada. was at Amherstburg, Chatham and Cobourg in 1838-40, painting a sizeable quota of local views. Artists of less competence were among Colonel By's Royal Engineers working on construction of the Rideau Canal during the earlier years of this third phase, but left an excellent topographical record of the district. The whole army phase extending over more than half a century in Upper Canada enriched the local art scene enormously.

Various temporary residents and visitors sketched the newly-opened wilderness during the province's earliest days. Mrs. Simcoe (1766-1856), wife of the lieutenant governor, worked on birch bark. One visitor to Newark implied that she could probably have accomplished more painting if her husband had not kept her so busy neatly copying his new survey maps. Tourists like Basil Hall (1788-1844) travelled through America. Hall worked with a camera lucida in 1816-17 making accurate sketches for publication.

Some early landscapes are unsigned and probably painted by unidentified English travellers. One shows Colonel Talbot's new settlement at Long Point, Lake Erie. Governor Simcoe after his return to England had assisted Talbot in obtaining a 5,000 acre grant on which the colonel began to build his new home in June, 1803. The first building to be erected was a log house of three rooms – store room, sitting room and kitchen; this was enlarged later into Castle Malahide. Here Talbot is said to have "baked his own bread, milked his own cows, made his own butter and cheese, washed his own clothes, ironed and dressed his own linen" until becoming more prosperous on arrival of settlers for the new township. The anonymous artist during the autumn of 1803 saw this new clearing as a kind of idyllic retreat, a feeling which he re-emphasized by using gentle warm colours and soft greens, blues and grays; he envisaged this early setting as a miniature paradise which is in contrast to the usual concept of the harsh struggle for existence to which the Upper Canadian pioneer was subjected.

One woman whose paintings were quite exceptional was growing up at Amherstburg. Catherine Reynolds (*c* 1782-1864) was born at Detroit while her father was barracks master of the fort during the years of English control. He moved across the border after Detroit's cession to the United States to build a new fort on the Canadian side. Following his death, Catherine lived with her younger brother Robert who was connected by marriage with the wealthy Montreal merchant group. Robert built "Belle Vue", an impressive Georgian mansion. Catherine had had a cultured upbringing; one of the first pianos in the province had been in her home. She was evidently largely self-taught as a painter, but achieved remarkable results considering her isolation from other painters. Her water colours have a particular fascination in subject matter for she turned to the local scene: one shows "Belle Vue" with its outbuildings, snake fences, solid massive oaks, her brother with a horse looking over his livestock in the attitude of a country squire, and the servant girl fetching the cows.

Upper Canadian society following the war of 1812 reached a point where painting commanded more attention. Warding off the Americans had instilled a new self-assurance and local pride. Richard Coates (1778-1868), a relative of Sir Joshua Reynolds, settled in Toronto during 1817 and became the town's first resident painter, but chiefly worked as a decorative artist. Charles Fothergill (1782-1840) arrived from Yorkshire about 1816 and took up land in Durham County. He painted numerous landscapes around Rice Lake and Port Hope in 1819. In these is the same idyllic interpretation of the new world as the anonymous painter gave to Talbot's clearing; both reflect an optimistic Arcadia which settlers expected to find. Fifteen years or more later, painting took on new directions when artists saw the countryside more objectively. Fothergill's gentle paintings would seem to indicate a poetic nature which contrasts strangely with accounts of an episode in 1821 when he led 150 drunken men singing "God Save the King" in protest at the malpractice of a partisan returning officer at the Port Hope election. He passed a busy life as king's printer, editor of newspapers and periodicals, and a keen student of natural history, but never lost his art interests and in 1835 proposed a Lyceum of the Fine Arts for Toronto.

Local artists in the capital were sufficiently numerous by 1834 to form the Society of Artists and Amateurs of Toronto for the purpose of sponsoring a first art exhibition in the province. There were seventeen associate members, including John Howard (1803-1890). Howard was a local architect, teacher of art at Upper Canada College for many years, and painter of local views. Captain Richard Bonnycastle (1791-1847) of the Royal Engineers was president. Most members exhibited portraits, many in oil, for it was the hey-day of the painted face before photography ruined the business of limners, silhouette cutters and portrait painters. There were also some landscape men, principally James Hamilton (1810-1896), Thomas Drury who was Paul Kane's first teacher, Kane himself but exhibiting as a copyist, Fothergill, Howard, and a few others. Some sent in original works but others copied European canvases in a day when the distant scene was really considered more fashionable than the local view. The exhibition included a total of 196 paintings, and was hung in the Legislative Buildings. The weather was hot; the cholera epidemic broke and the population was paralyzed with fear; attendance was consequently small. Further exhibitions were abandoned until hurt feelings mended, when the new Toronto Society of Arts held a similar show in 1847. There was an even larger proportion of portraits, but Young again showed landscapes and Cornelius Krieghoff (1815-1872) who had lived briefly in Toronto, showed some genre scenes. By this time, however, the Upper Canada Agricultural Society had come into being as a vehicle for public exhibition so that the Toronto show lost much of its earlier significance.

James Hamilton's was the most important name at this exhibition in terms of new local developments. His landscapes were both in oil and water colour. Hamilton had come from Cornwall in England and was the new accountant for the Bank of Upper Canada, living in a cottage which stood at Yonge and Wellesley Streets in Toronto. This house, surrounded by trees, was then in the suburbs, and the artist delighted in painting the distant city scape with foreground woods. His interest in atmospheric haze and objective approach parallels new interests of others in those years. The man might well have become a significant artist if he had turned professional (he did advertise as a landscape painter one year), but he preferred to remain a "Sunday painter", moved to London, and there led an active business life. Hamilton had the time to paint extensively only in retirement.

The new spirit of objectivity which first came into Canadian landscapes about 1830 or a little later echoes a new realistic approach to the social and economic conditions locally. As a part of the manifestation of this new attitude, paintings and prints of towns and the countryside became popular. Oil painting began to play a role, but original oils took more time to paint than water colours, were scarce and expensive, and could be bought only by the wealthy. On the other hand lithographs and engravings were cheap enough to grace the walls of many living rooms, so there was a great demand for prints from landscape sketches. This generation was awakening to their own country. There were new schools and colleges. Citizens looked around and with pride revelled in recent progress as typified by the new towns of Toronto, Cobourg, Kingston, Belleville and Niagara. They stood in what had been but recently a virgin wilderness. Upper Canadians were proud of the new roads and bridges, lake steamers, the Rideau and Niagara Canals, and the fine livestock farms achieved through a single generation of effort. Preferred landscapes were those which could be "read" as the eye examined every window, trade sign, chimney and portico; these were reminders of the new progress. Politically there was unrest over the Family Compact which was seen as blocking the common man's progress, and William Lyon Mackenzie's Rebellion erupted in 1837. The same awakening struck Quebec, the Maritimes and the United States. Everywhere was a new interest in the landscape as a mirror of progress.

Thomas Young (d. 1860) of Toronto was typical of the new realistic painters. He was an architect and schooled in setting down detail. Dr. Scadding in his book *Toronto of Old*, published in 1873, wrote an extensive antiquarian report describing each house, store, church and public building which is a literary parallel to Young's examination of each Toronto building in paint. But his expensive oils were beyond most pockets so he had them made into prints and advertised in the *Toronto Patriot* during May, 1836, that four views were available. They show the Government Buildings, a view of King Street, a general view of Toronto, and Upper Canada College. Each measured twelve by nineteen inches, had been lithographed in London, and sold for £1/10/– on Indian paper or £1 on regular paper. Naturally Young benefitted by royalties, but there was a mass spread of pictures to fill a local demand.

Others did the same. Samuel Tazewell rented a room in the Market House, Toronto, where in 1833 he made lithographs of Niagara Falls and other views from his own paintings. With sensible practicality he also published lithographic maps of the newly opening townships for which there was a great demand, but the cholera epidemic which struck in 1834 and ruined the painting exhibition, caused business to fall off so badly that he was bankrupted. John Gillespie's views of Toronto and Dundas of the late 1840's are known only from prints. City scapes of J. G. Sanders, a Toronto drawing master, were engraved in 1847.

Landscape artists, like contemporary portrait painters, often wandered from town to town throughout America. Several passed through Upper Canada. Prints brought in more income than did the sale of original works. Edwin Whitefield (1816-

1892) was an Englishman who had been in the United States but lived in Toronto during 1854. Some of his Canadian sketch books survive, neat thin booklets with soft covers decorated in typical marbled design. Inside are pencil studies of Port Hope, Belleville and Carluke, a post office hamlet near Hamilton. In going from town to town he sketched fine new farm houses and inns along the road. His precise pencil notes resemble little camera studies which he later fitted together like jigsaw puzzles into great panoramic prints of Canadian cities. Such large lithographs sold widely for everyone in Toronto, for example, could pick out in his Toronto view his own house or place of business.

Other artists worked for print makers. Coke Smyth, said to have been drawing master to Lord Durham's children in Canada during 1839, prepared a series of coloured Canadian views. William Henry Bartlett (1809-1854) made a Canadian sketching tour in 1838 and his sepia sketches were engraved for *Canadian Scenery*. Landscapes of Lucius O'Brien (1832-1900) into which he introduced Indians, were published in Toronto's *Anglo-American Magazine* during the early 1850's, while for the same journal Frederick C. Lowe (active 1843-56) engraved sketches by some local unidentified artist of the Toronto Yacht Club, of London and other centres. George H. Andrews (1816-1898) came out from England with the Prince of Wales, later Edward VII, and sketched in that year 1860 Kingston's new city hall, Hamilton's new Crystal Palace, and other local show places; these were engraved for *The Illustrated London News*. Such illustrations, the poor man's picture book of the Upper Canadian landscape, were pored over with the greatest interest and undoubtedly many served for home decoration.

Washington F. Friend was a wandering landscape painter with a special interest. He travelled from Niagara to Queenston, Toronto, Kingston, Montreal and Tadoussac on a three-year tour beginning in 1849. At each centre he made innumerable sketches. These were painted up afterwards into an enormous panorama on a canvas optimistically described as five miles long. This was exhibited widely, and a narrator described its wonders as it unrolled on the stage while Friend himself sang Canadian folk songs. Citizens for a small admission fee thus visited the whole country in their own city or town. The première of this particular panorama was in Quebec. A command performance in Buckingham Palace came as a grand finale, an occasion on which Friend enlightened Queen Victoria about her possessions in Upper and Lower Canada.

The spirit of progress prompted the annual Upper Canada Agricultural Society exhibitions which were initiated in 1848 and still survive as the Canadian National Exhibition. Shows were held in rotation at Niagara, Hamilton, Toronto, Cobourg, Kingston and Brockville, all readily reached by Lake Ontario passenger steamer; London was added to the group when the railway was completed from Hamilton in 1854. Amidst farm animals, flowers, grain, vegetables and all kinds of manufactured products was a section devoted to the fine arts. Leading artists were invited to exhibit so that the public would learn how to judge good paintings. The list of winners indicates that most of the more competent artists exhibited during the two decades immediately prior to Confederation. Critics objected to the preponderance of portraits in 1854 of which many were bad, and the landscapes were so inferior in 1855 that no professional prize was awarded. Despite this there were many impressive oil and water colour landscapes by permanent settlers, in contrast to the paintings by earlier army men and travellers who were simply painters "passing through."

Paul Kane (1810-1871), one exhibitor, was considered a truly native son even if born in Ireland. As a boy (at a time when Mississauga Indians still loitered in the muddy streets of York), he had acquired a love of art at the York Grammar School. He spent his early manhood in Cobourg decorating chairs, and painting portraits when he had the time. Then a European tour completely altered his style while George Catlin's paintings of Indians suggested new subject matter. Thereafter his only interest was to record Canadian Indian life. He left Toronto for the Georgian Bay district on June 17th, 1845, with nothing but his portfolio, paint box, gun and ammunition. That summer and autumn he painted little portraits and filled sketch books with pencil and water colour studies of the life of the Lake Huron Indians even if "filth, stench, and vermin made them almost intolerable." On a trip to the Pacific in 1846-48 he painted the western Indians. These romantic studies of Indians in the Canadian landscape made him justly a leader among artists. He won many prizes at the agricultural exhibitions from 1850 to 1857, and at the 1851 Brockville show, his tall imposing figure in the crowd was singled out as that of a celebrity. But when Kane requested a cash contribution from the government to help in his work, there was incredulous silence. Then parliament relented to the extent of commissioning twelve canvases. These were delivered after frustrating delays in 1856, and eleven are now in the National Gallery of Canada. The artist was very much Canadian-oriented; his greatest wish was to see his paintings remain permanently in this country. This was made possible when the Honourable G. W. Allan, his patron, bought one hundred which are now housed in the Royal Ontario Museum. Kane gradually went blind and died at his Wellesley Street home in Toronto in 1871. Many laudatory obituaries testified to the high regard in which he was held as an artist in those early Confederation years.

Immigrant ships by the hundred left British ports for America during the 1840's and 1850's, their steerage accommodation packed with young Englishmen, Irishmen and Scots looking forward to carving a farm from the backwoods or "doing well" in the towns. Among them were a sprinkling of professional men including a few artists. Four of these painters who settled in scattered communities, saw the provincial exhibitions as a vehicle for publicizing their works. Robert R. Whale went to Burford in 1852, William Nicol Cresswell settled at Harpurhaye near Seaforth in 1855, William Armstrong chose Toronto as a home in 1857, while Daniel Fowler bought a farm on Amherst Island opposite Kingston in 1843.

Robert Whale (1805-1887) painted in oil and had an immense repertoire of subject matter: landscapes, portraits, historical paintings, marines and still life. He catered to all tastes. Prizes were awarded to him during his first year in Canada. He copied and re-copied for cheap sale his views of Hamilton, Dundas and Niagara Falls, and his Hamilton landscapes were made into prints. An amusing canvas with maidens bathing in a rural Ontario pool contains possibly the first nude studies painted in the province, and it is questionable whether he ever dared exhibit it publicly. Whale's descendants describe how each autumn he and his nephew, John Hicks Whale (1829-1905), also of Burford and later of Brantford, loaded paintings into a buggy and toured the local country fairs at Paris, Burford, Norwich and other centres. The older man exhibited as a professional, the younger as an amateur, and they took home many prizes.

William Armstrong (1822-1914) was a Dubliner who studied art before becoming a practical railway engineer. Although living in Toronto, he travelled widely and so had a good opportunity to paint unusual subject matter in widely scattered places. His best known paintings between 1852 and 1862 when he exhibited at the agricultural shows, were his elaborate landscapes of the Prince of Wales arriving by ship in Toronto. But later he developed other interests, particularly a liking for painting yachts in summer and ice boats in winter on Toronto harbour, and the Indian life of Lakes Huron and Superior and the Rockies which he saw while an engineer working on railway construction.

Far removed from the practical Armstrong was Cresswell (1822-1888), a tweedy remittance man who lived like an English county gentleman, and divided his time between fishing and painting. He won prizes consistently between 1858 and 1862 for oils and photographs but today is known chiefly as a pioneer landscape and marine water colour painter. Many subjects were drawn from the shore of Lake Huron, especially the rocky coastline of the Bruce peninsula.

Undoubtedly the finest artist of the whole group for sheer sensitivity, beauty, and craftsmanship was Daniel Fowler (1810-1894) who had earlier worked in London as a professional water colourist. When threatened with consumption, he moved to Amherst Island and stopped painting completely until 1863. On resumption of his old craft in his island retreat, he exhibited as an amateur but was transferred to the professionals at the judges' orders in 1866. Fowler won prizes for his flowers and landscapes, marines, animals and genre in water colour, and for his pencil portraits, pen and ink studies, and crayon works. Years later, on the formation of the Royal Canadian Academy of Arts, it was suggested that this shy retiring man should be the first president but he declined.

Painters were becoming legion as Confederation approached, and all cannot be mentioned. However some other landscape winners at the agricultural exhibitions were Edward Bull, a Toronto art teacher, in 1849; Harriet Henderson in 1850-52 and Alexander Davidson in 1859-60, both from Hamilton; Ida C. Jones in 1851-57 from Brockville; and James B. Wandesford in 1850 from Goderich. The latter achieved some celebrity after going to California during the gold rush and becoming a well known western painter. Captain John Caddy (1801-1883) exhibiting from 1858 to 1866, was a retired army officer who had settled in Hamilton in 1850. He travelled throughout the area, to Niagara, Caledonia, London and the surrounding countryside, making water colour sketches.

Painting had seemingly come into its own when exhibition authorities built the Hamilton Crystal Palace, opened by the Prince of Wales during the 1860 fair. It contained the first room in the province especially designed as an art gallery and was

> 54′ wide and 64′ long, reserved especially for the exhibition of works of art. Three of its sides are close-boarded, and the light admitted through the centre of the roof by a lantern light extending the whole length; the glass is frosted, or obscured in order to diffuse the light.

Pictures were becoming a part of daily living. Artists were responding by recording for a proud independent people the changing face of the land in that burst of energy which brought about the new Dominion of Canada.

BIBLIOGRAPHICAL NOTE

Alexander, Sir James Edward, *L'Acadie; or Seven Years' Explorations in British America* (London, 1849).

Barteaux, E., "W. H. Bartlett, of 'Bartlett Prints'," *Dalhousie Review*, XXIV (1945), pp. 424-37.

Bonnycastle, Sir Richard Henry, *The Canadas in 1841* (2 vols., London, 1841).

Canada, National Gallery, *Catalogue of Paintings and Sculpture* (Ottawa, 1960).

Colgate, Sir William G., *Canadian Art; Its Origin and Development* (Toronto, 1943).

Harper, J. Russell, "Ontario Painters 1846-1867," Canada, National Gallery, *Bulletin*, no. 1 (1963), pp. 16-28.

———, *Painting in Canada: A History* (Toronto, 1966).

Howard, John G., *Incidents in the Life of John G. Howard, Esq. of Colborne Lodge, High Park, near Toronto . . .* (Toronto, 1885).

Hubbard, Robert H., *An Anthology of Canadian Art* (Toronto, 1960).

Jameson, Anna Brownell (Murphy), *Winter Studies and Summer Rambles in Canada* (3 vols., London, 1838).

Kane, Paul, *Wanderings of an Artist* (London, 1859; Toronto, 1925).

Kidd, Kenneth E., "Paul Kane – A Sheaf of Sketches," *Canadian Art*, vol. 8, no. 4 (1951), pp. 166-7.

Needler, G. H., *Early Canadian Sketches by Mrs. Jameson* (Toronto, n.d.).

Niagara-on-the-Lake Historical Society, *Catalogue of Articles in Memorial Hall, the Historical Building of the Niagara Historical Society Founded in 1895* (Toronto, 1911).

Robertson, John Ross, *Landmarks of Canada . . . A Guide to the J. Ross Robertson Historical Collection in the Public Reference Library, Toronto, Canada . . .* (rev. ed., Toronto, 1967).

Ross, A. H. D., *Ottawa past and present* (Ottawa, 1927).

Spendlove, F. St. George, *The Face of Early Canada: Pictures of Canada Which Have Helped to Make History* (Toronto, 1958).

Windsor, Willistead Art Gallery, *Catherine Reynolds (ca. 1782-1864)* (Windsor, 1967).

Wilson, Sir Daniel, "Paul Kane, the Canadian Artist," *Canadian Journal*, New Series, XIII (1871), pp. 66-72.

A Pallid Picture: The Image of Ontario in Modern Literature

William H. Magee

Readers around the world who form their picture of modern Ontario from poetry and fiction can hardly envision it as a very lively province. Not only have writers failed to reproduce any comprehensive or distinctive sense of either the city or the countryside, they have also failed to suggest the vigour and enthusiasm which have created a progressive civilization of great complexity in little more than a century. Nor would readers alter their picture if they added historical studies to their reading range, to judge by the scant treatment deplored by the editors of *Ontario History* in 1962. For well over a generation, since the first world war, Canadian poets and novelists have quite failed to capture the spirit of this, the dynamic centre of Canadian civilization. Yet they would be sadly off without southern Ontario. Almost all the publishers who give them a voice are Toronto firms. The majority of the readers who give them an audience and make their meagre royalties possible live in the two-hundred mile semicircle radiating north and west from Toronto. Several of the universities which give so many of them their living are located there.

Ontario is odd in having a faceless literature. In the English-speaking world an energetic society has typically created a vigorous literature. From the golden age of the Elizabethan explorers to the martial twentieth century, each wave of economic expansion or social progress has inspired a new outburst of great books in England. There has been no echo in Ontario. In the United States Mark Twain and his forceful and prolific contemporaries flourished in a society even more similar to that in Ontario, but also without echo there. In every decade of the twentieth century famous American poets and novelists have well reflected a way of life similar to that of the silent Canadians. Other nations in the British Commonwealth have shown the same vocal trend. A glance at the anthologies of short stories from Australia and New Zealand in the Oxford World Classics, as compared with the volume from Canada, shows how dull Canada must look to readers. It also reveals that Ontario is poorly represented. The thoughtful citizen must wonder why Ontario has offered so little of itself in poetry and fiction.

When it comes to estimating the vitality of a society through its writing, traditional literary classifications are not of much significance. A writer tends to rely on his own environment as a general background for his creations, whether they are lyric, narrative or dramatic, and even whether they are romantic or realistic. Writing based on such a direct reflection of the social and natural background can be called *representational*, whatever its traditional form. What is significant is whether a writer is representational or escapist. The escapist writer deliberately avoids his own society, often creating a dream world which seems to him more bearable. A third possible attitude, the satiric, in which the writer sets up a perspective between himself and his society, will be considered later.

The representational writer may use his environment in one of two ways. He may be so gripped by it as to create an inspired picture of it, or he may not find it interesting and therefore treat it in a perfunctory fashion. An inspired picture bespeaks an intense society, but a perfunctory one suggests a pallid society. In turn, the vitality of the background affects the total literary success of a work. Let characters be ever so forceful and incidents ever so moving, they can achieve full artistic power only against an inspired background. The pallid picture of Ontario in modern literature reveals writers handicapped in their art by their failure to grasp the force of their environment.

There was a time, in the rural years of the nineteenth century, when southern Ontario was the centre of Canadian literary activity. Ontario seemed vital to writers then, although circumstances resulted in a fragmentary picture of it. The styles of English literature popular in pioneer Canada did not foster representational literature. Yet within the limits of antiquarian novels in the Scott tradition and the romantic lyricism of nature poetry, the writers did as well by Ontario as many of their contemporaries were doing by England. As early as 1832 John Richardson dramatized the significance of the Pontiac Conspiracy in *Wacousta* (3 vols., London, 1832), the first worthwhile Canadian novel. That event, he claimed, was the cause of British domination in Ontario, and so the novel was vital to local patriotism. Significantly, however, Richardson made no attempt to describe the Ontario countryside in the long paragraphs customary in the Scott romance. He did this only in the chapters in which he makes a short excursion to Scotland. Such prejudiced attention to European scenery is not without parallel in modern Canadian literature, as in some novels by Morley Callaghan and Robertson Davies.

Canadian poetry in the nineteenth century did feature the Ontario landscape, although the dominant mood of romantic lyricism kept the typical life of the times out of most poems. In *The St. Lawrence and the Saguenay* (Kingston, 1856), the best pre-Confederation poem, Charles Sangster of Kingston showed that the lakes and forests of Ontario were as sensuously inspiring as Italy had been to Shelley, or England to Wordsworth and Keats. In the generation after Confederation the most representational writers in the new nation, Archibald Lampman and Duncan Campbell Scott, wrote about life in eastern Ontario. Lampman continued in the tradition of romantic nature lyrics, while Scott turned to narrative vignettes, a form which requires people and a description of their place in society. Although he confined his characters to pre-settlement Indians and traders, he did take Canadian literature a step closer to coming to terms with its civilization. The other best-known Canadian poets of the time, Sir Charles G. D. Roberts and Bliss Carman, began with some representations of rural life in the Maritimes, but by the turn of the century they were both living abroad and writing for foreign readers. Ontario remained the chief subject of serious poetry written in Canada.

At the turn of the century, when a very different form of local colour gradually began to monopolize Canadian fiction and poetry, the towns of southern Ontario came close to ousting the rest of Canada from literature. Writers then shared a pride in the special characteristics of their region with all local colourists; in addition they usually wanted to preach about the devotion of their heroes to hard work and a strict morality. The attitude was, in fact, provincial – a feeling that non-urban Ontario was the perfect society, and that all others fell short of it. Never have so many Canadian writers concentrated on one theme. The Glengarry of Ralph Connor's novels and of the short stories in E. W. Thomson's *Old Man Savarin* (Toronto, 1895), the New Jedboro of Robert E. Knowles' *St. Cuthbert's* (Toronto, 1905), and the Mariposa of Stephen Leacock's *Sunshine Sketches of a Little Town* (London, 1912) represent literally dozens of fictional treatments of small-town Ontario. The roll call which opens with them runs through many other writers like Marian Keith, Peter McArthur, Madge Macbeth, Isabel Ecclestone MacKay, Archie P. McKishnie, Adeline Teskey, and Joanna Wood, until it even includes L. M. Montgomery, who moved her setting from Prince Edward Island to Ontario for a late novel, *The Blue Castle* (Toronto, 1926). Some of the few faintly memorable treatments of other parts of Canada in this period also came from writers who were born and bred in Ontario, including Ralph Connor's and Robert E. Knowles' novels of the far West and Norman Duncan's stories of Newfoundland.

This impetus continued into the 1920's and even into the 1930's in long series by established writers like Ralph Connor, but only a few new writers joined them then, like Clara Rothwell Anderson (*John Matheson: A Wholesome Human Story of Canadian Rural Life*, Toronto, 1923) and Jessie L. Beattie (*Hill-Top: A Tale of Ontario Rural Life*, Toronto, 1935; *Three Measures*, Toronto, 1938). Consequently southern Ontario began to look outmoded in fiction after the first world war. Even during the most active years, local colour had represented only one vigorous aspect of society, the moral, and had generally ignored commercial, industrial, agrarian and political aspects. A notable exception is Mrs. Sara Jeannette Duncan Cotes' picture of the Imperial Federation movement as a political cause in small-town Ontario in *The Imperialist* (Toronto, 1904). If the scenes were usually pale or partial, the difficulty resulted from artistic weaknesses and a narrow vision rather than from any hesitation of the writers to find inspiration in Ontario.

After the first world war Canadian literature enlarged its range of settings and started to depict a complex and expanding society, in the poems and novels of more able writers who have been inspired by all parts of the country except Ontario. In 1923 Newfoundland inspired representational poetry of unusual force, and the West of the pioneers gave strength to the Canadian novel at last. Pratt's *Newfoundland Verse* (Toronto, 1923) not only describes village life in Newfoundland realistically, but it also captures the human energy and fortitude which have made society possible there. In the same way on the prairies the immigrant and pioneer novel brought to life the almost superhuman heroism of the settlers from Ontario or Europe. Starting with Mrs. Laura Goodman Salverson in *The Viking Heart* (New York, 1923) and culminating with R. J. C. Stead in *Grain* (Toronto, 1926) and Frederick Philip Grove in his Prairie Series, writers looked steadily and deeply at a Canadian way of life for the first time since Haliburton and his *Clockmaker* series in early Nova Scotia. Incidentally they saw neither moral prairie ministers as Ralph Connor had done, nor dashing Mounties. Meanwhile the distinctive colour of remote ways of life, such as the hardships of Eskimo life, brought a real Canada into some of Alan Sullivan's books, and into a dozen others by new local colourists who avoided old Ontario even if they lived there. Inspired literature thrives on grand events and human triumphs, as these writers have shown. Ontario ought to have been at least equally inspiring.

Three important writers did start out with typical Ontario settings in the 1920's and 1930's: Morley Callaghan described Toronto, Philip Child the rivers and towns, and Mazo de la Roche the large farms. The results are baffling as a reaction to modern Ontario. In six novels and two volumes of short stories in just ten years, starting with *Strange Fugitive* (New York, 1928) and culminating in *More Joy in Heaven* (New York, 1937), Morley Callaghan presented a faceless Toronto which he named "the city." He apparently could find no difference between it and a hundred other North American cities to the south. In one novel, *A Broken Journey* (New York, 1932), he went so far as to dismiss wild northern Ontario as sterile and of no use to the future of North American civilization. His novels reflect the modern American trend to realism and naturalism, in which social criticism provides the central theme, and a whole picture of a society the setting; and yet Callaghan's Toronto is neither distinctive nor vital. In contrast, his more recent novels written since the second world war do show an individual and forceful city life, but not in Ontario. In *The Loved and the Lost* (Toronto, 1951) and *The Many Colored Coat* (Toronto, 1960) he has moved his Canadian setting to Montreal, and there he has found the inspiration of a unique society.

Philip Child, in contrast, explored the unusual and unrepresentative in Ontario. He described the ideas and doubts of isolated, lonely people, familiar in the British novel in the 1920's. In *The Village of Souls* (London, 1933) a seventeenth-century voyageur paddling through the Great Lakes naturally yearns for companionship, but so does a conscientious objector in an Ontario town of the first world war days in *God's Sparrows* (London, 1937). Although even the latter, twentieth-century topic cannot be said to deal with a significant attitude in modern Ontario history, Child's British prototypes like Aldous Huxley have written vivid pictures of modern British life. More recently, in the nostalgic poems of *Victorian House* Toronto, 1951), Child suggests that Ontario society a century ago made sense in a way it does no longer, as he explores the misery of a mind longing for the good old days of the now-decayed family home. Such a longing may be a common human emotion, particularly among the elderly, but it offers no insight into the vigour of an expanding society.

In *Possession* (New York, 1923), Mazo de la Roche took a more direct look at the environment than either Callaghan or Child did. Her farming hero Derek Vale hopes to escape economic retrenchment when he moves from Nova Scotia to an Ontario estate which he inherits. Instead, he finds similar difficulties there too, as well as a crippling moral code. Although the setting is 1896, the challenge of declining profits from cattle and orchards, under competition from newer breeds and strains in the developing West, provides a vital conflict for the twenties. A neighbour goes bankrupt and Derek almost follows him. Derek lacks the individuality of the *Jalna* characters, and the novel lacks humour and a tight style, but *Possession* far surpasses the later books as a representation of its environment. Apparently feeling the practical future hopeless, or at least uninspiring in creative literature, Mazo de la Roche turned to frank escapism in *Jalna* (Boston, 1927) and its more than a dozen sequels. Here the large estate, a legacy from early Victorian days, can provide sufficient income to keep the family free of its neighbours, its province, and the life of its times, at least for the current generation. Successive whittlings at the estate can raise enough cash for the present (1958 in the last novel, *Centenary at Jalna*, Toronto, 1958). The *Jalna* novels deliberately avoid the real life of Ontario seen in *Possession* and offer an escapist dream of the past alive in the present.

Several less remembered storytellers of the twenties and thirties turned to a less typical Ontario to exploit the colour of some distinctive way of life. Madge Macbeth made her heroine an Ontario forest ranger in *The Patterson Limit* (Toronto, 1923), one of the few Canadian novels about the rights of women. Nina Moore Jamieson described education on the Bruce peninsula as niggardly in *The Hickory Stick* (Toronto, 1921). The many-sided Alan Sullivan chose the local colour of the new Ontario mining towns for *The Rapids* (Toronto, 1920). Starting with *The Trail of the Conestoga* (Toronto, 1924), Mabel Dunham reintroduced the historical romance into Canadian fiction with the early migrations of a special group, the pacifist Mennonites, into southern Ontario.

The discrepancy in good representational literature between Ontario and the rest of Canada has even increased since the second world war. The attractions of life on the Pacific coast have inspired some of Earle Birney's best poems and all of Ethel Wilson's five novels. The prairies look powerful in both Sinclair Ross's sombre tragedy, *As for Me and My House* (New York, 1941), and W. O. Mitchell's cheerful stories of childhood. A. M. Klein has made Quebec vivid in his *Rocking Chair* (Toronto, 1948) poems, while Morley Callaghan, Mordecai Richler and Hugh MacLennan have created an impressive picture of Montreal. In the Maritimes Nova Scotia seems particularly vivid in the poems and stories of Charles Bruce, Ernest Buckler, Hugh MacLennan and Thomas Raddall.

To set against this array, Ontario has produced a motley shelf of historical or sectional romances, several sharp criticisms, and the odd unhappy attempt of major writers from other provinces to give literary life to a setting there. Following Mabel Dunham's example in the twenties, Luella Creighton has depicted the Mennonites in perhaps the most sprightly novels set in Ontario since the second world war, beginning with *High Bright Buggy Wheels* (Toronto, 1951). Both Gladys Lewis (*Joshua Doan*, Toronto, 1956) and Grace Campbell (*Thorn-Apple Tree*, Toronto,

1942) have turned to the past to find something distinctive in the province, the former in the pro-American attitude of some early immigrants, and the latter in Ralph Connor's dear Glengarry. This approach to history is curiously antiquarian for writers in the mid-twentieth century. It suggests an abandonment of the currently relevant for a society organized according to a dream of ancestral ambitions. In Nova Scotia, by contrast, Will R. Bird and Thomas Raddall have given early immigrants the aspirations and loyalties of modern Canadians.

Recent poets have had less scope than the novelists to present an overall picture of Ontario, for they have inclined to short poems. Furthermore, the impressive James Reaney is a poet with the modern intellectual interest in myth, and is therefore not directly concerned with a specific society. His rhapsodies on the golden age of childhood and on Biblical energy have no close association with the province. Yet he has produced some noteworthy glimpses of rural southwestern Ontario, particularly in the Stratford area. It looks most distinctive in the occasional short poem; for example he contrasts the English name of the River Avon there with its peculiar, non-English characteristics. His long allegory on Canadians as geese destroyed in old world wars, *A Suit of Nettles* (Toronto, 1958), has its base in the Stratford area too, but it is national rather than provincial in scope. The wild geese fly away to a second summer, but not the tame Canadians – they are slaughtered. Here and in plays like *The Killdeer* (Toronto, 1962) Reaney captures an energy unmatched by other Ontario literature. It is an energy of violence and horror, in sharp contrast to the sedate earlier literary pictures of Ontario.

The poets have also done rather better than the novelists by Toronto, in short critical or philosophical poems in which they could only draw vignettes rather than develop long narratives. In particular, Raymond Souster has recorded a variety of realist situations, most of them depressing, in many volumes like *A Local Pride* (Toronto, 1962). Short poems like "Christmas Lights of Yonge Street" and "Junk Man on Front Street" describe familiar scenes briefly but sharply. Critical poems like "A Week before Christmas" analyze more fully the despair of the unemployed. Margaret Avison also finds modern Toronto dispiriting in several poems in *Winter Sun* (Toronto, 1960). "Grammarian on a Lakefront Park Bench" reproduces the dullness which for her typifies Sunday afternoon in Toronto. In "The Agnes Cleve Papers" she depicts at some length the desperate adultery of clerical workers deadened by their routine work. In "To Professor X, Year Y" she gives the future historian the picture of present-day Ontario as people waiting in doorways for buses. Yet all these vignettes miss the vitality which must lie behind a complex society. The glimpse of a future estimate of our society offered by Margaret Avison totally lacks the vigour which Vancouver aroused in Earle Birney's "Trial of a City." Earle Birney even found a force in the present to admire, in the person of his Vancouver housewife.

When Earle Birney and other major writers have moved their settings to Ontario, they seem to have fared as badly as the native writers. In *Down the Long Table* (Toronto, 1955) Birney never seems to come out into daylight in Toronto (or Vancouver), and his geographical survey of Canada in *The Strait of Anian* (Toronto, 1948) contains noteworthy lyrics about all regions of Canada except Ontario.

"Laurentian Shield" describes the power but lack of inspiration in the least populated part of the province, and "The Ebb Begins from Dream" suggests that Toronto is most memorable when one is asleep. E. J. Pratt has described the life of the Jesuits in old Huronia vividly in *Brebeuf and His Brethren* (Toronto, 1940), but the more modern parliamentary drama of Macdonald versus Blake in *Towards the Last Spike* (Toronto, 1952), though set in Ottawa, derives its inspiration from western Canada. Grove set *The Master of the Mill* (Toronto, 1944) in western Ontario, but any feeling of the actual environment is cancelled by the futuristic edifice of the mill soaring eerily up from the rocks to cast its shadow over the nation divorced from the province. A much more casual exercise, *Two Generations* (Toronto, 1939), must stand as Grove's representation of the region in which he wrote his four last books. Thomas Costain turned back to the 1890's in *Son of a Hundred Kings* (Garden City, 1950), but, by focusing on business rivalry and manufacturing in his small city of Balfour, he came closest of all to representing the strong heart of civilization in modern southern Ontario.

Hugh MacLennan tried to vivify Ontario in his weakest novel, *The Precipice* (Toronto, 1948), for another version of his general theme of becoming a Canadian. His earlier hero of *Barometer Rising* (New York, 1941) comes to understand what Nova Scotia and Canada mean to him through exile. In *Two Solitudes* (New York, 1945) and *The Watch That Ends the Night* (Toronto, 1959) a French Canadian and then an English Canadian in Quebec feel their way to the new nationality. In *The Precipice* MacLennan chose the small town stolidity of Ontario to define Canadianism, by contrasting it with the hectic and ruthless business and personal lives found in his American city. He tried to depict his heroine's version of the familiar strict morality as dynamic and progressive. The result is unconvincing because his small town society is no more distinctive of Ontario as opposed to New England or Upper New York State than Callaghan's earlier "city." Nor does the Ontario way of life depicted involve much beyond gardening and moral dogmatism.

The writers so far discussed have accepted Ontario as either unquestionably good, like the local colourists, or tragically evil, like Morley Callaghan. In contrast the satirist is too sophisticated to accept his society as perfect, and too urbane to regard human failings as evil. The satirist laughs at the shortcomings he sees, to persuade readers to correct them. By nature a critic, he sets up a perspective between himself and his readers on the one hand and the society he is criticizing on the other. Such critical distance prevents a writer from identifying with the force of his society and echoing it in powerful works of art. Instead, he accepts his society as being deficient in the highest force, but he determines to use that deficiency as the source of a lively laughter. According to Matthew Arnold (in "The Function of Criticism at the Present Time") a society lacking great literature can regenerate literary vitality through vigorous criticism. Perhaps it is not surprising that the most memorable twentieth-century writers in Ontario are satirists.

Stephen Leacock loved to laugh at his neighbours in Orillia, but he tried to reserve his satire for the city. More often an incidental funny man than a serious critic of society, Leacock developed an overall theme only in *Sunshine Sketches of a Little Town* (London, 1912) and *Arcadian Adventures with the Idle Rich* (London, 1914), which are consequently his best two books. The results here are significant for the historian. In *Sunshine Sketches* he took a probing look at the sharp civic leaders of his small Ontario town of Mariposa at the turn of the century. Although they are clearly dishonest, he portrayed them as essentially kind and even generous. Innkeeper Josh Smith seems almost disinterested when he burns the church down to provide a building fund from the insurance money. Judge Pepperleigh seems loyal rather than hypocritical when he orders the investigators from the insurance company out of town. In *Arcadian Adventures*, in contrast, the businessmen are crooked and ruthless whether they run companies, churches, the university, or the city hall. Like the local colourists, Leacock loved small-town Ontario, but by contrasting it with its evil counterpart in the city he gave perspective and depth to his preference. The old boys in the last chapter of *Sunshine Sketches*, who are longing for Mariposa from their armchairs in their city club, know that only small-town life provides the leisure for a long-range look at human objectives.

Despite Leacock's avowed theme of leisure, the attraction of Mariposa for modern readers is its comparative vitality and complexity. From the fight over renewing the hotel's liquor license to the election campaign, from the annual picnic to the church building fund, from a fling on the stock market to a scare over mythical bank robbers, life there has much of the bustle and energy to explain a growing civilization. And Leacock has depicted an unusually varied range of social concerns, including business, politics, and sermons. Yet his omission of industry, farming and education detracts from the force of Mariposa society, for they have been essential to expansion in Ontario. His satire of the city in *Arcadian Adventures* omits industry too, but by describing the financial magnates in action it produces the most cohesive picture of city life in Canadian literature. The city is not Canadian, however, but vaguely American. Like MacLennan, Leacock may have regarded the city as somehow un-Canadian.

The few satires of Ontario life published between the wars look rather unrepresentative. *The Land of Afternoon* (Ottawa, 1924) and *The Kinder Bees* (London, 1935) attack the pettiness found in social partying in the parliamentary group in Ottawa, but the healthy points of view presented are western or French Canadian rather than from Ontario. Madge Macbeth complained about the lack of cultural interests in Ottawa; and Fred Jacob depicted that lack as the essential trait of his supposedly typical Toronto hero, a Canadian novelist, in *Day Before Yesterday* (Toronto, 1925) and *PeeVee* (Toronto, 1928). When Francis Pollock searched for meaning in the apparently city-oriented society of the thirties in his two serious novels, he produced only a bored beekeeper in a decaying village, and a speed-demon in Toronto (*Bitter Honey*, Toronto, 1935; *Jupiter Eight*, Toronto, 1936).

Following Leacock's tradition of cheerful criticism, Robertson Davies has provided the most searching and lively treatment of Ontario since the second world war. His three novels expose the deficiencies and yearnings of his modern small Ontario city of Salterton. A numbing materialism makes his thinking and artistic citizens seem totally alien there; consequently their dramatic and publishing goals produce absurdly inappropriate results. In *Tempest-Tost* (Toronto, 1951), an amateur production of Shakespeare's fanciful and mature last comedy, *The Tempest*, suffers from regular community friction and from actors who confuse their real life and acting roles. *Leaven of Malice* (Toronto, 1954) dramatizes the distractions facing the editor of a would-be serious newspaper by besetting him with a libel suit over a false wedding announcement. Apparently the society wilfully neglects the one thing necessary to make it civilized, that is, culture. Perhaps it can hope for a vicarious salvation in *A Mixture of Frailties* (Toronto, 1958), in which it sends one of its young geniuses to England to study music. Unfortunately she stays there.

In these three novels the social picture of Salterton becomes increasingly more serious and broad. *Tempest-Tost* is confined to citizens with considerable leisure time – professors, well-to-do wives, and the odd teacher or librarian. Although *Leaven of Malice* chiefly describes the same group, they are involved with more typical and crucial small city concerns. By *A Mixture of Frailties* Davies broadened his scope to include a working family and their fundamentalist pastor, in that part of the novel still set in Salterton. Yet although Robertson Davies' picture of modern Ontario is unusually representational, it is misleading if taken too seriously. In real life such people lack the aims and the naiveté which Davies attributes to them, and they have others which they can come closer to realizing. Davies' scope at best is narrower than Leacock's, for it omits politics, government, and the professions, as well as industry. The same insistence on cultural salvation to the neglect of existing dynamic pursuits has produced a similarly narrow effect in Ralph Allen's ironic study of radio broadcasting in Toronto in *The Chartered Libertine* (Toronto, 1954), and in Selwyn Dewdney's Babbitt-like criticism of high school teaching in *Wind Without Rain* (Toronto, 1946).

Neither urban nor rural Ontario has been adequately represented in modern Canadian poetry or fiction, in sharp contrast to the rest of Canada. The best of Canada's writers from every province, in all kinds of media from nature lyrics to satire, have failed to react dynamically to a civilization which is dynamic. A true southern Ontario, perhaps focussed on the industry and commerce which express its vitality in daily life, remains to be dramatized or even recorded memorably in Canadian literature. The story is there. *The Financial Post* of March 23, 1963, can describe the imagination behind the Macdonald-Cartier Freeway and even find a hero (William Joseph Hamilton, formerly chief surveyor for the Ontario Department of Highways), and it can record the dramatic change in the lives of thousands of citizens resulting from the highway. Apparently, Canada's creative writers cannot.